STAYING POSITIVE IN A NEGATIVE WORLD

GETTING THROUGH THE 2020 PANDEMIC

Sermons from the Pastor
Dr. William H. Jarrett, Ph. D.

Copyright © 2022 Dr. William H. Jarrett, Ph. D.

No part of this book may be reproduced or transmitted in any form or by any means: graphic, electronic, or mechanical, including photocopying, recording, taping, or by any information storage retrieval system without permission, in writing, of the publisher or author.

Published by:
Lowbar Publishing Company
905 S. Douglas Ave.
Nashville, Tennessee 37204
615-972-2842
Lowbarpublishingcompany@gmail.com
www.Lowbarbookstore.com

Author: Dr. William H. Jarrett, Ph. D.
Typist: Deborah Reese
Editor: Eunice
Format Artist: Fiverr
Graphic and Cover Design Artist: Fiverr
Printed in the United States of America

ISBN: 978-1-7329202-8-6

For additional information or to contact the author for workshops or seminars, please email the author at, williamjarrett@att.net or Lowbar Publishing Company.

Table of Contents

About the Author	v
Dedication	vii
Expressions Of Support	viii
Foreword	xvi
Does God Forsake the Righteous?	1
How Long Is the Night?	12
The Colt and the Crowd	25
Who Will Roll the Stone Away?	40
A Life Lesson in the Wilderness	54
But Prayer	69
They Have the Word	88
A Mother's Faith in the Time of Crisis	106
The Battle Is the Lord's	123
Consider Our Challenge	143
God Is Able	160
Living the Abundant Life	177
Unity	188

A Father with a Purpose	204
Staying Positive in a Negative World	222
Too Blessed to be Stressed	242
I'm Down, But I'm Not Out	259
For the Glory of God	277
Zacchaeus's Conversion	294

About the Author

William H. Jarrett was born and raised in Lauderdale County, Tennessee. He currently serves as Pastor of the St. Mark Baptist Church Henning, Tennessee. He is married to Rose Marie Jarrett, and the father of two daughters.

Educated in the Lauderdale County School System, Pastor Jarrett holds degrees from Dyersburg State Community College, Union University, and Trinity Theological Seminary.

As a committed and dedicated member of the community in which he lives, Pastor Jarrett's service includes, but is not limited to the following: board member of the Alex Haley Museum for (5) five years; Chairman of the Board for the Lauderdale County Water District; Vice- Chairman of the Delta Human Resource Agency Emergency Food & Shelter Board; the Lauderdale County Zoning Board.

Pastor Jarrett has served as Moderator of the West Tennessee Baptist Missionary and Educational Association for (8) eight years, Western Regional Vice- President of Congress of Christian Education for (4) four years, Western Regional Vice- President of the Tennessee Baptist Missionary and Education Convention Incorporated (8) eight years, and Chairman of the Trustee Board for the Tennessee School of Religion Memphis, Tennessee.

Pastor Jarrett is a Retired Reservist of the Military with twenty years of service.

Dedication

This book is dedicated to my lovely wife Rose Marie Jarrett, who stood by my side each Sunday during the entire Covid 19 pandemic as the Minister of Music. She used her gift of singing Hymns of praise to the glory of God. I want to thank her for support and love.

Also, I want to thank my entire family my mother Gloria Miller, she listened to my messages each Sunday by phone. Then there were a great host of Facebook friends from around the Country that worshiped virtual with us each week, love you Facebook friends.

With a deep and abiding love, I want to dedicate this book of Sermons to the best Church in the world, St. Mark M.B. Church. You did not miss a beat nor wavered, thank you, to all the ministries and entire congregation.

Lastly, I want to thank God for those members and friends that departed this earthly life, to their eternal abode during this time. I will forever remember you in my heart for the great work you did among us.

Pastor: William H. Jarrett

EXPRESSIONS OF SUPPORT
For My Beloved

It is with great exultation that I express my gratitude towards this project to my Pastor, Husband, and Best Friend, William H. Jarrett.

I am truly thankful and grateful to God for allowing you to remain vigilant during these difficult days. I am so honored to have witnessed the work and time spent by you preparing to share weekly with the congregation God placed before you, the community you serve as well as people all over the world, preaching and teaching the unadulterated Gospel of Jesus Christ.

It is with the utmost respect that I say "Thank You" for your untiring service to the Kingdom of God. I "Thank You, God" for allowing your servant to remain *steadfast, immovable always abounding in the work of the Lord.*

Your Loving Wife,
Rose

EXPRESSIONS OF SUPPORT cont'd

Spiritual Guidance is a necessity in our daily walk of life, for both good and bad times. In March of 2020, Christian Church Worship was significantly altered due to a Global Pandemic caused by the Coronavirus (COVID-19). "We are in a bad time!" The normalcy that we once knew had shifted drastically. The CDC took unprecedented steps and mandated all churches and non-essential businesses to close their doors immediately to combat the spread of this deadly virus! 1 Corinthians 3: 16 says; *Know ye not that you are the temple of God, and that the Spirit of God dwelleth in you?* My husband and I knew that not being at the church did not stop us from being the church, but the fear of what was going on around us was troubling and having the sanctity of collective worship taken from us brought a jolt to our spirit. Our faith was not shaken, but we were still in need of our Spiritual food – the Word.

Praise be to God for Pastor William Jarrett and his beautiful wife First-Lady Rose Bonds-Jarret, who from their home used online broadcasting as an Avenue in which to bring Sunday Morning Worship Service and Wednesday night Sunday School Class to the Congregants of their St Mark Baptist Church Family. With God, their online ministry reached further than the confined walls of their church family and entered the homes of many, from coast to coast. "Look at God".

Each Powerful Message given by Pastor Jarret and each song heard from the Anointed Voice of First-lady Rose was a balm that soothed, healed, and consoled sad and broken hearts caused by the death of loved ones and friends. They administered peace to troubled spirits and offered comfort and Spiritual encouragement by echoing; "have faith over fear, hold on, don't give up even though our world is a dark place, God is still in control; a change is going to come".

God thank you for choosing and using Pastor William and First-lady Rose Jarret as beacons of light needed for this unprecedented time of uncertainty. They are a truly a Spiritually Divine Duo, Anointed and Designed by You for such a period as this!

Love,
Jimmy and Anna Morgan.

EXPRESSIONS OF SUPPORT cont'd

As we were going through a dark period unlike anything we've experienced in our lifetime, we knew we needed the Word of God to ground us. The only way we could make it through COVID-19 was to listen to inspirational messages, along with prayer and meditation. One Sunday, God led my husband, William Bradford, to tune into your Facebook Live sermon. We listened together. Through your motivational and comforting sermons, we found more help each Sunday morning to strengthen us. Your sermons gave us what we needed to continue to trust in God, after all, He is in charge of all things.

One sermon that impacted me was on July 26, 2020. In that sermon, you reaffirmed that "We must go to the Word of God." We must have faith in God because we can do nothing on our own. You pointed out that God is Good, Holy, and righteous. Most of all, God is a bridge over trouble waters.

As we watch the news and witness all the lives that are lost and are still being lost by COVID-19, we are certainly going through trouble waters today. However, we know God is our bridge over these troubled waters. We know we are going to be alright if we follow the rules and continue to trust God, as you always say at the close of each service. We know not to put God to a test, just to see what will happen to us.

Nevertheless, with the Word of God, provided by you, Rev. Jarrett, we have a foundation to stand on. We know God loves and cares, and He is with His children all the time. This virus is only a test for God's children to strengthen their faith in Him. With God, and the preaching of His WORD, from you, Rev. Jarrett, we have nothing to fear. Keep preaching God's WORD. He's using you to help his sheep make it through these trying times.

The Bradfords

EXPRESSIONS OF SUPPORT cont'd

During this time of Covid-19 and safer at home order, I had to go back to my foundation and reconnect with God, through listening to Rev Jarrett and Mrs. Rose Jarrett's church service via Facebook live. I started watching in late March 2020 where he gave several passages of encouragement: Psalm 37:25, Philippians 4:18, and Psalm 23. These all are testaments that God is going to take us through trials and tribulations, but God will never forsake us. We are going to have difficult times, and God is working everything out. We just have to keep the faith.

I was so moved by this sermon, and I immediately texted my family in our group chat that I wanted them to start watching service with me every Sunday. The only time my family has attended church together unfortunately was during the funeral of my grandmother and grandfather. This was a great way for my whole family to also connect with God together. Every Sunday I share the link in our group chat and love seeing my family log in and showing that they are watching too. Even with social distancing and safer at home orders, my family is able to connect together in watching Sunday service too.

Every Sunday Rev. Jarrett gives a word of encouragement/devotion and these along with his sermons have really helped me during these times. 1 Peter 5:7 - this is not the time of doubting. I need to let things go and not worry. This is the time to worship and give it over to God to handle. Roman 8: 38-39 - nothing can separate us from the love of God. His sermon on that day was **But Prayer** coming from Acts 12: 1-12. We must have a Purposeful Power Prayer and pray without ceasing. Matthew 7: 24-25 - the rock of my salvation has a great foundation. Ephesians 2:8 - the grace of God that worked out favor for me. Christ did the work for my salvation. He always ends his sermon with the testimony that Jesus Christ died for our salvation and the importance of having the ABC.

Melody Pearson

EXPRESSIONS OF SUPPORT cont'd

To God Be the Glory, for All the things he has done. From my humble beginnings I know God is Able. I am the great-granddaughter of Doc & Mary Bell Bates, grandfather, Robert Bates, mother, Jean Doris. For me the end of 2019 with the loss of my dearest cousin, Lee Alice, going into a pandemic, racism, and other negative evil sources that we've dealt with, it is an honor to express my thoughts on this fruitful journey with the Reverend Doctor William Jarrett, my cousin. He is such an anointed man of God. He is an outstanding professional peer to the Lauderdale Community and a Spiritual driven pastor. He loves his church family as well as his real family. Reverend Dr. Jarrett has an anointed wife Rose, with a voice of an angel, as well as wonderful children and grand babies.

Rev. Dr. Jarrett's sermons during this pandemic, made God's word a huge feast on our tables. You can pick any sermon and it will bless you. I listen to June 28, 2020 when he preached ***STAYING POSITIVE IN A NEGATIVE WORLD***. The theme came from Philippians 4:6-9. That was food for my soul. I'm so proud of Rev. Dr. William Jarrett for these outstanding sermons that will bless this negative world.

Be Blessed
Euphenia A. Watkins, Louisville, Kentucky

Foreword

I give all glory and honor to God for blessing our congregation with Rev. William H. Jarrett. In 1979, at the age of 24, Rev. Jarrett became the Pastor of his Church family, St. Mark Missionary Baptist Church in Henning, Tennessee. This appointment had to be anointed by God because he has held this assignment for forty-two years.

I cannot begin to share how blessed I am to be a congregant under his leadership. During this time, I have had the privilege of being counseled, corrected, and challenged to be my best self by this man of God. He has ushered our congregation through births, graduations, weddings, family celebrations and crisis, and loss of loved ones, countless times throughout the years. Our congregation has prospered spiritually and financially because of his leadership.

In March 2020 our congregation entered a new normal which continues to evolve daily. We have not missed a Sunday morning worship service because of his love, dedication, and obedience to the Holy Spirit. He prepares for Sunday morning worship and bible study with the same vigor as always.

As you read this book, you will be reminded of the roller coaster of emotions, specifically anxiety and depression, which communities have faced and still face throughout the world because of the Covid-19 Pandemic. But from the opening remarks to the closing prayer of each worship service, you will find the messages are filled with hope, peace, and God's never-ending love for us all. Pastor Jarrett is well in tune with the impact of the Covid-19 Pandemic on the members of his congregation and community. Because of his diligence we are a well-informed congregation which stands ready to keep others well informed through these difficult times.

This collection of sermons is timeless and must not be viewed as a onetime read. You will be compelled to pick it up again and again. I am grateful that he is sharing this compilation of sermons born out of the Covid-19 Pandemic. These sermons will continue to minister to your spirit no matter what the circumstance.

Ministering to a congregation through such times has not been easy for any Pastor. However, the members of St. Mark Missionary Baptist Church have not been denied access to the preaching and teaching of the Word. He has continued to check on our sick, encourage those of us struggling with anxiety and depression, and help make peace with saying goodbye to loved ones in a different yet sometimes unsettling manner.

The words of encouragement and the message of hope have been crystal clear. Only a man of God could continue under these circumstances. I would be remiss not to acknowledge First Lady Rose M. Jarrett who has been by his side every step of the way. She has ministered to our congregation through songs which enhanced the messages being delivered. In them God gave us a strong spiritual team.

St. Mark loves Pastor Jarrett. We appreciate the love he gives to our congregation. I know that he has covered our Church Family with prayer. There is no amount of money that can adequately compensate him, but we ask God to never let us be caught not honoring the service he gives daily.

Who knew that our world would be turned upside-down? It is good to know that God made provision for the unexpected. We thank

God that he is a part of that provision. We pray God's blessings upon him and his family.

Deborah L. Reese, VBS Director
B.S., M.A.T., M.Ed.

Does God Forsake the Righteous?
Sunday, March 22, 2020

CALL TO WORSHIP

Good morning! Good morning! Good morning to the St. Mark Missionary Baptist Church Family and my Facebook Family and friends. This is the day that the Lord has made, I will rejoice and be glad in it. Thank God for His faithfulness. *Great is Thy faithfulness, Great is Thy faithfulness, Morning by morning new mercies I see. All I have needeth Thy hand hath provided, Great is Thy faithfulness, Lord unto me.*

OPENING REMARKS

I am live streaming with you this morning from my home. Thank God for technology, social media that allows us to share and communicate and especially the Gospel of our Lord and Savior Jesus Christ. I am appreciative of the great help I received, which allowed me to come to you live on Facebook. The Church house at St. Mark in Henning is empty, however, the Church has gathered because the Church is in us. Thank God we are the Church.

WORDS OF ENCOURAGEMENT

Let's keep in prayer members of our Church family and our neighbors, and certainly those in nursing home. Let's also pray for our nation and our world because we are hampered with corona virus, and it has taken the lives of so many across the world. We want to pray for the leaders of our nation and world leaders as they try to bring this virus under control. But most certainly we want to pray for those who are on the front line like our doctors, nurses, and other health workers. They are going to need our prayers, because we want divine intervention in this bad situation that we find ourselves. And I have come to learn that in crisis that Our Lord and Savior Jesus Christ is good for every crisis.

So, this morning we want to remember all the persons that have been affected by this dreadful disease, and certainly those families who have lost loved ones. So, let's pray, and let's pray mightily. Let's pray hard that God through His Sovereign Power will do something great, will do something wonderful for the land. I am reminded of 2 Chronicles 7:14 where He *says that if my people that are called by my name would humble themselves and pray, and seek my face and turn from their wicked ways, then will I hear from heaven, and forgive their sins and I will heal the land;* and certainly my brothers and sisters our land needs healing.

At this time, I am going to ask my wife who is in service with me this morning to come now and sing us a song and get us ready for the word of the Lord.

SELECTION

If It Had Not Been for the Lord on My Side by Margaret P. Douroux

Thank you so kindly for that beautiful rendition. If it had not been for the Lord who was on my side or our side, where would I be? Where would we all be? Thank God that He is on our side. He is in control. He is operating even in the midst of crisis. Thank God. Thank God for our Sovereign God.

At this time, we will go to the Throne of Grace, where we get our strength and solace in time of need. I am going to ask *each one* to bow your heads as we approach the Throne Room of God. Thank God that He has allowed us to come boldly to the Throne of Grace. This morning we want to come to the Throne of Grace. I know I don't deserve it; but thank God, He gives me what I don't deserve. So, let us pray.

PRAYER

Our God, our help in ages past, our hope for years to come, our shelter from the stormy blast, and our eternal home under the shadow of Thy Throne still may we dwell secure, sufficient in thine arm alone, and our defense ensure.

Our Father, we come to Thee this day with a deep and abiding trust, and Thy might and Thy power to sustain us. Today you are the same as you were yesterday and will be tomorrow and forever according to your word. Thy steadfast love is made real day in and day out because you are ever near us. We feel Thy sustaining grace; it woke us up this morning as we start this day's journey. Help us to look always to you. Give us a childlike faith, a humbling faith; faith without faltering and without failing even in trying times.

Our Father, strengthen our weak and feeble hands, thy will grant unto us the capacity to overcome any doubt and fear. The doubts and fears that sometimes so easily beset us. But we hear you say in your word that we should lay aside every weight and sin that so easily besets us, and let us run the race with patience, looking to you oh God who is the author and finisher of our faith.

We know that dark clouds will come into our way, but that Thou art near. And when you are so near to us, dark clouds roll away and sea billows cease to roll. Hold to our trembling hands as we try and place our little hand into your big hand. So many times, we close our hands, but you never close your hand to us even in darkness. Be with us in our dark moment, lead us and guide us to an eternal light and a truth that will always prevail.

And God we pray for our nation. We pray for our world. Jesus, move like only you can. Do what only you can. Heal those who have been affected by the virus. Heal those families who have lost their loved ones. We just thank you now, we praise you now and we worship you. Thank you for a personal relationship with you, for confidence you have given us and the will to worship a God who is worthy to be worshipped and praised. We thank you now and we ask it all in the precious, promising, and powerful name of Our Lord and Savior Jesus Christ, and we pray with thanksgiving. And all the people said Amen.

Thank you for sharing in that prayer with us. And we just believe that God is going to do a great thing in the life of his people. We pray for change, but most of all I pray for salvation for those who don't know the Lord, because we know that God sent His Son that we might have life, and that we might have it more abundantly.

SERMON

Thank you once more as we prepare now to go into the word. This morning I want to share from the Psalms. Psalm 37:25. And this Psalm the Lord put on my heart and in my spirit this week to share with you this morning. It's one verse, but I love the whole chapter. This is the Psalm of David. David says, *I have been young, and now I am old, yet have I not seen the righteous forsaken, nor his seed begging bread.* In our text this morning, **Does God Forsake the Righteous?** David makes an incredible statement. What is his statement? He declares that he has never seen the righteous forsaken. What David is witnessing to God is that God is faithful to him and to those who have a right standing with him. He in essence reminds us that he was once a young man, but now he is old and gray. Between youth and old age, he had never seen the righteous forsaken, nor his seed – his children - begging bread.

Just last week across the country, after the schools were shut down, the school and community came together to gather food to take to children that would have been out of school, without food during their day. That just shows me that God will take care of those who belong to him. He will not allow His children to go without daily necessities. And this is what David is saying to us in the text this morning. He's saying that God will not allow His children to go begging for the basic needs of life.

David, the old man, will tell us this morning, "Don't judge me by my statement. Only hear me out. Let me tell you who the righteous are. Because I told you I have never seen the righteous forsaken." Who are the righteous? The righteous are those who have a personal working relationship with God. They are the ones who serve the Lord. They trust God with their whole heart, soul, mind, and strength. I like the way Solomon says it. Solomon says when they have a right relationship with God, they lean not to their own understanding, but in all their ways they acknowledge God, and God directs their paths.

Let's look at the old patriarch Abraham. Abraham was man that served the Lord and trusted in the Lord despite all of the many events and challenges that he would come his way. But do understand that Abraham did not get it right all the time. We don't get it right all the time either, but the Lord continues to bless us despite our failures and our shortcomings. God is interested in the fact that we trust Him, so trust Him. When I trust God that means that I'm leaning solely on Him who is able to do anything but fail. And because Abraham believed God, it was counted or was imputed, or it was credited to him as righteousness.

Abraham was not perfect, he wasn't flawless, and he failed. We fail. All of us have fallen at some given point and time in our lives. You remember when God promised Abraham a son, he and his wife were getting older. They felt that they had to give God some help for the promise to be fulfilled. And we know that Sarah influenced Abraham to go in with Hagar to bring that promised child that God never imposed upon Hagar. The promise was made to Sarah and Abraham. They were impatient and took matters into their own hands. As a result, the child was born. And later the child and his mother brought bitterness and tension to the family. And eventually Hagar and her child were expunged from Abraham and Sarah's home.

But listen at this, history tells us that in-spite of Abraham's imperfections and impatience, he went down in the annals of history as a friend of God— The Father of the Faithful. And God honored Abraham because he trusted God and that made him righteous. Today, we and all the families of the earth are blessed because of Abraham's faith. So, when David says that he has never seen the righteous forsaken, he is saying he has never seen those who put their trust in God and lean totally on God ever forsaken. I know it seems like things can come to us unannounced and unseen. And it can hit us so hard that we feel like we have been forsaken by the Almighty God. But David says, "*The righteous are never forsaken.*"

David is saying, "I was young. I was following my father's sheep. And God was with me in times of crisis, in my fights. I had a fight with a lion and a bear. But I was able to with my bare hands, with God's strength, I killed the lion and the bear. Let me tell you what God did," is what David is saying to us. "He protected me. And if you think that was something, let me tell you what else he has done. I was coming into the camp of the Israelites. The Israelites were on one side of the valley, and the Philistines were on the other. And as I came into the camp, I came upon a giant blurting out 'send me a man!' His name was Goliath, and he was threatening my people."

My Brothers and Sisters we are threatened today by a giant. And this giant is worldwide. It is called corona virus. And it has people scared. They are afraid. Many don't know what they are going to do, or how they are going to make it. Many people think or feel that they are forsaken. But I come by to tell you this morning that there is nothing too big that God cannot handle. The Israelites were afraid. They were afraid to go out and challenge their giant. But God gave a little boy named David the courage and the wisdom to slay the giant. That was not all, God told David, "David you have a slingshot. Go down by the brook, pick up five smooth stones. Use your slingshot and slay this uncircumcised giant." God will give you victory. My brothers and sisters David obeyed the God that he had a relationship with. He knew that God was going to enable him. The giant in front of David was not bigger than the God inside of him. In the same way the Covid-19 that we face now is not bigger than the God we serve. Now that's what we must do. We must humble ourselves. We must pray. We must seek His face. God says that if we do what we are supposed to do, this is what He will do. He said that He will forgive our sins, and He will heal the land. There is no giant bigger than God. I don't care what kind of giant it is.

There are people in society today that are skeptical when they read the Bible situations where God's people have been in bad times. They went through unbearable conditions, and they asked the questions: "How could God allow them to suffer? Is that not considered forsaking his people? I got an answer. NO! Yes, we are going to incur things. We're going to come up against some inconceivable odds. That doesn't mean that God will forsake us. James says that we're going to be tested. We're going to be tried. But he says that the testing or the trials we go through is to work something out in us. What is God trying to work out in us? God is saying to us be patient. God is trying to work patience in us. We're in a hurry, running to and fro. Seemingly, we don't have enough time in the day to take time to spend time with God. And God says that I'm sending some testing. No, No. God never tempts us. The devil tempts us, but God takes the temptation and allows it to become a trial so it can work out patience in us. And if we don't understand what God is trying to do for us through patience, He says if you don't have the knowledge or understanding, James 1:5 says; *if any man lacketh wisdom, let him ask God.* If you don't understand the testing or the trial of your faith which is trying to work out patience in you, then let a man ask God. We need to be asking God to give us wisdom on how to get through what we are going through, because testing and trials are coming.

Another writer says, they are just light afflictions. Paul will tell us, "I went through so many trials and testing of my faith. I was beaten. I was placed in a Philippian jail, but you know what I did while I was going through that time in jail? We were on locked down, I and Silas. We made the best of the situation. We prayed and sang. And those around us heard us. The prisoners heard us. Not only did the prisoners hear us, but God heard us. And God came to our rescue through nature. He allowed and earthquake to come and shake the jail and allowed the shackles on our feet and hands to come *a loose*." God will come if we pray.

The beloved disciple John will tell you, "I was carried out on a lonely isle called Patmos. I was threatened even with death. I was in isolation." And many of our American citizens are separated in isolation. But it does not matter where you are if you know the Lord. He won't forsake you. He'll come to you wherever you are. John will tell you, "I was in the spirit on the Lord's Day. And he heard the voice of God." Are we listening for the voice of God amid this situation? David said that he's *never seen the righteous forsaken*. David never said that the righteous would never face troubles, trials, and tribulations. He never said they would not have to face death. But this is what David said, *I've never seen the righteous forsaken*. The New Testament can help us better understand this. Paul in 2 Corinthians 4:8 says *we are troubled on every side, yet not distressed. We are perplexed but not in despair. Persecuted but not forsaken.* I really like this part. *Cast down but not destroyed.* Praise God. Paul reminds us that God allows us to face difficulties, but through it all God never forsakes.

And as I come to a close, David says something else in the text. *I've never seen the righteous forsaken, nor his seed beg bread.* Won't God feed you when you get hungry? Growing up in a Baptist church, listening to the warriors and saints of old, they would say it like this, *He's bread in a starving land. He's water in dry places. He's shelter in the time of a storm.* He is our defense mechanism. I hear Jesus say this. He says *I am the bread of life.* Thank God He is our bread that came down from heaven. The disciples asked the Lord once, to teach them how to pray. And one of the petitions in the Model Prayer says *give us this day our daily bread.* I like Psalm 23, one of my favorite Psalms. David says *the Lord is my shepherd, I shall not want.*

Paul says in Philippians 4:18: *but my God* (personal) *but my God shall supply all of my needs according to his riches in glory.* Now when you have a relationship with God, you can say what your God can do and will do for his children. How many of you, this morning, are His children? Is He your father? A father has obligations to take care of his children, to protect his children, to provide or make provision, he won't forsake his children.

I know sometimes when things become heated, and when things come to ravish us, we feel forsaken. Can I tell you this morning, it was one dark Friday, Our Lord and Savior Jesus Christ hung on an old, rugged cross. And one of the seven last sayings I heard Jesus say, *My God, My God, why hast thou forsaken me?* But can I tell you this morning, those were not His last words. It may have been one of the last, but not the last word. His last word was *Father into thy hand I commend my spirit.* That's not the end of the story. God did not forsake Jesus. Nor did God allow Him to remain in the grave after death. God did not forsake Him because, guess what, early Sunday morning...I say early Sunday morning, God raised Jesus up. What did God do in reality through this process of death and burial? You know what? God vindicated Jesus' righteous life. He vindicated Him. What else did He do through this process? He justified His sacrifice by raising Him from the dead. And guess what He did? He gave Him a name above every name. That makes me want to shout there now; "A name above every name!" *And at the name of Jesus, every knee must bow, and every tongue shall confess that he is Lord.* Thank God for the name. There's no name like the name of Jesus.

My Brothers and Sisters, God won't forsake us. This too shall pass because I just believe God is going work it all out to our good. God is going to get what God deserves: praise, worship, respect, and honor. So, God is going to bring good out of turmoil, he'll do it every time. I've watched Him. He's done it before. He'll do it again. God is God and we need to recognize Him as God.

CALL TO DISCIPLESHIP

If there is anyone out there that doesn't know this Jesus that I'm talking about, I beg you, I plead, I adjure you, accept Him as your Savior today. All you got to do is just believe in your heart that God raised Jesus from the dead, and confess it with your mouth, believe it in your heart that He did raise Him you shall be saved. I pray that you will ask him into your heart and say Lord save me. I'm a sinner and I need salvation. Guess what God will do. He will reach way down and touch your soul and give you this gift called salvation. Paul says *you are saved by grace through faith lest any man should boast.* I pray that you will accept him today. Let's pray.

PRAYER FOR SALVATION

Eternal God, our Father, we thank you for this day. We thank you for this opportunity to minister to your people once more. Many are listening in faraway places. Thank you for tuning in today, and we pray that the message has been strength, encouraging, and gives you hope in what seems like a hopeless situation. But our hope is in our hope that is in Jesus Christ the hope of Glory. Lord anybody out there listening today that is unsaved, we pray that they'll come under conviction and realize that they need a Savior in such a time as this. Prick their hearts. Touch them right now. And let them come to a Savior who loves them. We lift once more our sick, bereaved that you will touch them today. And now God we just want to say thank you for this another expression of your love and kindness toward us. For we do ask it in the precious, promising, powerful name of Jesus Christ our Lord. Amen.

We're going to have another song, and we hope and pray that you will enjoy this next number. We're going to Sister Jarrett one more time. Thank God for her voice and I know that this day is going to be a good day because the Lord made this day.

SELECTION

Battle Hymn of the Republic **by Julia Ward Howe**

CLOSING PRAYER

Oh Lord Our God, we thank you for another privilege of worship even though we are not assembled in a church house. But as we have fore stated, the Church is in us; and wherever we are, the Church is gathered. And now may the grace of God, the Love of God and fellowship of the Holy Spirit, may He rest, rule, and abide in the hearts of your people now and forever, and we can all say simultaneously, Amen.

How Long Is the Night?

Sunday, March 29, 2020

OPENING

Good morning! Good morning! Good morning to St. Mark Baptist Church Family and my dear friends and community, Facebook friends. We welcome you to another worship experience. St. Mark I am missing you greatly. These past two weeks have been lonely without being with my Church family. But thanks be to God that we are the Church, and the Church is the temple of the Lord. Our bodies are the temple of the Lord. And we thank God that we can worship Him anytime, anywhere, and any place as long as we are in Christ Jesus.

CALL TO WORSHIP

Well, the Lord is in His Holy Temple, let the earth be silent before Him. To God be the Glory for the things that He has done. He has done great things. He has done marvelous things, magnanimous things. The Lord is still in control.

We are live streaming again, and certainly we want all our good friends to come in and join us for this service today. So, if you are out there and you are listening, go ahead and just give me a thumbs up, or a high five however you want to do it this morning. We're going have a message for you and pray that this message will be a blessing in your life as we go through this crisis that is in our country and in our world. Again, we thank God for Facebook, we thank God for media outlet, as we can still get out and reach our people in wonderful ways.

WORDS OF ENCOURAGEMENT

We are in continuous prayer for our country, our nation, and for people in general. These are difficult days, and these are dark days in which we live. But we thank God that we serve a living Savior and for that we ought to just give God a little praise right now. Give Him a handclap of praise right where you are.

    This morning, I'm going to have my lovely wife come to bless us in music ministry. The Bible does tell us to come into His presence with singing. And know that the Lord He is God, and it is He who has made us and not we, ourselves. So, we come into His presence with worship through praise through song. Singing is worship. Praying is worship. Preaching is worship. Giving is worship. So, this is a worship day. The Lord has given us six days, and He says on the seventh day we ought to rest and give Him praise. So, you know the Lord may be telling us something- greatly! We have been ignoring, we have overlooked the Lord in so many ways. So, He says "well I'm going to get my day, I'm going to get my praise". And so here we are this morning ready for another worship experience.

    Come on Sis. Jarrett and bless us with a musical selection, and then we will come back with prayer for the country, for our leaders, for those who are doing a great work during this great crisis we find ourselves in. Amen.

SELECTION

I Will Bless Thee Oh Lord – Lyrics: Anonymous; Recorded by Various Artists

Thank you so kindly. I will bless thee oh Lord with a heart of thanksgiving. Now let us go to the Throne of Grace. This is praying time. And we need prayer today. All over the world prayer is needed. So, let us petition, now, the Throne of Grace.

PRAYER

Oh Lord, my God, when I in awesome wonder consider all the worlds thy hands have made. I see the stars, I hear the rolling thunder, thy power throughout the universe displayed. God of our weary years, God of our silent tears, Thou who has brought us thus far on the way.

Dear God, we come now into your presence. We ask you now to forgive us of our sins and our transgressions. We present ourselves before you with one plea. Out of a heart of thanksgiving, we look ever to you for your amazing grace. Thank you for grace that awakened us this morning. Thank you for a pleasant night of sleep and slumber. Thank You, Lord that no danger or harm came to our doors. As our nation and world reel and rock, yet, faced with a virus that has taken lives and many are being affected. They are affected hourly. The numbers are rising daily.

And oh Lord we pray for our presidents, prime ministers, governors, policemen, firemen, doctors, and nurses that are working tirelessly day and night. Bless those families that are quarantined waiting to recover. And Lord we pray that you touch those who are disobedient to rules and laws. We pray that they become awakened. Look upon those who are in nursing homes, unable to see their family members, those that are in hospitals yet being treated. Amid our lives we commend them unto you into your lovely hand.

And God as I share your word, we pray it will be encouraging, thought provoking, uplifting, and even convicting. We pray that it will change someone's thoughts, change their hearts, and transform them into new creatures in Christ Jesus. And today, Oh God, we just pray and commend all these things we ask you for in this prayer to our Great Comforter. And we pray it in his name with thanksgiving, and everyone can say right where you are, Amen.

God bless you. Thank you for sharing in that prayer.

SERMON:

At this time, I'm going to invite you to another Psalms. We shared from the Psalm last week. Last we shared from Psalm 37, Verse 25. On today we are going to share with you from Psalm 30. But I'm going to read the entire chapter. There are twelve verses in this chapter. But there is one particular verse that I want to lift and bring a word from. But let's begin at Verse 1;

1. *I will extol thee, O Lord; for thou hast lifted me up, and hast not made my foes to rejoice over me.*
2. *O Lord my God, I cried unto thee, and thou hast healed me.*
3. *O Lord, thou hast brought up my soul from the grave: thou has kept me alive, that I should not go down to the pit.*
4. *Sing unto the Lord, O ye saints of his, and give thanks at the remembrance of his holiness.*
5. *For his anger endureth but a moment; in his favour is life: weeping may endure for a night, but joy cometh in the morning.*
6. *And in my prosperity I said, I shall never be moved.*
7. *Lord, by thy favour thou hast made my mountain to stand strong: thou didst hide thy face, and I was troubled.*
8. *I cried to thee, O Lord, and unto the Lord I made supplication.*

9. *What profit is there in my blood, when I go down to the pit? Shall The dust praise thee? Shall it declare thy truth?*

10. *Hear, O Lord, and have mercy upon me. Lord, be thou my helper.*

11. *Thou hast turned for me my mourning into dancing: thou hast put Off my sackcloth, and girded me with gladness;*

12. *To the end that my glory may sing praise to thee, and not be silent. O Lord my God, I will give thanks unto thee forever.*

This morning I want to lift Verse 5 for the premise for our text today. And shall I read it once more.

5 For his anger endureth but a moment; in his favour is life: weeping may endure for a night, but joy cometh in the morning.

I want to talk today from this subject, **How Long Is the Night?** People all over the world are asking perhaps this question today. How long is the night? How long is this coronavirus going to last? I hear it in the news. People are asking and wondering, when will it be over? How long is it going to last? In our text this morning I want to raise that question: How long is the night? But first and foremost, let's look back at Psalms 30:1-12. I want to not just browse and skip some pertinent things that lead up to verse 5 and that which follows verse 5.

David says in Verse 1: *I will extol thee, O Lord; for thou hast lifted me up.* In essence he is saying he is experiencing some antagonizing things in his physical vernacular. When I read that verse it implies that David had been in great distress and nearly overwhelmed by his enemies. And so, he's extolling, he's exalting, he's magnifying God for having lifted him up and having preserved him from the cruelty of the adversary. When I look at Verses 4 through 6, David says that he has been brought into great prosperity; trusting in what he had received and forgot to depend wholly on the Lord. David was looking at all the success, the prosperity that he had, but he was not looking to God. So, David incurred some things.

Verse 7 David says the Lord hid his face from him. And David felt that he had been brought into great distress. In Verses 8-10 he feels his loss, and so now he makes earnest prayer and supplication. He needs divine intervention. And of course, God will through his providential powers intervene in our situations. Look at Verse 11. He says that he is restored to the divine favor, and he is filled with joy. God will come and restore favor and give us joy in the midst of our distresses.

In Verse 12; He *purposed,* David *purposed* to glory in God alone and to trust Him forever. And that is wonderful to know that when we have experienced our night's season and we come out of it, we are to purpose in our heart to trust the Lord forever. Now let's go to our central verse in the text. This is what David says, "*for his anger endureth but for a moment.* His anger endureth for a moment. *In his favor is life. Weeping may endure for a night but joy comes in the morning.* Now this scripture of all scripture is a scripture of hope and confidence. *For his anger endureth but for a moment. In his favor is life. Weeping may endure for a night, but joy comes in the morning.* Can't you see the hope and the confidence of a man saying in essence, "I'm coming out of this"?

Better yet it is a testimony of a man who knows what it is like to be in a dark situation, to be in a valley, or to be pressed against a wall. It's a testimony. Now a testimony, or in order to have a testimony, one has to have been in a test. David was tested. But listen to his testimony. For God's anger *endureth but for a moment. In his favor is life. Weeping may endure for a night, but joy comes in the morning.* This is a testimony of one who had lingered in that valley and the shadow of death. David felt like his soul was ready to go to the pit. But David cries out to God and says, "How can I praise you from the grave?" In essence, "God, I need you to raise me up." Oh, what a testimony.

David says *his anger endureth for a moment.* In the Hebrew text this is the literal translation, *for a moment in his anger lives favor.* Let's look at that word *favor.* Favor is something done or granted out of good will rather than from justice or compensation. Favor is a kind act. That's what favor is. It is a kind act. People don't have to do anything for you. God doesn't really have to do anything for us. And all the things God does for us it is out of his favor. Favor is that kind act. A favor is kindness out of God's will because He is a loving God. It is not because we deserve it, but because of a loving God.

God is good. He is so good that he cannot delight in the depression or the ruin of His people. Even if He afflicts us, it is for our advantage. Why? It is because we may be partakers of His goodness and His holiness. The believer cannot be condemned with the Word.

Did you hear David? Even if He is angry with us, it's but for a moment. *His anger endureth but for a moment.* When we have reconciled back to Him and seek His face, His favor can be obtained. Therein lies in that favor today for the life that is now and the life that is to come in the next world. Let's interrogate this verse further. When weeping comes, it is only to spend the night. The verse says: *Weeping may endure for a night.* Reading further; *But joy* and singing *will* surely come in the morning. America and the world are weeping now. But let me say it is just for a night. I said last Sunday, this too shall pass. It's just for a night. Allow me to tell you this. We can't always know the why of national crisis or national disasters and calamities. Even when God doesn't reveal the reason, He reveals himself. And I just wonder how many really see the revealed Christ of the times that we are experiencing.

To see God and define the strength to endure, we need to be sure of who we are. We need to be sure that we are in a relationship with Him, by praising Him in midst of our circumstances, understanding with whom we are walking by faith, and focusing on him we can find the strength to endure. See, we need to know who we are. We need to know where we stand with God in midst of this. And we need to be walking by faith and focusing on him. The just live by faith. Walking doesn't mean you are taking steps. It's a way of life. It's the way we live, and we ought to be focused.

As I look at this Psalm, the Psalms were literally sung by the Old Testament warriors. The lyrics of this Psalm could only be sung by a person who had some moments of weeping. The Psalmist also suggests that our tears are just temporary, and joy will come. My Brothers and Sisters tears are not going to last always. But let me tell you what will last, the joy of the Lord.

The joy of the Lord is permanent. "How long is the midnight?" Many times, in life we don't know how long the night. But David assures us that the morning is coming. Oh yes morning is coming after this dark crisis that we are experiencing. Morning is coming. Morning is coming, and we as humans ask how long because we want to know. We want answers. We ask the questions: How long are we going to cry? How long are we going to weep? How long is this sorrow that we are experiencing? How long are these frustrations? How long? These questions are asked. But can I tell us today, many stories in the Bible hinge on the night situation.

This leads me to suggest that maybe God does some of His best teaching through encounters in the night. God does His best teaching in our night seasons. In the 19th Psalm David says something profound. He says, *The heavens declare the glory of God and firmament sheweth his handiwork.* See this; *Day unto day uttereth speech, and night unto night sheweth knowledge.* God is teaching even through nature itself. And most time people never pay attention to anything that is going on around them whether it's day or whether it's night. He says *day unto day uttereth speech*. God is speaking. God is talking. But how many are listening? How many are giving heed to what the Lord is saying? Some of our best teaching comes through our night seasons. Sometimes God has to press us against the wall to get us to see. Let's look at a few Biblical scenarios of night.

You remember Jacob, the twin brother of Esau, the son of Isaac and Rebecca. There is a long story behind this family. I dare not to try to tell the whole story. Let me just mention Jacob's night with the Lord out in the middle of nowhere. Jacob wrestled with God all night long. God and Jacob wrestled. Jacob and God wrestled that night, and Jacob would not allow God to get away. And God in essence was saying to Jacob turn me a loose. And Jacob *said I will not turn you a loose until you bless me.* And you know God blessed Jacob. God changed his name. You know Jacob was called a trickster, a swindler. And sometimes we've got to wrestle with God in our night, in order, to receive our blessing in the morning. Bless the Lord.

You remember that dreadful night in Egypt when God told Moses to tell the people to move into their homes and place the blood over the mantles, for the death angels were coming through the city. It was in the night. Those who did not have the blood over the door posts, the death angel would come and take the first born. But those who were hid behind the blood lived. The death angel would pass over, which was our representation of Christ. Christ is our Passover from death into life. It was in the night.

You remember the king of Babylon, whose kingdom divided, saw the handwriting on the wall. Guess what? It was in the night while he was lying on his bed. God was writing a word, a message unto him in the night. And he did not understand the handwriting. But the prophet of God, Daniel, gave him the interpretation of the handwriting on the wall. It was in the night. God has a message for us in our night. Night doesn't have to be the blackened sky. Night can be circumstances, trials, and tribulations.

You remember the disciples who fished all night long and had caught nothing. But guess what? Jesus shows up and asks them, "Brothers are you having any success?" "No Lord. We have been out here all night long and we have caught nothing." They replied. And I just believe Jesus said in so many words, "Well you're not fishing right." "What do you mean Lord we're not fishing right?" they asked. "You've got your net on the wrong side of the boat. Put your net on the right side." Maybe God is teaching us through this process that we need to fish from the right side of the boat. When they dropped their nets to the right side of the boat, they had success. They had more fish than they could handle. They called out to other brethren, "Come help us because our success is in abundance."

Paul and Silas were in jail. It was at night. As Silas and Paul prayed and sang. We can do the same thing. We can pray and sing, and God will open the door so that we can get back out again. He's got it. He's got it in his hand. You remember Jesus. Jesus prayed in the Garden of Gethsemane. It was in the night. He prayed three times. Jesus was going through a period of oppression. He was being pressed because Calvary was dangling in the wind. He was praying saying *Lord let this cup pass.* That was His human, mystic side. He was God and man. But the God man would rise up and say *not my will, but let thy will be done.* My Brothers and Sisters let the Lord's will be done.

As I hurry to a close, *Weeping may endure for a night, but joy comes in the morning.* That someone is saying I know there is a better day coming. A better day is coming. I know God moves in mysterious ways and his wonders to perform. All I know is that God is going to work this thing out. He's going to see us through this. We're going to have our night, but morning is going to come. *I know that all things work together for good to them that love God.* How many of you, out there, love God today? I know I need *to wait on God and be of good courage.* I know that *earth has no sorrow that heaven cannot heal.* I know that He knows just how. The old warriors use to sing I know *He knows just how much we can bear.*

I have learned something about night. I've learned that there are times you can't run through your night. You just can't run through it. Zip. It's over. I've learned that you just can't skip over your night. I've learned there are some things you just can't avoid. Some things you've just got to go through. You just got to endure the night. Do you hear David? *Weeping may endure for a night.* Endure. I know that prayer changes things. But I've also come to know, and I say this all the time, prayer doesn't change things always. But this is what prayer does; even if it doesn't change it, prayer will see you through whatever you're going through. It may be God is giving us a teaching moment to get us to pray. And eventually He will see us through this. And even if He doesn't do it right now, that doesn't mean He's not able. That's what Shadrach, Meshach, and Abednego said. He may not deliver us right not, but that doesn't mean that He is not able. We're going to still trust Him; yet trust Him in-spite of all that my come our way.

And remember this; the same God who closed the curtains of our night is the same God that opens the curtains of our morning. God will allow His sunshine to shine through a dark and stormy night. Last night we were under tornado watch, tornado warning. A neighboring state experienced a tornado, it did some severe damage to our neighboring state Arkansas, and it came across to Tennessee. Storm, rain, wind, lightning but look at March 29, Sunday morning, the sun is shining. Behind every dark cloud there is some sunshine. God will send some sunshine. He will open the curtains of the morning. God is going to open the curtains of the morning through this Corona virus. He's got His time. Time is in His hand. Just remember, you can't run through it, you can't skip through it. You just got to endure it until morning. But be faithful and stay focused, God is going to keep us in his keeping power. Thank you. I hope you got something from the message today. I just want to pray to God and ask him to give you the blessings of today. May he give you peace in midst of a crisis. Shall we pray?

CLOSING PRAYER

Eternal God Our Father, we thank you for this day this beautiful Sunday morning. We thank you for allowing us to experience the joy, the peace, but most certainly the fellowship of the Holy Spirit. God we just pray blessings upon your people everywhere all over the land. We pray for those who are bound by strongholds, that you will break all strongholds. Break the chains that have them shackled for whatever reason. And Lord we just pray that you will deliver and set free. Oh Lord, allow your presence to be made known, that they may know that you are God and God alone. Shower now your choice blessings and your special graces upon your people all over the land. We thank you now, we bless you now and we praise you now in the matchless name of Our Lord and Savior Jesus Christ. Amen.

CALL TO DISCIPLESHIP

If there is anyone out there unsaved and don't know the Lord as your personal Savior, I say to you today, it's time. It's time. It's time. Don't let this valuable moment pass you by. Don't just not pay attention to what's going on around you, it is time to draw nigh and closer to the Lord. It is time to be still and know that God is God. And if you hear His voice today, I pray that you will give attention to that voice.

If you're a sinner and unsaved, tell the Lord that "I'm a sinner and I need salvation." Lord, save me. He will come right to where you are. It doesn't matter where you are behind your locked doors. You may be out in the opened fields. Wherever you are, you can stop right now and say, "Lord, come into my heart and save me." This is what God will do. He will come in, and He will make you a brand, new creature. *If any man be in Christ, he is a new creature. Old things are passed away, behold all things are become new.*

If you don't know Him, accept Him right now. Ask Him in your heart. And after this is done and the Church doors are open, find a Church where you can come and worship. You don't have to come to St. Mark, but we invite you to come. Wherever you go, we are all in this thing together. We're just trying to get people to see that Christ is real and that He yet lives.

It's time to get in the house. This is not time to be lollygagging and wasting. It is time to get in the house. Get behind the blood of Jesus. Thank you so much.

We're going to ask Sister Jarrett to come sing another song. As she comes, we continue to encourage you to support the Church financially because the Church is still on the move. We're just not congregating in the building, but the Church is still on the move. The Church is on the move. The Church is here today. Nothing can destroy the Church. Jesus said upon this rock I build my Church and the gates of hell shall not prevail against it. He never said that the Church wouldn't catch it. But He said it would not prevail against it. This shall not prevail over the Church. The Church is you and I. God bless you. Thank you, Sis. Jarrett, will you come, and we'll come back. Have a blessed day.

SELECTION

***I've Decided to Make Jesus My Choice* by Harris Johnson**

CLOSING PRAYER

Father God, we thank you once more for a worship celebration. Thank you for the anointed voice of Rose who helps us so tremendously. And God we just pray that your saving grace will continue to hover over us as we continue to go through day by day. I know you're going to work it out in your own timing. And now God, may your grace, love, peace and the sweet communion of the Holy Spirit rest, rule, and abide in the hearts of your people everywhere, all over the world in Jesus' name. Amen.

Be blessed. Take care. Be safe. Remember to wash your hands and stay 6ft apart. Let's do it so we can get over this crisis in Jesus' name.

The Colt and the Crowd

Sunday, April 5, 2020

OPENING REMARKS

Good morning, St. Mark Baptist Church, and a good morning to our friends around the country. Praying that all is well with you. This is a beautiful Sunday morning. The sun is shining bright.

WORDS OF ENCOURAGEMENT

This is Palm Sunday, Holy Week. As we reflect more than 2,000 years ago, Our Lord and Our Savior Jesus Christ was triumphantly led into Jerusalem. My friends this is a great time of celebration as we enter this advent season even though the clouds are hanging over our nation and world. Some of you are under curfew, and others are told to stay home until our warfare is over. We are in the middle of a medical warfare. Not only a medical warfare, but we are also in the middle of a spiritual warfare. I am reminded of the Apostle Paul's words to the Church at Ephesus there in Chapter 6. There are about three verses that really tell us what we are in - Verses 11, 12, and 13. These are going to be words of encouragement for somebody that's under curfew or has to stay at home orders. We studied this in our Bible Study for more than a year.

Paul says in Verse 11: *Put on the whole armour of God, that ye may be able to stand against the wiles of the devil.* Verse 12a: *For we wrestle not against flesh and blood.* But these are the things he is telling us we are wrestling against. There are approximately five things in that passage that Paul says that we are wrestling against. We are wrestling against powers, against the rulers of the darkness of this world, and against spiritual wickedness in high places. But see he says we should do: *Take unto you the whole armour of God that you may be able to withstand in the evil day.* Today is an evil day. Yet, it's a good day. It is evil that is happening in our world. And Paul says *having done all to stand.* In spite of it all we still got to keep standing. Every morning you are awakened, put on your war clothes. Dress up for a fight.

We are in a spiritual fight. We are in a medical fight. These are the things we must do; put on our helmet, put on our belt of truth, put *on the breastplate of righteousness,* the sword of the spirit, and have our *feet shod with the preparation of the Gospel.* That's how we must suit up for this warfare we are in. And as we fight against this medical war, I'm going to add this one: put your mask on. So, the fight that we are fighting is a fight of faith. We have got to keep the faith in-spite of what's going on in our world. I've learned a winner never quits, and a quitter never wins. This is my encouragement to you this morning.

CALL TO WORSHIP

As we prepare for worship today, let me say as the scripture says, *"The hour is come that and now is when the true worshiper shall worship the Father in spirit and in truth. For the Father seeks us to worship him. God is a spirit and they that worship him must worship him in spirit and in truth.* Let's start our worship for today.

As we make ready now to petition the very Throne of God, we have the privilege as saints of God to come boldly to the Throne of Grace. We have a great High Priest. His name is Jesus who fixed the way and made it possible for us to come into His presence. So, this morning we want to come into His presence to worship and to give Him praise and thanks.

OPENING PRAYER

Oh Lord, Our Lord, how excellent is thy name in all the earth. Who has set thy glory above the heavens? Lord, you have been our dwelling place in all generations. Before the mountains were brought forth, wherever thou has formed the earth and world, even from everlasting to everlasting you are God Lord.

We thank you for this beautiful Sunday morning. We thank you for last night's sleep and slumber. We praise your great Name. We lift you up. We worship you for who you are, and you are worthy above all else. There is nothing or no one like you. Thank you for saving us by your saving grace. Thank you, God for Jesus who made our salvation, secure. And as we enter the advent season, this holy week, we know you made your triumphant entry into Jerusalem to offer yourself as our Messiah, our king, and our Savior. Mankind rejected you and crucified you. Even now men are rejecting you, and you continue to offer salvation to them.

And God I pray that as we go through this crisis that we find ourselves in, that some good will come to those who don't know you as a living Savior. We pray that lives will be changed, transformed, and the Kingdom of God will increase. Lord, we pray for your covering over your people. In the name of Jesus, we plead the blood even now. We know that the blood that Jesus shed for me, and others *will never lose its power. The blood reaches the highest mountains, it flows to the lowest valley; the blood that gives me strength from day to day,* the precious blood, the sanctifying blood of the lamb, thank You Lord. And today oh God, continue to bless our nation and the nations of the world. Heal them in Jesus' name. Bless my Church family, bless this community, continue to feed them, keep them comforted, and keep them well. And now

Lord as we end this prayer, bless your Word that is about to come forth, and we pray it in Jesus' name with thanksgiving. Amen. Amen. Amen.

TODAY'S SERMON

Thank God for the power of prayer, and it is a privilege to pray. The old hymnologist said, *What a friend we have in Jesus, all of our sins and griefs to bear, What a privilege it is to carry everything to God in prayer. Oh, what peace we often forfeit, Oh, what needless pain we bear, all because we do not carry everything to God in prayer.* It's a privilege my friends, it's a privilege to take everything to God. *Oh, what peace we often forfeit.* We forfeit our peace by dwelling on the things that are going on around us. The pain, it's needless to bear this pain when we can take it and put it in the Lord's hand, everything. Amen. Amen.

This is Palm Sunday, and I want to speak to us around the idea of that great subject of Palm Sunday, Holy Week. Shall I call your attention to Matthew Chapter 21, Verses 1 through 11.

1. *And when they drew nigh unto Jerusalem, and were come to Bethphage, unto the Mount of Olives, then sent Jesus two disciples,*
2. *Saying unto them, Go into the village over against you, and straightway ye shall find an ass tied, and a colt with her: loose them and bring them unto me.*
3. *And if any man say ought unto you, ye shall say, The Lord hath need of them, and straightway he will send them.*
4. *All this was done, that it might be fulfilled which was spoken by the prophet, saying*
5. *Tell ye the daughter of Sion, Behold, thy King cometh unto thee, meek, and sitting upon an ass, and a colt the foal of an ass,*
6. *And the disciples went, and did as Jesus commanded them,*

7. *And brought the ass, and the colt, and put on them their clothes, and they set him thereon.*
8. *And a very great multitude spread their garments in the way; others cut down branches from trees, and strawed them in the way.*
9. *And the multitudes that went before, and that followed, cried, saying, Hosanna to the Son of David: Blessed is he that cometh in the name of the Lord; Hosanna in the highest.*
10. *And when he was come into Jerusalem, all the city was moved, saying, Who is this?*
11. *And the multitude said, This is Jesus the prophet of Nazareth of Galilee.*

From these series of verses, I want to use a subject, the simple subject, **The Colt and the Crowd.** Jesus told them to go into the city, the village and untie the colt. The Bible talks about the multitude that went before him and spread their garments - that's the Crowd. So, I want to talk about **The Colt and the Crowd.**

In our text today, Jesus and his disciples are approaching Jerusalem into Bethpage and Bethany, proceeding to the Mount of Olives. This would be Jesus's last and final visit to the city He loved. Jerusalem was the capital, the Holy City, the Mother City. She was the heartbeat, the seat of worship of Jehovah God. Now Jesus is paying this visit, and this visit would mark the beginning of the end. Yet we must keep in mind that it was a new beginning also because Jesus would enter Jerusalem and he would be arrested. He would go to trial, and from trial to crucifixion. All this lay ahead after all there would come the Resurrection, Pentecost, the birth of the Church.

You would have to imagine Jesus taking His last journey into Jerusalem. Thousands upon thousands of people were gathered to celebrate the Passover, a Jewish celebration that God established in the book of Exodus. It would mark the deliverance of the children of Israel from Egyptian bondage - The Passover. They were to celebrate the Passover, and Jesus kept the traditions and the customs of his Jewish heritage. So, He is about to celebrate Passover with the disciples. The Crucifixion to be outside of Jerusalem in just days would become a symbol of the Passover. This suggests to us today, if we accept Jesus' death, His burial, and His resurrection, and if we would just look to the Cross of Calvary where He died for our sins, we too can pass from death unto life eternal. The triumphant entry of Jesus into Jerusalem is about to take place, and Jesus is preparing His twelve disciples.

Notice in the text the disciples, a colt or a donkey, and specific details. Jesus informs His disciples, "I want you to go and fetch me a colt and bring him to me." But also, we have to consider the crowd, because the crowd would be chanting praise and waving their palm branches. But better yet the children seemingly were wiser because they all ran and praised the Lord. Let's look at the colt in verses 2 through 7. Jesus gave the disciples some details or instructions saying, *"Go into the village over against you, and straightway ye shall find an ass tied, and a colt with her: loose them and bring them unto me. And if any man say ought unto you, ye shall say, The Lord hath need of them.* Jesus gave the disciples some instructions, strange details: *Go to the village, find the colt and ass, they are tied in the street, loose them, and bring them to me.* Look at the detail, the instructions. Then he says, "Now if you are questioned by anyone as to why you are *losing* the colt, tell them the Lord needs them."

I have a question there. Have you ever considered that you have something that the Lord wants or that the Lord needs? When I read the scriptures, I hear and I see so many things that the Lord wants, or He needs from us, or He requires of us. The Lord wanted a virgin by the name of Mary to be His mother. The Lord had need. He divested Himself of His eternity, His divinity and came through human flesh. He needed a human body, and Mary was needed. She was the chosen one to be the mother.

Jesus wanted twelve disciples to follow him to become learners. They would later spread the gospel into the world and turn the world upside down. He needed twelve men. So, He called twelve disciples. The Lord needed them because He knew He only had a short time on earth. He wanted Peter to feed the sheep of God and the lambs.

"Peter lovest thou me?"

"Yea Lord."
"Feed my sheep."
"Peter lovest thou me?"
"Yes, Lord I love you."
"Feed my lambs."
"Peter lovest thou me more than these?"
"Yes, Lord you know that I love you."
"Feed my sheep."

The Lord needed Peter.

He wanted Mary of Bethany to anoint His feet for burial. When others had indignation because she took that precious ointment and put it on Jesus' feet, disciples said to Jesus, "You should have taken this precious ointment and sold it and given the monies to the poor." But Jesus said, "The poor you will have with you always, but I will not be with you very long." And then Jesus says something else that is profound. He says that wherever this gospel is to be preached, "This woman is to be remembered for this act that she has performed upon me."

Jesus healed ten lepers. So, He wanted ten lepers to tell Him thank you. But only one returned after they were healed to tell the Lord thank you. The Lord needs somebody in the crowd this morning to tell the Lord thank You. Thank You for how He's been keeping us, shielding us from danger, disease, and whatever. I'm just talking about the Lord needed them. The Lord needs us.

He wanted Paul to preach the gospel to the Gentiles. He needed Paul. We have thirteen Epistles written by Paul because the Lord needed him.

Can I tell the Church, this morning, God wants a worshiping Church? God needs a worshiping Church amid the disease that the country and the world are experiencing - this new virus, coronavirus, many are calling "Rona". But God wants worship in the Church today. Even though many of us are not in the Church house, we can worship in our own houses. He's saying to us there hasn't been a whole lot of worship going on in our own home. The Lord says that He wanting to see some worship in our homes. He wants us to get back to some very basic things - prayer and worship at home. The old Warriors said it, "Charity starts at home and spreads abroad."

God wants a worshiping Church. God is saying to Pastors that I need you to preach the Gospel. What is the Gospel? It is the good news of Jesus Christ. Paul says *I am not ashamed of the Gospel for it is the Power of God unto salvation to everyone that believeth.* Preach the Gospel. There are several words in that word, 'preach'. There's the word 'preach', but then there is another word that says 'reach'. Then there's another word 'each'. We are to preach, reach, each. Preach Jesus, reach somebody. Everybody needs to hear the gospel.

I just believe in this dark period in the history of our world that God is saying you have left me out. You have not been looking in The Book. Too many of us have been on Facebook. We've got a Facebook page, but we have not looked at The Book which is the Bible. Everybody is seemingly on Facebook. It doesn't matter whether you are young or old. He's saying, "I can fix it now so everybody can hear the gospel. It won't be in the pulpit, but it may be on Facebook. Pastors, reach them through Facebook. They don't have Bibles, but they do have Facebook." Maybe, this is God's way of getting our attention to let us know, "I need you. Untie them. Bring them to me."

In our text Jesus wanted a donkey to carry him through the streets of Jerusalem. This donkey was important because it had not been used by another before. There are some people out there that are in the streets and the Lord is saying, "I want to use you. But the problem is you're tied up. Somebody got to *loose* them and bring them to me." The donkey had not gone through rough times. It was special because Jesus said, "It's been set aside for my use." This donkey had not gone through rigorous riding or tremendous work. He did not know anything about carrying rough loads, heavy loads, and rough times. He was innocent. But Jesus said, "I can use it because I need it."

Jesus wanted this donkey. He was able to use it for His glory. God wants to use us; he needs us for His glory. Regardless of who you are or what gifts or talents you may have, can I tell us that God has a special task just for us, for you and for me. God has use of us. We must have a willing mind and an obedient heart. Jesus says, "Whosoever will let him come." God wants a willing mind and obedient heart. In other words, obedient just means simply follow. Do what you are told. Do what's asked of you. Obedience, God has not asked a whole lot. God asks so little of us. God says, "Just lend me yourself. If you lend me yourself, you can bring Glory to me."

The Lord never requires more of us than we are able to do. What He does --- is to prepare and equip us for whatever we need to carry out His will faithfully, deliberately. All He wants is a willing and obedient heart and mind. Yes, I know we have failed. This is a time of reflection as to what we have not done that the Lord wanted done. All the Lord wants is a humble and low creature; humble, meek, a donkey that had not been used before. Humble. You don't have to be afraid. When I read this text, it says something so profound. Let me just share it with you. It says Jesus told these disciples to go to the village, untie this colt (this foal) and this ass. Then He says bring them. In other words, this little colt had a mother. Perhaps when unloosing the little colt, the colt perhaps would not have followed the disciples freely. So, Jesus is saying allow the donkey, the ass to come along. By her trotting alongside the little colt, it would cause the colt to feel that he is not alone. *I see my mother coming along with me.* He came humbly as a little low creature. If a lowly animal can be honored and used by Jesus, He can use me. He can use you.

He can use men and women of low position. You may have a bad background; however, God can use you. Society may use your background against you, but Jesus can forgive your background. All of us have been forgiven of our past. Don't allow your past to become an excuse for you not being used of God by saying, "God can't use me because I've done this." God says, "I can wipe clean. I can fix that. I can straighten that out." He fixed that at Calvary. He blotted out all our transgressions. I've been saved. I've been cleansed. I've been washed. I've been justified. Because I've been justified, who can condemn me? Nobody. Not only have I been justified by faith, but I've been justified by His blood. So, Jesus does not look at our backgrounds. God looks at us as being servants He can use. He can use you because the Lord needs all of us. He can forgive a background. Paul had a background. Paul hated Christ. Paul hated the Church. Paul hated the things that the Church stood for. But God said, "I need him to preach the gospel to the Gentiles."

Not only was the little colt humble, a low creature, but this colt was a symbol of peace. If a king came riding upon his stallion, guess what? That king was coming to wage war, to annihilate, to destroy not only humans, but infrastructure. But look at Jesus as He comes riding on this colt. This colt symbolizes peace. So, Jesus came riding on this low, humble creature, but He didn't come to wage war. He came with a peaceful solution. *I didn't come to destroy. But I come to fulfill all righteousness.* That's why Christ came on that little colt. The colt was a symbol of service. My brothers and sisters, all of us have some service in us. We can do what we each have been designed to do. No, we all can't do the same thing, but we all can render service and give the Lord ourselves.

Not only was the colt a symbol of service, peace, and humility, but it was also a symbol of sacredness. He had been set aside just for Jesus to ride upon. We are symbols of the colt. We are to be set aside to be used of God. Oh, it's wonderful to be used of God. Whatever we do for God, the songwriter says, *Only what you do for Christ will last*. All of this other stuff is temporal. Only what you do for Christ has lasting effect. It will take and follow us into eternity. However, before God can use any of us, we first got to be loosed. And you know what, as I look at the times in which we live and as I look at what we are experiencing, people never allowed themselves to become vessels that God could use or speak through. We were attached, we were tied to some things. We were tied to our jobs. We were tied to a man. We were tied to our money; we're tied to women. We just held on to that stuff and we couldn't give God the worship that he was due, the praise that he so richly deserved. God says, "Some of ya'll, I'm gonna put you off your job for a while. I'm gonna to *loosen* you. I'm gonna to loosen you from that man. I'm going to *loosen* you from the money."

What is it that you must be loosed from? Let me say this to our young people, and I hope they can hear me all over the world. We're going to have to be loosed from the streets. The streets are symbolic of places, some people, and some stuff. Some of you got some street buddies that you need to be loosed from. Some places you go, you must be loosed from. There are some people you must be loosed from. There is some stuff you must be loosed from. This is a wakeup call for the world. From heads of state, down to people who are in low places; from the highest to the lowest, you must be loosed. Jesus says, "I'm loosen you so I can use you."

So, when those who don't hear you ask you *why am I not seeing you anymore*? You can tell them, "I've been loosed from the streets. I've been loosed from some places. I've been loosed from some people. And I've been loosed from some stuff." They may ask, "Where have you been? I haven't seen you in a long time". "I've been loosed. I've been set free."

Last thing I want to speak to you about is The Crowd. We've talked about the colt. Let's talk about the crowd a little bit. When they had cut down the palm branches, the crowd spread their garments. The crowd, the multitude spread their clothing before Jesus. They placed the palm branches along the way. What did the crowd do? The crowd praised the Lord. That's what the crowd did. They praised the Lord. What were the sentiments of their praise? They chanted, "Hosanna to the son of David." Hosanna means save Lord, save now. Even in this season, in this time, this advent season as this event is happening in our country and in our world, I believe everybody where you are right now just ought to shout, "Hosanna! Save Lord! Save now!" That's what we ought to be shouting right now. "Save Lord! Save now! Change now Lord! Change some people! Change some minds! Change some hearts!" Their chanting continues. They say, "Blessed is he that cometh in the name of the Lord."

Notice now they pumped Jesus. These entire thirty plus years that Jesus had lived and walked among men, seemingly this is the first time, He ever received any praise or pump. All the other times He was talked about. They called Him a wine bibber. He was the prince of devils. They even said He wasn't the Son of God. They even said, " how could any good thing come out of Nazareth? Who is He? Who does He think he is? We see in our text that this is the only time He is really getting some praise, or He's being lifted and pumped up. "Blessed is he that cometh in the name of the Lord! Hosanna! Save Lord! Save Now!" Listen to all that emotion. Listen to all of that enthusiasm.

Let me say something else about crowds. Crowds can become fickle sometimes. They become fickle in their praise. Same crowd, same folks. The same folks that said *blessed is he that cometh in the name of the Lord, blessed is he that come the Son of David,* the same fickle crowd that gave the praise soon turned praise into jeers. Soon the blessing became boos. Soon the crowd started chanting not save Lord, but "Crucify Him.

Get rid of him. Get him out of here." It isn't always the crowd. Jesus didn't pay attention to the crowd. The people were moved with what they saw. And those who were bystanders saw this entourage of cheers and blessings coming. The question was asked, "Who is this?" And somebody in the multitude said, "Y'all don't know who this is? This is Jesus. The prophet of Nazareth, of Galilee."

Notice they had said earlier in His life *how can any good thing come out of Nazareth?* But now they are saying, "This is the prophet of Nazareth of Galilee. That's who he is." But they really didn't' know who he was. This is God's only Son. This is Jesus. This is the Lamb of God. This is the Savior of the World. This is *Jehovah-jireh*. This is *Jehovah-nissi*. This is *Jehovah-shalom*. This is the Sovereign God.

CALL TO DISCIPLESHIP

If you are out there today and you don't know the Lord as your personal Savior, this is a good time for you to come to the realization that Jesus does exist. He is real. Just believe that He is the Son of God. Just believe that He died for your sins. If you can confess your sins, God is faithful and just to forgive you of your sins and cleanse you from all unrighteousness. Right where you are you ought to ask the Lord into your life. Say Lord come into my life save me. I'm sorry for my sins. Forgive me and give me eternal life. And you know what? He comes in at the snap of a finger. *That if thou shalt confess with thy mouth the Lord Jesus, and shalt believe in thine heart that God hath raised him from the dead, thou shall be saved. With the mouth confession is made unto salvation.* If you can pray that and ask God, you are saved. And as soon as we get back into Church or Church houses, you can come and make a public profession of faith that you received Him, and then from there to baptism and from baptism you are a part of the family of God.

This is my message to you today. I'm not at the pulpit of St. Mark, but I am in the confines of my own home. I'm locked in. I'm locked down. I've got my own keys in my pocket. I'm locked in, but I'm not locked out of the Church. God bless you today.

On Wednesday night, join me for Bible Study. We are going to use our Sunday School material. We don't want our Sunday School material to go to waste because it looks like we are going to be in the house for a while. We're going to study our Sunday School lessons and get use of our books. So, join me on Wednesday between 6:30 and 7. I just want thirty minutes of your time. I'll try to get through it, but y'all know that time and I don't get along. So, if you will, use your Sunday School material for our Bible Study.

As we prepare now for another selection, I hope you will enjoy this next selection. Come on Sis. Jarrett.

SELECTION

Thank You, Lord by Judy Marshall of the Marshall Family

CLOSING REMARKS

Thank You Lord. Thank You Lord. Somebody out there ought to give Him a big hand clap of praise and say Thank You. Lord.

You can't have worship without giving. We encourage our members to use Givelify. If you want to mail your gift to the: St Mark Missionary Baptist Church, P.O. Box 493, Henning, TN 38041. Some of you have been so wonderful in your contributions, and we want you to continue, as long as the Lord blesses you.

The Lord is doing great things even in these tough times. So, I want to say to my members, be safe, and put your mask on. Wash your hands. And if you don't have to go anywhere stay at home, so that this Corona Virus can get out of our communities, our nation, and our world; so that life can get back to a sense of normalcy. But it's going to take all of us working together. So, I encourage our young people, stay away from each other. Stay six feet apart. We don't want anybody to become affected by this dreadful disease. So be obedient, and we all will get along. As we prepare to close out today's worship experience, I hope and pray that you have been blessed. I pray that you have been uplifted. I pray that you have been challenged through today's message. I just bid you God speed; and I want to say to St. Mark and to the community, and to all of the people who are listening to me from all over the country, I am proud of you, I love you, and you can't do one iota about it.

CLOSING PRAYER

The Lord Bless you and keep you, The Lord make His face to shine upon you, and be gracious unto you. The Lord lifts up the light of His countenance upon you and gives you peace both now and forever. And let all the people of God say Amen.

Who Will Roll the Stone Away?
Sunday, April 12, 2020

OPENING REMARKS

Good morning, St. Mark! Good morning, Faith Community! Happy Easter Day, Happy Easter to all the children out there that are listening to us this morning. To all our friends around the country who have been giving me a thumbs up saying that they have been watching and they are enjoying our services. We are glad you can join us from so many parts of our Country. This is a celebrated day. We celebrate a Risen Savior who triumphed over death, hell, and grave and declared He has all power in His hand. My Brothers and Sisters that call for celebration right where you are you ought to just give the Lord a great big Amen or a hand clap of praise. This is a joyous time. This is a joyous season to know that we serve a Risen Savior. We're not in the Church house. We're in our homes, and we thank God that the Word can continue to go out in-spite of where we are. This is my second time ever in my ministry that I have not been in Easter worship.

Let me tell you the first time that I was out of the Church house at Easter. I remember it very vividly as if it were yesterday. In 1991, I was in Desert Storm serving our country, and I was there on Easter. And you know what? We had Easter service in the desert. I had a great audience that morning, members of the 95th MP Brigade out of Germany. We had the 93rd MP Brigade that was there, the 705 out of Puerto Rico, and 268 MP Company. I tell you we had a mass worship in the desert. It was not just only on Easter, but it was every day. We had devotion, and I was blessed to serve the young men and women from all those units while even at war. And even as we are at war now, we're not at Church on Easter, but guess what? We're still having Church. This is my second time, but we're still having Church, even from our homes. My brothers and my sisters, this is a great time to be alive in-spite of.

WORDS OF ENCOURAGEMENT

Let me just share a word of encouragement with you before we move directly into our morning worship. There is a passage of scripture found in Jeremiah Chapter 29:11. And this is how the passage reads:

> *For I know the thoughts that I think toward you saith the Lord. Thoughts of peace, and Not of evil. To give an expected end.*

The Lord promised the people that His plans for them were not to harm them, not to do them evil. God gives to them to understand that His love was moved toward them to bring them peace and prosperity. Know that God's plan offered them a bright ray of hope for their future. If the people placed their trust in the Lord, He would deliver them from their captivity in Babylon and return them to the Promised Land, to their normal way of life, their normal routines. That was God's promise to them. You see God could have promised them no greater hope and a future than to bring them back to their native home and to give them peace and not evil. We all are encouraged by our leaders who stir us to move ahead. Someone who believes we can do the task that He has given to us, and who will be with us always. God is that kind of leader. He knows the future, and He has a plan for us. And that plan is a good plan. And that plan is full of hope. God who knows the future has already provided an agenda; and that agenda goes with us as we fulfill the plan that He has given to us. We can have endless hope in spite of. This does not mean that we will be spared pain, suffering, or a few hardships along the way. But the God that we serve will see us through to a glorious end. This is my encouragement to you this morning as we prepare now for worship.

CALL TO WORSHIP

The Lord is in His holy temple, Let the earth be silent before Him. Holy! Holy! Holy! The Lord God Almighty! Early in the morning our song shall rise to Thee. Holy! Holy! Holy! Merciful and Mighty; God in three Persons, blessed Trinity.

At this time, Sis. Jarrett is going to come and open with a beautiful song, and we pray that this song will be a blessing to you as you listen to it. Let's start our worship. God Bless.

SELECTION

He Looked Beyond My Faults and Saw My Needs – Lyrics by Dottie Rambo (Tune Oh Danny Boy)

Thank you, Sis. Jarrett for that beautiful number. I'm so glad that Jesus looked beyond my faults and saw my needs. The Lord will meet our needs, even in difficult times. When we were yet in our sins, God sent His Son to meet our needs. He knew that we needed so great a salvation. And my brothers and sisters, let us prepare now to move to the Throne of Grace to lift up prayer before Our Almighty God who is able to do that which is exceedingly, abundantly above all that we can imagine or think. Amen.

OPENING PRAYER

Dear Heavenly Father I come to you at this moment in time to say *Lord have thine own way. Lord have thine own way. You are the potter. I am the clay. Mold me and make me after thy will, while I am waiting yielded and still. What is man that thou art mindful of him and the Son of man that thou visiteth him for thou hast made him a little lower than the angels and has crowned him with glory and honor.*

Dear God, today we place at thy feet, by the Throne of Grace, the problems of this world for there are many: sickness, death, hunger, pain, fear, mental challenges, and joblessness. Lord your people want to know when is it going to get better? Many people feel like motherless children in a strange land.

But God we will not lose faith in you because you are from everlasting to everlasting. You're the beginning and the end; you're the first and the last. So, God we pray today that you will stabilize your people's worry. Calm their nerves as we walk through these dismal days. Teach us to build our hopes on things eternal and to hold to your unchanging hand. You alone, Oh God, have all power, you alone are all knowing, and you alone are everywhere at the same time. Touch them now in the name of Jesus. We bless you now for you *are able to do that which is exceedingly, abundantly above all that we can imagine or think.*

We thank you for your victory today, your victory over death and the grave. You alone --- defeated it --- all! Now we your people have the same victory through Jesus; so, all of us today can sing Victory is Mine! Victory today is Mine!

While we pray Oh God, we pray that you keep your hands upon our leaders and those who are working in the medical field. We pray today for nations around the world for we're suffering. But God we know that you've got all power in your hand, and we know when you move everything is going to be alright.

Oh God as I come on this Easter Sunday morning to speak your word, speak Oh Lord through these clay lips. Hide me behind the Cross that your Son, Jesus may shine forth. When we will have finished this worship today, we will know that we have been revived. For it's in the precious and the promising name of our Christ that we pray with thanksgiving. And all the people of God said Amen, Amen. Thank You Jesus.

TODAY'S SERMON

As we make ready to move into the Word, I want to call your attention to the Gospel that is recorded by St. Mark, Chapter 16, Verses 1 through 10. Here is what the passage reads:

1. *And when the sabbath was past, Mary Magdalene, and Mary the mother of James, and Salome, had bought sweet spices, that they might come and anoint him.*

2. *And very early in the morning the first day of the week, they came unto the sepulchre at the rising of the sun.*

3. *And they said among themselves, Who shall roll us away the stone from the door of the sepulchre?*

4. *And when they looked, they saw that the stone was rolled away: for it was very great.*

5. *And entering into the sepulchre, they saw a young man sitting on the right side, clothed in a long white garment; and they were affrighted.*

6. *And he saith unto them, Be not affrighted: Ye seek Jesus of Nazareth, which was crucified: he is risen; he is not here: behold the place where they laid him.*

7. *But go your way, tell his disciples and Peter that he goeth before you into Galilee: there shall ye see him, as he said unto you.*

8. *And they went out quickly, and fled from the sepulchre: for they trembled and were amazed: neither said they anything to any man: for they were afraid.*

9. *Now when Jesus was risen early the first day of the week, he appeared first to Mary Magdalene, out of whom he had cast seven devils.*

10. *And she went and told them that had been with him, as they mourned and wept.*

My subject this morning is in the form of a question, and it comes directly from the text. **Who Will Roll the Stone Away?**

We live in an exciting time, but it is a critical Church age. It is a time of great opportunity and possibilities. Yet, it is a time of spiritual decline and a falling away from God. But I got good news for you this morning. Our risen Savior has created a Resurrection story that is good for critical times, and it will never grow old. His story is renewed in every sermon, in every prayer, and every song. It is renewed in every born- again soul that believes on the name of Jesus. But wherever we see a Church that is dedicated to the worship of Christ, it ought to remind us of the resurrected power of Jesus. For it has brought salvation and hope to millions, and it will continue to bring salvation to millions or more. It's a story that has never changed, though it is not fully understood by many, yet it gives faith and hope and stability to mankind in every generation. It matters not what the nation or the people are going through.

The resurrection of Jesus from the dead serves as proof of God and that God was pleased and totally satisfied with what was accomplished at Calvary. My Brothers and Sisters what happened at Calvary, it paid the price of our redemption. Jesus paid that price with His blood. But His resurrection also means that the Church does not worship a dead Savior on a cross, or in a tomb. But rather a risen resurrected Savior who has now been seated at the right hand of the Father. He is interceding for us right now. Even in midst of difficulty He's interceding for us. I want you to know this morning, somebody is praying for you. But better yet, Jesus said in John 14: 19 *Because I live you shall also live.* And I believe that He meant for us to live now and not in the hereafter. We need to be living now. Living now, don't be afraid to live. Do not wait until I get over there and say I'm living the life. I want to live now. And then I want to live then once we reach our eternal abode. The Lord intends for His Church, for His people who are called by His name to become revived, renewed by His power, the power of God.

The problem is --- my brothers and sisters, we just got to be loosed. We got to be loosed like Lazarus who laid in the grave for four days. Jesus came to Lazarus grave and called him up and told him to rise-up. Come forth. My Brothers and Sisters, we just got to rise-up and live. We got to continue to live and not die. What do we need to rise-up out of? We need to rise-up this morning out of our discouragement, rise-up out of our doubts and our fears. Jesus wants us to rise-up out of our tomb of idleness. We've been idle too long. Jesus is saying to us, "You need to rise, get up, come back, get involved in the Kingdom building and Kingdom work. Rise out of the tomb of death into life." In John 10:10 Jesus says *I come that you might have life, and that you might have it more abundantly.* That's what Jesus came for; to give us life. Then there is another individual He points out in the same verse and text. *But the thief comes but to steal, kill, and to destroy.* He wants to destroy us. But I come by to tell us this morning choose life. Choose Jesus. Choose Jesus.

Something else He's telling us. He's telling us that we desperately need to come out of the tomb of defeat into victory. That's what Jesus did on that third day. He came out the tomb of defeat into the victory. We need victory today. How many of us are willing to come out of our tomb of defeat? The enemy thinks we're defeated, but I come to serve notice on the enemy this morning we're not defeated. We're serving a victorious God, and He has given us the victory also.

Something else about Lazarus and Jesus, Lazarus came out of his grave wrapped in his grave clothes. Jesus said to those grave attendants *loose him, let him go.* Jesus got out of the grave. He left the grave clothes, not that the grave clothes could hinder Him. He wanted to leave the grave clothes for those who would come behind looking for a dead Savior, and they would discover the grave clothes and say, "He's not here. There are the grave clothes."

Jesus wants us to *lose* some stuff. He wants us to pull off some stuff that hinders us: everything that would confine us, everything that would limit us, everything that would hinder us from fulfilling God's purpose in our lives. My brothers and my sisters, we don't need anything or any person to hinder or retard our spiritual growth, nor our worship of God. When we sing, when we pray, or even when we preach, we don't need any hindrances. We do these things because we have been crucified with Christ. We have been raised with Christ. How? In the power of His resurrection. I'm glad I've been raised with Christ.

As we look deeper into this text this morning notice in the text the early visitors. Mary Magdalene, Mary, and Salome were about to give their last ounce of devotion to the Lord. They loved the Lord. They trusted the Lord. Nothing could stop them or hinder them from loving the Lord, even in life and even in death. Calvary and the crucifixion had not destroyed their love for Jesus. He left on record before Calvary that He would be killed and in three days He would rise again.

But notice these women. Here they are, bearing spices to anoint a dead body. And as the women went toward the tomb that morning, their minds were filled with problems that they faced. Maybe somebody out there this morning mind is filled with the problems they face as Mary, Mary Magdalene, and Salome. They thought they had a problem. You look at the text closely. It says that they thought about the heavy stone that was in front of the tomb. They asked the questions, "How are we going to remove the stone and anoint Jesus' body? Who will roll the stone away?" Little did they know that God had already taken care of that situation. Sometimes we worry about stuff…How are we going to do this? How are we going to make it? Who is going to do this for us? God has already gone ahead of us and made the way, paved the way for us, yet we have all of these questions in the back of our mind. First, you should have known in advance that Jesus said, "They are going to kill me, they are going to crucify me. But in three days I'm going to get up."

They should have been anticipating a Christ that was already risen. But they were going to anoint a dead body and asking questions along the way, "How are we going to roll that stone away? Who will roll it away for us? It's too heavy for us. We can't handle it." But our God is able to handle what is too big, too heavy for us to handle. My Brothers and Sisters this is how we are in these times in which we live. We go along looking at our problems, which are not ours to handle in the first place. And you know we always looking for the ones we have, and then we are looking for the ones that we are expecting to have, failing to realize God has already solved it. This situation we that we find ourselves in on this Resurrection morning, can I tell you God has already got it solved. I don't know when, I don't know how He's going to do it, but I do know this, He's got it solved.

To their amazement, Mary, and the others, when they arrived at the tomb, discovered the tomb not to be a place where Jesus' body remains. They discovered the tomb to not be a place of death, but a place of life. It wasn't a place of death. It was a place of life. They discovered that Jesus is not dead. He's alive. He's up. Matter of fact, He's gone. Now *they're* discovering something else. It is not a place of despair. Now it has become a place of hope. Look at all that discovery this morning at the tomb where Jesus once laid. Let me tell you something else *they* found when they got there. They found the tomb to be a place of comfort. *They* found comfort. How do you know *they* found comfort, Reverend? I'm glad you asked. The angel said to them, "Be not afraid." Isn't that comforting? Isn't that comforting when you've been told don't be afraid? Don't be afraid. That's comfort. And then he goes on to say, after he tells them be not afraid, he says, "I know who you are seeking. You seek Jesus who was crucified. He is risen. He is not here. Look where He laid."

Can I tell you something else *they* found? *They* found it to be a place of hope. The hope was the stone was rolled away. Resurrection is not just a promise. But it's a fact. It's a fact. It's a fact that Jesus lives, and it's a place of hope. It's a time of hope. It's a time of comfort. It's a time not to despair. This is not a time of death. But this is a time of hope for all of us.

There are so many things these women found. And as I come to a close, there are several more things they found at the tomb. At the tomb the women found new power. They found a new outlook. *Y'all,* hear that. They found new power. They found new energy. The energy now is that you've got a task, you've got a new vision, and you've got a new outlook on Kingdom building, Kingdom work. They had a task to perform. The angel says to these women He's not here. See where He laid. Now that you have a new-found discovery, you got a new outlook, and you have new energy, go and pass that new look, new outlook, that new energy to some fellows. Tell the disciples. Tell the ones that you know best. Tell the disciples, but not only the disciples but specifically tell Peter that Jesus is gone before you into Galilee. Now! *Y'all* go see Him. Go see Him. Go see Him. Go see Him.

We must start to roll away the stone which hides Jesus from the world. We must start to roll away the stone which hides Jesus from the world. How can we Reverend roll away the stone that hides Jesus? What do we have? Well tell others what you saw when Jesus gave you a new heart. Go tell somebody. Go tell the story of how He *ros- up* in your life, gave you a new hope, gave you a new power, and gave you a new outlook. Now you got to go tell somebody. Tell the ones that you know the best.

Maybe it needs to start right now as we are on lockdown in our own houses. Maybe we need to start right at home. Isn't that what Jesus said to the twelve when He gave them the Commission? Go to Jerusalem first, go home. And once you get home right spread out a little bit. Go to Judea and outer regions. Better yet, then go to the folks that you have issues with, the Samaritans. Tell them, they need to know. And then don't stop there, go to the uttermost parts of the world. We got to tell somebody that Jesus is alive. Tell them just how you felt when His love came into your life, and gave you hope, and gave you glory. Tell those who are yet in their sins that God can roll the stone away from their hearts, and allow Jesus to *ris- up* and come in.

We must roll away the stone by telling what we have heard as Jesus shows up in our lives every day. He *rose-up* in me right early this morning, and I just come to tell somebody this morning He's been good to me. He watched over me last night. He dispatched His angels around the corners of my room and house. Yes, He watched over me. But not only did He watch over me, He awakened me this morning. He has given me new life and new vision. Most of all, we must show the change that's in our lives. Now that we have all of this, we must show that a change is in our lives. And how do we show a change in our lives? We show the change by the way we live each day. By the way we live, by the way we give, and the way we talk, that shows the change that is in us. I'm not what I use to be. And all of us can just shout right now and say Thank God I'm not what I use to be. A change has come over me. Oh, what a wonderful change that has come. Thank God that the stone was rolled away. Now we've just got to tell somebody.

Easter is a good time to proclaim the good news of Jesus Christ. Proclaim that the author and finisher of our faith is alive. Regardless to what the critics, the skeptics, the atheists, and whomever else that are out there, we've got to tell them He is alive. Even the doubters, we've got to tell them. We've got to declare that He is alive.

We've got to tell those that are out there that Resurrection Sunday is more than a springtime holiday, with Easter bunnies, Easter rabbits, or Easter candy, and all that good stuff. We've got to tell somebody that Resurrection Sunday is more than a time of just fun and fellowship. It is deeper than that. It's deeper than that. It's because our Savior lives, and He lives in us. Resurrection Sunday is more than dressing in a suit and a brand-new dress and attending Church. Many of us are not in the Church house. We're not dressed up with our Easter frock, but we're dressed up on the inside. We're fixed up because Christ has dressed us up with his Holy Power.

Maybe God is trying to tell us something on this Easter. Maybe God wants us to come back and see that Resurrection Sunday is the foundation or the foundational truth that distinguishes Christians or Christianity from all the other hoopla that we hear from all angles. Resurrection Sunday is the foundational truth. I stand on it because that's where my hope lies. Paul says I don't want to know anything among you except the power of Christ's Resurrection. The power of His resurrection. The power of His resurrection. And my brothers and sisters, as I get ready to leave you, we owe it all to Jesus. I said we owe it all to Jesus. And I'm so glad that Jesus thought enough of me that He would give His life for my sins.

CALL TO DISCIPLESHIP

I don't know who is listening out there, but there may be someone listening nearby, far away, that has not met this risen Savior, Jesus. I want to offer Him to you today. I want to tell somebody that He can save anybody. If you're out there today and you have not accepted Christ as your Savior, you're living in your sins, let me say to you now, salvation is free. It doesn't cost you anything but a contrite, broken heart. That's all it cost you. Just feel sorry for your sins, believe, and come to know that loves God you. But He wants to save you, to give you His saving grace and mercy.

If you would, just right where you are, say, "Lord I'm a sinner. I need saving. Lord, come into my heart. Cleanse me. Wash me thoroughly. I'm sorry for my sins. I believe that you died for my sins, and that you were buried, and you were raised the third day with all power in your hand. I believe that in my heart."

If you can confess it and believe in your heart, you can be saved right where you are. Ask Him now, and watch my God move swiftly into your heart. He said today if you hear my voice, He said I will come into your heart and save you. Today is the day of salvation. Now is the time. Now is the acceptable time. We don't know when the Lord might come and call us. We don't know when our number is up. But one thing for sure, I'm fixed up right now. I'm fixed up. God bless you. Thank you so kindly.

At this time, we're going to ask my lovely wife to come back once more and bless you with a number. And I'll come back and close us out.

SELECTION

Jesus **by Shekinah Glory**

CLOSING REMARKS

Come let us give the Lord a hand clap of praise right where you are. What a beautiful number. Thank God for Jesus. Jesus! It's just Jesus *y'all.* It's just Jesus.

This has been a glorious moment for me. My heart is just rejoicing. I tell you I miss you guys, and I pray that we all can come together real soon where this kind of worship will continue. We can look at each other eyeball to eyeball. That's what I'm praying and hoping for in the very, very, very near future.

Well, just let me make my morning appeal again. We have **Givelify** at our Church. Many of you have been giving through **Givelify**. We appreciate all your giving. Those of you have even mailed some of your tithes and offering to the Church, we encourage you to continue so that things can continue to move swiftly.

I want to say to all my friends around the country, Detroit – and I might mess up trying to name all the cities, towns, rural far and near. You know who I'm talking about. We've had calls from so many. We've had correspondence – mail. We've had so many people I didn't know. They know St. Mark now. They know Pastor Jarrett. I've had friends from the Convention that have been watching us, they have shared how they have been truly blessed by the messages shared over the last few weeks, and for this I am truly grateful.

My Brothers and Sisters, I want you to remember that Wednesday night is Bible Study. We're going to utilize our Sunday School material, and we will see you then. So, allow me now to come forth with the Benediction. Then we will have a little music to take us on out. Amen.

CLOSING PRAYER

And now the Lord will bless you, and keep you, the Lord make His face to shine upon you, and be gracious unto you, the Lord lifts the light of His countenance upon you, and give you peace both now and forever, God Bless. Have a great rest of this Resurrection Sunday together. Be Blessed. Stay safe. Obey the rules. Wash your hands.

A Life Lesson in the Wilderness
Sunday, April 19, 2020

OPENING REMARKS

Anybody out there holding on to God's unchanging hand? Oh, I thank God this morning that He has an unchanging hand. Good morning Church, Family and Community. Good morning around the country. Good morning around the world. It's good to be alive, and to know it. That's so important to be alive and know it. I'm glad to be on top of planet Earth, and planet Earth is not on top of me.

I am excited to be a witness on this Post-Resurrection Sunday. Last Sunday was an exciting day. We celebrated Easter, and I just know that messages that came forth from Church Pastors and leaders, letting the Saints know that we yet serve a risen and living Savior. As I was looking back over this week and thinking about all the great things that God has done through the Resurrection story, I was reading in Matthew's account in Chapter 28. The scripture says after Jesus' Resurrection, the eleven disciples went away to a mountain where Jesus had appointed them. The Bible says that when they saw Him, guess what they did? They worshipped. They worshipped Him. But some, the scripture says, doubted. This is not a time of doubting. This is a time for worshipping, and wherever God has appointed you to meet Him, as He appointed the disciples to meet Him in this mountain area. Wherever God appoints you to meet Him then worship Him. Worship Him. Even if it's on a mountain top, or it may be in the valley low, worship Him. And many of us are in our homes this morning, even right where you are in your home, worship Him.

Now this season we find ourselves in today, is not a time for doubting or procrastinating. It's time to learn what it means to worship God, in spite of… in spite of inclement weather… in spite of a pandemic virus. Just worship and praise God even in midst of. Know that this is a season of praise, worship, and thanksgiving.

WORDS OF ENCOURAGEMENT

Now I have a word of encouragement for you this morning. And there is a passage of scripture that is found in 1 Peter 5:7. We all quote it so often. It says *Casting all of your care upon him; for he careth for you.*

Now there are interesting words in this passage. The first word 'cast'. What does cast mean? Cast means to throw. It means to hurl. It means to abandon or to toss something away that you no longer need or want. Simply, it's saying to us whatever it is, whatever that something is, get rid of it. Cast it away. You have nothing else to do with it. Instead of trying to deal with it, throw it away. It's of no use.

Now, the word care means, also, anxiety, stress, distractions, and worry. It suggests the kinds of thoughts that trouble us or keep us from a peace of mind. There is nothing like a piece of mind. You know what, Jesus used this word also. He used it when He said to His disciples *take no thought or be anxious for your life*. It's in Matthew 6:25. That says to us what worry does. God aims to take from our backs, and He places it upon himself. He will carry it for us. So, He is saying to us there is no need for you to worry. There's no need for you to be anxious for your life. I've got this, give it to me. My brothers and sisters, cast, hurl, abandon whatever that something is, and allow the Lord Himself to carry it, because He cares for us. Aren't you glad this morning He cares? Which means not just today, but He cares about your life from birth through death. He cares. There isn't ever a time that God is not caring. This is my encouragement to you this morning. Amen.

CALL TO WORSHIP

So, God bless you. And we're going to move further into this worship experience today. I'm looking for a great worship and we know the Word of God is so relevant for our time. I don't care whatever else we do. If we don't hear from God, then we don't have all that we need to complete our worship. The worship is the apex, and the preaching of the Word is the apex of worship.

We're going to ask Sis. Jarrett to come and lead us in song. And we'll come back, and we will share with your further in this worship experience. So, at this time, let's give Him a hand clap of praise right where you are. You have hands. Put them together. If you're happy and you know it, clap your hands.

SELECTION

I Love You Lord Today **by Edwin Hawkins**

My heart is filled with praise on this beautiful Sunday morning. Let us now go to the Throne of Grace and seek God's presence, power, and provision in our lives for this moment. Let us pray.

OPENING PRAYER

Most Gracious God, Our Father, Creator, Sustainer of all living things, we come now humble with a submissive spirit. We come seeking your forgiveness of sin. We confess that we have not always done your will. We come to say that we love you. We love you for who you are. And we bless your name. We don't have anything or own anything to bless you with, because you are everything and you own everything, *the Earth is yours and the fullness thereof.* All I have, and all we all have we owe it to you. You want our praise and worship. For you alone deserve our heart, our soul, our minds, and strength.

Thank You Lord for all things. And we pray that you give us this day our daily bread. And Lord while we pray, we pray for the sick, the shut-in, the hospitalized and all places and manner of sickness, all over the land and country. We pray for those that are suffering for their lives. I heard you say in scripture, *there is a Balm in Gilead to heal the sin sick soul. There is a Balm in Gilead to make the wounded whole.* Lord, we heard the prophet say in the Word, *but they that wait upon the Lord shall renew their strength; they shall mount up on wings as eagles, they shall run and not be weary, walk and not faint.* So, we pray today that you lift-up those broken in spirit. Deal with them gently in their worn and torn bodies. We pray today that you meet every soul's need: the hungry, the least, and the left out.

Lord, there is death all over our world, even in our communities. Bless families that have lost loved ones, look on the families as they experience bereavement. And then God I pray that you keep our Church family. Keep our Church community. We ask that you bless every need. Comfort everyone.

We pray that you continue to lift the leaders of our nation and our cities. Keep our medical personnel healthy as they minister to others: police officers, firemen. Lord we just pray for everybody. Bless our pastors, our leaders who lead in their specific churches. We pray for their strength. We pray that you continue to minister to them that they may continue to minister to your flock.

And God we pray today, that all I've asked you will grant it. And God we will forever give your name praise and glory. Amen.

TODAY'S SERMON

Thank you. And as we make ready now to move into the Word, we pray that our message for today will be a blessing to you today and onward. There's a passage that is found in the Old Testament in the book of Exodus, Exodus Chapter 16. And I want us to give Verses 1 through 8 our attention. Here are the verses:

1. *And they took their journey from Elim, and all the congregation of the children of Israel came unto the wilderness of Sin, which is between Elim Sinai, on the fifteenth day of the second month after their departing out of the land of Egypt.*

2. *And the whole congregation of the children of Israel murmured against Moses and Aaron in the wilderness.*

3. *And the children of Israel said unto them, Would to God we had died by the hand of the Lord in the land of Egypt, when we sat by the flesh pots ,and when we did eat bread to the full; for ye have brought us forth into this wilderness to kill this whole assembly with hunger.*

4. *Then said the Lord unto Moses, Behold, I will rain bread from heaven for you; and the people shall go out and gather a certain rate every day, that I may prove them, whether they will walk in my law, or no.*

5. *And it shall come to pass, that on the sixth day they shall prepare that which they bring in; and it shall be twice as much as they gather daily.*

6. *And Moses and Aaron said unto all the children of Israel, At even, then ye shall know that the Lord hath brought you out from the land of Egypt:*

7. *And in the morning, then ye shall see the glory of the Lord; for that he heareth your murmurings against the Lord: and what are we, that ye murmur against us?*

> *8. And Moses said, This shall be, when the Lord shall give you in the evening flesh to eat, and in the morning bread to the full; for that the Lord heareth your murmurings which ye murmur against him: and what are we? Your murmurings are not against us, but against the Lord.*

From these verses this morning I want to talk from this subject: **A Life Lesson in the Wilderness.**

There are serious challenges in life that impact us from day to day. There are all types of challenges that come against who we believe in, why we believe in and what we believe in. We are challenged by Satan. We are challenged by problems. We are challenged by things. However, the seriousness of the challenge that comes at us to impact us from day to day, there is often one experience after another. Many times, we don't have time to rest, to adjust ourselves or collect our thoughts for the next event because the challenges just keep on coming one after another.

When I was a young boy, I would hear older people talk about things that happened in the community and around the world. Challenging and mind-blowing things. And they could not wrap their mind around things that were happening, nor could they make sense of the effect it may have or had on people. But this is what I would hear them say as a result of the challenges and the situations. They would say it like this: *if it ain't one thing, it's another*. My Brothers and Sisters while life seems to impose upon us experiences that we didn't ask for, we forget that God is just setting us up, to instruct us, and to remind us that He is the Lord. He is the Lord.

That word Lord in the Hebrew means Yeshua! Yehovah! From Yehovah, we get the word Jehovah. Jehovah means *The Existing One*. Jehovah is the proper name of the one and only true God. He's the Lord. God is trying to remind us that He is Lord. He's Lord over everything.

Now in the Greek it means *Kyrios* which suggests to us that God is Lord over all. We cannot become the Lord of our own lives. If you are on the throne of your life, ruling and reigning, let me ask you to do me one favor. Step off the throne of your life and allow the Lord to mount the throne that is in your life because He is boss. He's Lord over everything. He is Lord of Lords. He is King of Kings. And this is what the prophet Moses is trying to convey to the children of Israel this morning. He is Lord. He's *The Existing One*. He's Jehovah. That's His true name. Jehovah. Israel needed to understand that. And my brothers and sisters, we need to understand that even in our time in which we live. We need to realize, recognize that God is Lord. He is Lord.

Upon God's delivering of the children of Israel from Egyptian's bondage, He led them into the wilderness. The text says the wilderness of sin. The wilderness of sin, He led them. He's taking them to a place. Where's He taking them? He's taking them to a land of promise. He's taking them to their inheritance. And God had made this promise to their forefathers. He made this promise or covenant with Abraham, Isaac, and Jacob that He would lead His people into a land of promise. As He was leading them through this wilderness the text implies to us that God was testing them. God was proving to them that He is God. He is Lord. He is *The Existing One*.

But in the thick of things, as they lodged in the wilderness, some things happened. Some challenges came to impact them. What was the challenge? The challenge was their food and water supply ran out. They were hungry and thirsty. But look what happened in the text. They started to murmur and to complain over the fact that they did not have water or food to eat. They started looking back at their slave days when they received their daily rations from the flesh pots. They remembered the way things were there. But they could not recognize where God was taking them. They started complaining and murmuring. We often move from one complaint to another but listen to this; we forget who has the last word about all circumstances. God was about to teach a life lesson in the wilderness.

This lesson taught that the wilderness was meant to cause them three things. These are three outlines of the lesson that I want to share with you from this text this morning. The first lesson that was taught in the wilderness was 'to **believe God's promises**.' Believe in His promises to us. Do you think God brought them out of bondage into this wilderness of sin to destroy them and cause His promise to Abraham, Isaac, and Jacob to be null? God does not renege on his promises to us. Never would God renege. God stands on His promise. Can I share this with you? The promises of God are 'Yes and Amen'. All that the Lord gave to Moses and the children of Israel for the journey after the deliverance was promises. All Israel had to do was to say, 'Yes and Amen, Amen Lord'. *Amen* means so be it. Whatever you say Lord, that's what I'll believe…that's what I'll do. Amen.

I'm taking you to an inheritance. I'm taking you to houses you didn't build, I'm taking you to trees you didn't plant, wells full, and vines that you didn't plant. I'm taking you somewhere. This is just a test to see how you will view me in your circumstances. Will you depend upon me? The thing for the believers, in our walk with the Lord and desire, is better life.

The better life hinges on the promises of God without murmuring, and without complaining, and without asking why or an explanation for the things that the Lord does. Just trust my promise to you. We may never be able to explain how or when God gets ready to do what he promises. All I know is that we can trust Him to do it. God says, "I will make a way for you. I will supply all of your needs. I will make your enemies leave you alone. I'll never forsake you or leave you alone. I will heal you." These are the promises of God. All we need to do is say, 'Yes and Amen'. But you know what? Despite their complaining God responded with His grace and mercy. Thank Him for mercy, not murmuring and complains. The first lesson is to believe His promises.

The second thing I want to lift from this passage this morning: **experience His provision**. Believe the promise. But experience His provision. Do understand what God promised them is a miraculous provision not for their complaining. They didn't deserve it. But He did it anyway. We need to see that what God does for any of us we don't deserve it. And I'm glad He keeps on doing what He does. But what He does for me and I'm sure you feel the same way this morning. I don't deserve what God is doing for me in this season and in this time. He's supplying my needs, He's making a way, and He's keeping my enemies back. He's not forsaken me; He has not left me alone in this thing by myself. I'm glad He keeps on blessing me. And I just keep on experiencing His provisions for me.

Yes, they're in the wilderness. And you know the wilderness is a dry place. Nothing grows there. But can I tell us this morning that God can allow us to come to our dry places only where He and He alone can provide and work miracles for us. And I've seen God work in places where it seems like nothing will prevail. Thank God that I've had some dry places. I watch God provide. I've watched God work miracles. He's getting ready to work a miracle now. He knows what their needs are, and God is going to provide. God is going to make the provisions.

What did He do even after their complaining? And you know God is so gracious. Even in our complaining and our murmuring and wishing for the worst even on ourselves, God just keeps on showering and showing us that He is Lord, and He has power. What did He do? God sent manna from on high, sweet bread. When they needed water, He supplied water from a rock. I used to hear the old warriors and grandma say it best; He is bread in a starving land. He is water in dry places. He's shelter in the time of a storm. He's a friend for the friendless. He's a company keeper in a lonely hour. He's a doctor in a sick room. He's a provider. He makes provision for His people. He gave them enough of what they needed. And God is going to give us just what we need in this season that we're in.

I don't care what the stock market says. God is not governed by stock markets. God is not governed by any laws of this land. But God is the Great law giver. We need to line up with what He has designed for us because whether we know it or not the whole world belongs to God. God is ruling. Yes, He's above everything. We've got our people who lead whether it's in the social world, political world, or religious world. God is in control of it all. I would hate for God to say, "I'm going to remove my hand." If God had removed His hand, none of us would be here this morning. The whole world wouldn't be here. But He's still in control, and I'm glad He's controlling, He's at the helm of the controlling system. When God speaks, everything must listen. This is not just a lesson on Him keeping His promises, and on how He provides. But it's also a lesson **to test our obedience**.

Are we going to be obedient? Let me say this. What we have to do is change our perception of God. Israel had to change their perception. See, what we know about God determines how we see and respond to God. We've got to learn to know God. And the way we know God is to study God like we do anything else. We study it. We know what God likes, what God dislikes, what God requires, and what God does not require. What we know about Him determines how we see and how we respond to God. For Israel, they were coming out of bondage. They really hadn't had a great relationship with God. God is now teaching them how to develop that relationship. These folks are fresh out of bondage. God has brought them through the Red Sea. Now He's leading them through this wilderness of sin up to Sinai so He can give them His laws and His precepts as to how to live as a people, how to live as a nation, and how to get along with one another. They had to come to know God and know how to respond to God. The first four laws of the Ten Commandments were concerning God and last six of the Ten Commandments are how we ought to live with each other. What we know about God determines how we see Him and how we respond to Him.

Do understand that nothing takes God by surprise. He knows us better than we know ourselves. He watched Israel's behavior. What was the kind of behavior that they were distributing? Here it is. When there was no bread and water, what did they do? Complain. They wished their own demise. We've got to watch our behavior. He sees us. He sees how we act. But God already had things figured out for them. He knew that. He didn't bring, as we sing in a song; *He didn't bring me this far to leave me now*. He didn't bring me out here to destroy me. God didn't have to figure out how to meet their needs. He didn't have to figure out, He already knew that.

It reminds me of John's gospel when the writer talks about how Jesus took two little fish and five barley loaves of bread and fed a multitude of men, women, and children. He asked them to feed the crowd, and they said "We ain't got that much money to feed these folks." Jesus knew that they didn't have the sufficient funds to buy food for everybody. For the scripture says *He knew what He was going to do*. He knew what He was going to do. God has got it already figured out what He's going to do. He knew that the bread was going to be short. But God had already made the provision.

All Israel had to do was change their perception on life. He led them by the way of the wilderness so they could see him better *and for who He is*. That's why the question for us today is how much of God do we know? How much of His power do we know? *He can do that which is exceedingly, abundantly, above all that we can imagine or think*. How much of His power do we know? In Verse 7, listen to what Moses said, "In the morning you shall see the glory of the Lord." If you don't know by now you just wait until in the morning. You're going to see God in His splendor because that's what glory means. Glory is the splendor of God. It is the awesomeness of God.

As Moses is trying to say, "You haven't seen anything yet. Just wait. Wait 'til in the morning. Wait another day. And I want you to see God. And when you see Him, He's already heard your murmuring against the Lord. And what we are that you murmur against us. God going to show you just who He is, and when you see Him it's going to change your perspective."

Hallelujah! And when we have our life challenges, circumstances and situations come up against us, stop looking at the situation and start putting your perception on God and look to Him. When you look at God, He will change your perspective about Him. You look at your situation and say, "Oh shoot, that's nothing compared to the glory, the splendor, the awesomeness of our God." That makes me happy right now!

God has a track record. God has a reputation like none other. He's great, a great teacher. He's a great deliverer. He has power to move any obstacle. He has power to meet every challenge and need that we have in our life. Just take it as a life lesson with little stuff that we go through. He can handle, He can handle our crisis with no problem. Why? It is because He's able. He is able. Yes, God is able.

I'm going say this and I'll be out the way. He handled our sin problem at Calvary. If He can handle our sin problem at Calvary, what makes you think, or anyone think that He can't handle these other little minute things. I see them as little minute things. If He can handle that, He can handle anything else. He can handle me. He can handle everything. Yes, He handled our sin problem. Where did He handle it at Reverend? He handled our sin problem at Calvary. Yes, He took the nails. He took the spear in the side. He took it. He handled it, He died, rose early Sunday morning with all power in His hands. Tell me that He can't handle our situations. He handled it. I say He handled it! He didn't need my help. He didn't need nobody's help. He did it all by Himself. Just trust Him today for whatever it is.

Even when you can't trace God or see which way God is going, all you need to do is just trust in His power. There *were* so many times that I couldn't see where God was going with some things. I couldn't trace Him. My mind, my finite mind was too feeble to ascertain this infinite God that I serve, because He is big. But I trusted Him. I told the Lord have thine own way. And you know what? He fixed that thing, whatever was challenging me.

As I said in my prayer this morning Isaiah 40:31, *but they that wait upon the Lord*, it didn't say 'might', but *shall renew their strength, they shall mount up on wings like eagles, they shall run and not be weary, they shall walk and not faint*. Mount up in this wilderness that we are going through. It seems like a wilderness. It looks like things are drying up. But I come by to tell you, my God is able to handle the challenges that we face even in the 21st century. He handles it.

Can I just go on and tell you He handled it a long time ago! I'm just walking in destiny. He chose me for such a time as this. I could have been born in another generation, but He said no. I know the generation I want you in. I know I need your voice. And I'm not here by happenstance, but I'm here by divine providence. And so are you. Yes, it's a lesson in the wilderness. How many of you are going to adhere to the instructions or the lessons in the wilderness? As I leave you, I want you to know God got you. God got this. May God bless you and forever keep you.

This is my message to you today. Oh, I'm excited. I feel good now. You know; it's always good when we can share from The Holy Writ. His Word is life. His Word is living. It is a living Word. Thank you, God for the Living Word. God Bless you today.

CALL TO DISCIPLESHIP

Sis. Rose is going to come and sing. And what I'm going to do is extend an invitation. I know we're not in each other's presence, but I can feel you in my spirit. I want to appeal to anyone out there this morning that is not saved. I pray, I beg you, I plead to you accept Jesus Christ as your Savior. Believe that Jesus died, that Jesus rose from the dead. If you can believe, yes, you may be going through some things in your life, maybe through this wilderness experience that we are all experiencing. You've had some questions. You've been murmuring. You have been complaining about this and that and the other. God can handle it. He's already handled your salvation.

So, if you can believe that Jesus died, was buried, and raised the third day, if you can confess that with your mouth wherever you are, just tell God I'm a sinner, I need saving. I confess my sin. I repent of all. I want to be a saved person. I want to be a Christian in my heart. He can save you right now. Just ask Him, "Lord, come in and save me." And guess what? Today salvation will have come to your house. If you can believe it, receive it today.

And when this pandemic is over, I encourage you get in a fellowship. Unite with somebody's church, because it is time for the world to see the Church is God's business, His *redemptive* business of saving souls. And if you believe that today, confess in your mouth, believe it in your heart and you're saved. Thank you. Sister Jarrett, will you come.

SELECTION

In Times Like These **by Ruth Caye Jones**

CLOSING REMARKS

Praise the Lord. Be very sure that your anchor holds and grips the solid rock. We know who the Rock is. The Rock is Jesus and this morning it is encumbered upon us to get anchored with the Lord. This is going to bring us to a close of another worship experience. I'm still excited and I miss you guys. I wish that we could be together every Sunday. But for unforeseen reasons we're not meeting. It doesn't look like it's going to be soon. But I pray to God through divine intervention will find a way to bring His Church family, His people back in fellowship, back into communion with one another. And I want you all to know that I love you. I love you with a passion, and I hope that you love me.

I pray for you day and night. I pray God's covering over our Church. I specifically pray for our Church. I specifically pray for the Church, the universal Church. I pray for our country. I pray for the nations of this world because we all stand in need of prayer. And we need the Lord to move in the Earth like He's never moved before. So, I just want to encourage you, stay faithful, stay prayed up, and let's love one another. Let's love one another. Those of you who don't mind, you've got the time, you're at home, let's reach out to our Church Family, let people know that we are thinking about them to see how they are doing and make sure that their needs are taken care of. And we will continue to do that. Have a blessed rest of this Sunday, be safe, remember to wash your hands, stay 6ft. apart if possible, and keep your mask on. We're going to beat this. I just believe God is going to take care of it all. So, my last words to you, be blessed, stay safe.

CLOSING PRAYER

God, we thank you for this day. We thank you for this fellowship by way of technology. We thank you for each person who has listened, tuned in to the message today. We pray Lord that you will keep them. Bless them. Keep them oh God in perfect peace. And now the Lord bless you and keep you, the Lord make His face to shine upon you and be gracious unto you. The Lord lifts the light of His countenance upon you and give you peace both now and forever. Amen.

But Prayer
Sunday, April 26, 2020

OPENING REMARKS

It's going to work in your favor. God is working even as we speak. He's working everything out in our favor. Good morning, St. Mark Church Family! Good morning, Church, Community and those friends and family that are watching us across the country. We want to just thank God for you today. This is a beautiful bright Sunday morning. The sun is shining so bright outside and it just feels refreshing. This morning I am so happy. I feel like the Apostle Peter today when he said, "Lord, it is just good for us to be here." And I'm sure you all feel the same way. You're just glad to be here. You're in the land of the living. Are you thankful this morning that the Lord has allowed you another day? If you are thankful, then you ought to just give Him some praise right now. Go ahead. Give Him some praise right in your home. Give God the glory for this beautiful Sunday morning. And I pray that everyone is well and good this morning. We thank God we have not heard of any tragedies or anything of that nature. We just thank God that He dispatched His angels around our dwellings and allowed us to see this beautiful Sunday morning. We have a beautiful worship lined up for you today, and we hope that you'll enjoy it. You'll be blessed the rest of this day and even into the rest of the week.

WORDS OF ENCOURAGEMENT

Well, I've got a word of encouragement for you. The entitlement of our words of encouragement to you this morning is **Nothing Can Separate Us from The Love of God.** That is the word penned by the Apostle Paul in Romans Chapter 8, Verses 38 and 39. He says, *For I am persuaded, that neither death, nor life, nor angels, nor principalities, nor powers, nor things present, nor things to come, Nor height, nor depth, nor any other creature, shall be able to separate us from the love of God, which is in Christ Jesus our Lord.*

What is Paul saying to us this morning in these *two* verses? Well, first of all he's saying to us that nothing can separate us from the love of God. That means that Christ protects His believers from the most extreme experiences and forces that come at us. This is blessed assurance of His deliverance. There is nothing in the Earth that can separate the believer from the love of God which is in Christ Jesus our Lord. The believer can be fully persuaded of these facts even as Paul lays it out so prevalent in the text.

Just consider the experiences and forces that Paul mentions in those two verses. And most of them begin with the word *not*. You just hear that repetitive *not*. What can separate me from the love of God? Not death. Confronting death and leaving this world cannot separate us from the love of Christ. What else? Not life. No trial, no pleasure, no comfort of this world can separate us from the love of God. What else? Not angels, principalities, or powers, no heavenly or spiritual creature shall be able to separate us from the love of God. Not anything present or anything to come. Nothing. No events. No events of the present. No events of the future. No being or thing shall separate us from that great love of God. Absolutely nothing in existence or anything in our foreseen future can cut us off from Christ and His love for us. What else Paul? Not height, or depth, nothing from outer space, nothing from beneath the Earth can separate us.

This is the grand finale here. He says if there be any other creature than the ones that are named in the text, it can't separate us. Even corona virus cannot separate the creature from the love of God which is in Christ Jesus. This is my word of encouragement to you from the inerrant Word of God Himself.

CALL TO WORSHIP

It is time for worship, and as we proceed into this worship experience today, we want you to just give God the Glory, give God the praise for another opportunity to worship Him in spirit and in truth. May I say to you the Lord is in His holy temple, Let the Earth be silent before Him.

Sister Rose is going to come and lead us in a song to prepare our hearts for the worship of today. I will come back and lead us in an intercessory prayer.

We need prayer in our world today. We need prayer in our communities, in our homes. We need prayer in government. We need prayer in all entities that exist today around this world. Sis. Rose will you come now and lead us in a song.

SELECTION

Sanctuary by Randy Rothwell

Lord, make me a sanctuary for you, a living sanctuary. Anybody out there this morning wants to be a sanctuary for the Lord that He may dwell in us? That the Holy Spirit may dwell in us? We'll be cleansed from sin and all the ills of this life and world. You want to be a living sanctuary. As we prepare now to beseech the very throne of God where we can find strength, we can find all that we need in the Lord. It is a privilege to pray. Thank God for prayer. So, my brothers and sisters if we would, right where we are, take this moment to bow, and to come boldly to the throne of grace, and petition Him for every one of our needs and the needs of our world. Shall we pray?

PRAYER

Most Holy, and All Wise God Our Heavenly Father, we come now recognizing that *the Earth is the Lord's and the fullness thereof, the world and they that dwell therein, for you founded it upon the seas. You established it upon the floods.* Be with us as we prepare our hearts to worship you. We thank you that you are everywhere at the same time. We ask for the blessings of the Holy Spirit to pour out upon us the Spirit of worship. Lord, we want to hear from you. Send a word for your people.

Lord, we bless every congregation that has gathered in your name on this Lord's Day. Lord, we lift every pastor, preacher, teacher, and saint. Shower them with your special graces and your choice blessings. Keep them as your ministering flames during this time in the history of our Church. Keep the sheep, the shepherd to feed them with your word.

Heal the sick, comfort the lonely and the bereaved. Supply every one of their needs whether it's food, medicine, or just a roof over their head.

I pray you keep a watchful eye on our nation and our leaders from the national, to the state, even to the local areas. We pray that they seek you and call upon you for answers to our nation's problems. As we pray for them to hold up, to be held up, lift their hands, lift their minds, lift their thoughts in midst of Covid-19. We realize our leaders are human and have their human frailties. We know they don't have all the answers. You have the answers to all our problems. So, we are saying to you today, Oh Lord, have your way. Have thine own way as we are yielded and still.

Keep our medical workers. Keep your arms around them. Keep them protected. Look upon our police officers, firemen. We pray for every entity today. And bless our children and our grandchildren. Bless like only you know how to bless God, and we will forever give your name praise and glory, for it's in Your Son Jesus' Name we pray with thanksgiving, Amen and thank God.

SERMON

Thank you for sharing in that prayer moment with us. We believe in prayer. Now it's time to hear a Word from the Lord. Pray for me as I bring a Word to you this morning. And if you have your bibles where you are, we're going to ask you to turn in your bibles to the book of Acts; chapter 12. We're going look at the first 12 verses of that passage. There are several points that I want to bring out in that passage; those 12 verses. I pray that it be a blessing to you today and the rest of the week. Let's read, starting at Verse 1.

1. *Now about that time Herod the king stretched forth his hands to vex certain of the church.*
2. *And he killed James the brother of John with the sword.*
3. *And because he saw it pleased the Jews, he proceeded further to take Peter also. (Then were the days of unleavened bread.)*
4. *And when he had apprehended him, he put him in prison, and delivered him to four quaternions of soldiers to keep him; intending after Easter to bring him forth to the people.*
5. *Peter therefore was kept in prison: but prayer was made without ceasing of the church unto God for him.*
6. *And when Herod would have brought him forth, the same night Peter was sleeping between two soldiers, bound with two chains: and the keepers before the door kept the prison.*
7. *And, behold, the angel of the Lord came upon him, and a light shined in the prison: and he smote Peter on the side, and raised him up, saying, Arise quickly. And his chains fell off from his hands.*

8. *And the Angel said unto him, Gird thyself, and bind on thy sandals. And so he did. And he saith unto him, Cast thy garment about thee and follow me.*

9. *And he went out and followed him; and wist not that it was true which was done by the angel; but though he saw a vision.*

10. *When they were past the first and the second ward, they came unto the iron gate that leadeth unto the city; which opened to them of his own accord: and they went out and passed on through one street; and forthwith the angel departed from him.*

11. *And when Peter was come to himself, he said, Now I know of a surety, that the Lord hath sent his angel, and hath delivered me out of the hand of Herod, and from all the expectation of the people of the Jews.*

12. *And when he had considered the thing, he came to the house of Mary the mother of John, whose surname was Mark; where many were gathered together praying.*

My subject is going to come from Verse 5. As a short subject; **But Prayer**. That's my subject this morning, **But Prayer**. Peter was kept in the prison, but prayer was made without ceasing of the church unto God for him. Somebody ought to just say it, **But Prayer**.

As we make ready to move into this message this morning, I want to say that there is nothing in life that can push the Church and the believer into the winning column like purposeful, powerful, penetrating prayer. Nothing in life can push the Church and the believer into the winning column like purposeful, powerful, penetrating prayer. Prayer is a communication that, first of all, begins with God and it ends with God. Prayer is from God the Father, in the Son, through the Holy Spirit. In other words, prayer is not our idea even the worst or most horrible situation. There's nothing like prayer. Even Jesus said in scripture that when we pray, we pray to the Father. And when we pray purposeful, powerful, penetrating prayer and make our petition known to the Father, we ought to conclude our petitioning by asking God to do it in Jesus' Name. So, prayer is from God the Father, in the Son, through the Holy Spirit in the worst of situations. Prayer is a divine idea that prevails because of its origin and the will of Him who is the answer to our prayers. God hears prayer. He answers prayer.

Andre Crouch penned the song years ago entitled "*Jesus Is The Answer For The World Today*". That song is more than 30 years old, but you know it is even relevant and vital in our times thirty years plus later. Jesus is still the answer for the world's problems today. For many believers those who have not matured in the faith often respond and say these things about prayer: *What is the use of praying? Why should I pray. Nothing is going to change.* The problem is there is nothing wrong with praying or prayer. The problem is they have a pessimistic outlook that is rooted in what I believe is an inconsistent walk with God. When you are not walking in step with God, living in God's will, living on purpose with God, guess what? Nothing's going to happen. You must be in fellowship with God. But most of all you must have a personal relationship with God. It seems that the immature person of faith in their minds the situations they are going through are lasting too long. How come I'm going through this over this long period of time? It appears, they would say, God is not listening to them. You've heard it said in the Church, God may not come when you want Him, but He's always on time. That's what I like about my God. Even when I pray, sometimes it seems like when we're praying God is silent. God is not doing anything. God is not going to do anything. See God is waiting on us to pray to Him and when God feels the tug or the urge then God moves when God gets ready to move. He may not come when we want Him, but He's always on time. You just got to trust Him. You've got to give Him time.

I believe the immature Christian, when it's all said and done, they conclude that prayer doesn't work. Prayer can't work, *it not going to work*. But if you are a believer in prayer, you know that God may answer our prayers in one of three ways. And it behooves us to learn these three methods or ways that God answers our prayers. He may say yes, He may say wait awhile, or He may even say no.

If God answers yes, that means that God can answer our prayers instantaneously or spontaneously. God answers right on the spot. He's done that so many times. Have you ever been in a situation where you couldn't seemingly get a prayer through? All you said was, "Lord, Have Mercy" and God just stepped right-in, at the moment you needed Him the most. He said, "yes". Then He may say, "Wait a while". You see sometimes by telling us to wait a while, God has got to work some things out in your favor. See, whatever you are praying for, whatever you are desiring in life, whether it's a job, whether it's a spouse, or whether they're things that pertain to living, we want it right away. You know we're living in this microwave age where we want things done in the snap of a finger. But God may be telling us wait a while. That job you want, you want it right now but see God says, "Wait a while". Let me work on the management. Let me work on who is doing the hiring. So, yes, their heart is a little stiff right now. Let me work on it. Let me soften the heart up. Then when it's time, I'll move you into the job with ease. Wait a while. God might be telling somebody out there right now; "Wait a while. Let me work out some dark places. Let me work out some rough places you can't see right now". There may be some things that you're praying for; you're asking God for that you can't handle right now. And God has to mature you in order to bring you into what you are asking for. You can't handle it right now.

Well, let's look at the third step. God may say no. There may be something you're asking God for that may not be to your benefit. It might be destructive. See God knows our hearts. He knows our minds. So, God knows that if He gives us what we ask for right now we won't act right. We won't do the right thing. We won't honor God. We won't honor the person who is in our life because we got something, and we pride it over others. Whether it's a relationship or whatever the case may be. God says, *no you can't handle this right now. So, no. Let me mature you. Let me groom you. Let me grow you to that point and level in your life when you can handle it. You might be destructive with it. You might destroy yourself. You might destroy someone else.* So, these are the ways that God answers some prayers by saying yes, wait a while, and no.

Let's move into our text this morning. In Acts, Chapter 12, it shows us, the believing Church, was united in prayer with one purpose in mind. What was that united purpose in mind? Well, they were praying, in order, to get Peter out of jail. See, you must believe in what you're praying for. But my first point, I want to make today --- is the **purpose of the prayer**. See! They were praying one specific prayer that was get Peter released from jail.

Well, what's the backdrop of the text? What's going on in the text? The Church was under spiritual and political attack. Yes, persecution was happening to the Church community because Pentecost had come, and the Church had received power. The Church had gone out in power. They were preaching and souls were saved. Miracles were being wrought. But there were those who were anti-Christian, anti-Christ. So, they started a revolution to change what was about to take place. The Church was under spiritual and political attack. Can I tell us today! I do believe our Churches today or the Church in general is under a spiritual and political attack. This attack started with the stoning of Stephen. Even Paul, who before he became Paul was Saul, and we know Saul was an anti-Christian. He was anti-Christ. And even Saul at that time stood as the Jewish people stoned Stephen to death. He held their garments. Chapter 9 will bear it out to us. But even at the stoning of Stephen. Its flames continued to grow against the Christian Church.

If you will listen to the text this morning in Chapter 12, Verse 1 the text says Herod stretched forth his hands to vex certain of the Church. Interesting word in that passage – vex. To vex means to oppress. Vex means to accuse. Vex means to harm. It means to oppress, to do evil against. Who are they doing all this evil and harm to? The text says certain leaders. Certain leaders were on Herod's hit list. Know this, if you are saved, if you are Christian then you are on Satan's hit list. He wants to attack you. He wants to oppress you. He wants to harm you. He wants to do evil against you. Yes, this oppressive and harmful evil was like a flame. It was continuing to grow against the Church. For in the passage, it says James the brother of John had been killed with a sword. They come and get Brother James out of the pulpit, dragged him out and killed him with a sword. And the Bible says because it pleased the Jews. The devil is pleased to destroy us. He's happy to destroy us. He does not want to see us saved. He does not want to see us praise God. It pleased the Jews. It was a pleasure to the hearts of the Jews who were against Jesus and the Church. My Brothers and Sisters the world doesn't love you. They hate you. Jesus said the world will hate you because it hated Him first.

Just naming Christian, or saved, people look at you differently, wrongly. The text says James was killed. But now they have captured Peter. Peter was in jail, and he's waiting for his fate, really awaiting his death sentence because he was on Herod's hit list. And I'm sure this has gotten the attention of the other Church members. And I'm sure that they were pondering in their minds, they were asking questions: Who will be next? Stephen is gone. James is killed. They got Peter locked up. But I like Verse 5. But prayer. But prayer. When the enemy is determined to divide and to diminish and to destroy, can I tell you what works? Prayer will work. Prayer will work. But prayer. Prayer will work. Not only will prayer work, but prayer is work. Prayer is work. My Brothers and Sisters if we are going to overcome the ills, the anti of our day, we're going to have to learn the power of prayer and know that prayer works. And prayer is work. We're going to have to spend some time in prayer. We're going to have to develop some camel knees. We're going to have to get on our knees. We're going to have to get some calluses on our knees. We've got to bow because prayer works. And if you don't know that prayer works, you need to learn like the disciples. When they came upon Jesus, and they saw Jesus praying and they saw John pray, they said Lord, "Teach us to pray". Prayer is work. You got to work it.

Not only is prayer work, but prayer is warfare. It's warfare. You've got to fight to pray. You've got to push to pray. And you better armor up with prayer. If we're going to fight through stuff, we the Church and Christians are facing in the 21st Century, we are going to have to have some prayer in warfare, and not only prayer in warfare, but prayer and worship. We've got to worship, pray, work prayer, let prayer work for you, then do warfare, but in the meantime do some worshiping because all these yield results. And I'm looking for results. And when I pray, I want results. I want to see something happen with the prayers that I pray. I'm not just praying to be seen, and to be heard. But I to pray to make things move. When I look at the word, *pray*; pray until something happens, PUSH until something happens.

The second thing I want to lift in the text is the **persistence of the prayer**. In the prayer that the Church is praying for Peter, there is persistence in it. It says the Church was praying without ceasing. You've got to be persistent. You've got to believe what you are praying for. You've got to believe what you are praying about because Verse 5 emphatically tells us. But prayer! All that had happened to the Church is clear. James is killed. Stephen is killed. Peter is in jail. It is clear the Church's outlook and protection looked dark. It was threatened. It looked scary. Peter is in jail. Go back to Verse 5. *But prayer* was made without ceasing, and they were praying unto God for Peter. They were persistent in the prayer. As I look back and as I read continually in the text, Peter had gotten out and went home and went to Rona's house, guess what? It said it was many in the house. So that suggests to me that the whole Church was praying. The whole Church was praying. The Church was doing all it could do, praying specifically for Peter's deliverance.

I want to interrogate this word *ceasing*. Without ceasing means they were fervently and earnestly continuing in prayer. Ceasing! Without ceasing means fervently, warm, hot. They were not praying these cold prayers. They were praying fervently. Their prayers had some bite to them. Their prayers had some heat to them. Their prayers were hot. They believed in their praying. They believed in what they were praying about. So, the idea is that they were in intense prayer. Prayer captivates and focuses on a person's concentration. They knew what they were praying about, and they knew to whom they were praying. It said the Church was praying to God. They weren't praying to be seen and to be heard and to be patted on the back and say oh man, you are praying go on and say it. No, they were praying with fervency and earnestly, hot prayers.

This root word *praying without ceasing* means that they were stretched out. The picture is that the Church was stretched out. Her face was before the Lord, earnestly, fervently crying out to Him for God's deliverance of Peter. Lord, we want Peter. The Church is under attack. It's under spiritual attack. It is under political attack. And God, our beloved leader, the one who led us at Pentecost, the one who preached that sermon, and 3,000 souls was added to the Church. Lord, we are praying for our beloved preacher. Church, let me just say pray for your preacher, because he's under attack. He's under attack. And if a Pastor/Preacher is under attack you better believe or know that the Church is vulnerable. If he gets your leader, he's got you. So, the Church was praying for his deliverance. The Church could do nothing as they knew it. Peter's only hope was God. And the Church's confidence was in God that God would deliver Peter.

I want us to look at Verse 6, because there is something in Verse 6 that I want to lift. And I'm almost done. Verse 6 says Peter that same night; what was he doing? He was asleep. He's asleep the night before his execution. But the Church was praying. They had a purpose for praying. They had a persistent prayer. But they were praying while Peter is asleep. And while they were praying, God Himself was meeting Peter's needs. God had him surrounded with His grace and His peace. Can't you just see Peter, you know, lying between two soldiers, surrounded by God's enemies at the gate, at the jail door, guarding the door. They got him under quarantine. But guess what? But Peter is asleep. Yes, he's surrounded by soldiers, but he's also surrounded by God's grace and peace because the Church is praying. What I like about it, he's asleep. And the word says they are thinking about the next day because they are going to put him to death. But he's asleep. I don't know if Peter had prayed before he went to sleep. You know when I thought about that as I was preparing this message for you this morning I thought about when I was a kid and before I graduated from this little prayer to the Lord's Prayer and then really knowing how to pray, knowing that prayer works, we were taught to pray this little prayer. And I don't know if Peter had prayed this prayer or not. And this little prayer goes like this: *Now I lay me down to sleep, I pray the Lord my soul to keep, If I should die before I wake, I pray the Lord my soul to take.* Anybody know anything about that? I just believe Peter was asleep, but he had a sense of trust that the Lord was caring for him. Even in jail God was taking care of him. Guess what? The Church is praying.

God's got Peter surrounded with grace. He's got him covered. Peter doesn't have to worry about anything. Seems like he's not worried about anything, he's asleep. This is what God did. What did He do? He sent an angel, and the angel shined a light in the jail and smote Peter on the side. When I saw the words *smote on the side,* it meant that He didn't just touch Peter with a little finger. Peter, wake up. Peter, wake up. Peter was so deep into his sleep that the angel said this guy is sleeping so hard that I can't just touch him, I need to hit him. He hit him. Boy! Was he sleeping? Praise the Lord. Yeah, Peter was so into his deep sleep, the angel had to smite him to wake him up. That's a man to me that is in confidence that everything is going to be alright. You can lie down and go to sleep. And if you know that the Lord got you, and you serve the Lord, you don't have to worry about sleeping. You go on to sleep, because the record is that the Lord Himself neither sleeps nor slumbers. And if the Lord is not sleeping, I go on to sleep and let the Lord stay awake because I know He's watching over me. Go on to sleep. Go on to sleep. Sleep on sleeper. Sleep on Peter. Peter was asleep. But he had to smite him. I am not worried about this thing. God got me. God is not through with me yet. When He gets through with me, then I shall come forth like pure gold. God wasn't through with Peter. Can I tell some of us this morning that God is not through with you yet? He left you here for a reason. He left me here for a reason. When He gets through with me, then I too like others must quit this old walk of life. I don't care what the spiritual attacks are. I don't care what the political attacks are, But God.

Let's see further what the angel tells Peter after he smites him and wakes him up. The angels told Peter get up quickly. And the Bible says, *and the chains fell off his hands.* The angel said put on your shoes. He put on his shoes. He said now put your clothing on you. He put his clothing on. He says now follow me, and Peter followed him. Look at all these directives. Look at the obedience of Peter. You got to be obedient. See, in order, for the Lord to deliver you and to bring you out, you got to be obedient. You got to take orders. You got to listen. When God sends you His deliverance, follow the action. Peter followed. And the record is he did not know whether this was true that was done by the angel. God can do some miraculous stuff that blows are minds sometimes. And we don't understand how God is doing it. I don't believe Peter really knew that the Church was in prayer. But thanks be to God that God knew the Church was praying. Not only did He know it, but He heard their prayers, and He sent the answer to their prayers. He delivered Peter.

Peter did not know. Peter didn't realize that it was true. Am I dreaming? Am I in dreamland? He thought he saw a vision. But this was the divine hand of God working things out in the favor of the believers. After Peter realized that this wasn't just a vision or a dream, the record goes on to say that Peter and the angel past the first and second ward, passing by guards. They are probably all asleep too. See God will put your enemy to sleep so that they can't see you. They're wondering which way did they go? How did he get out of here? How did he get delivered? Who delivered him? The guards didn't even see Peter and the angel being led out of the jail. It says and they came to the gate, the iron gate that led to the city. The gate opened on its own accord. Peter didn't have a remote control or sensitive device to get him out. God did it. Look at Go! It was open. Why was the gate opened? It was opened because prayer was being made for Peter. Look at God's deliverance. Somebody ought to say won't He do it right there. Won't He, do it? Won't He, do it? Won't God deliver? Anybody out there been delivered? And you are yet trying to figure out how God did that. How did He do it? *I was sinking deep in sin, far from the peaceful shore.* God can do it because He has the power to do it. And when the church prays, the church has power. This was just a few believers praying fervently and earnestly. They weren't praying those dead prayers, hot prayers.

We've talked about the purpose of the prayer. We talked about the persistence of the prayer. Now let's talk about the **people of the prayer**. Who were these people? Rhoda, Mary. I remember when I was a teenager, we were in revival one year. This was back in the 1960s (I'm telling you how old I am). Our pastor then was Rev. P.H. Baker. He brought a pastor from Memphis, Rev. Crutcher. I never will forget him. One night in revival he preached from this text: **Prayer Meeting at Big Mary's House.** Big Mary and Rhoda and other believers were at the house. These were the people of prayer. The Bible doesn't give all their names. They were praying. When prayer is offered, it should be constant, and it should be fervent by the Church. Paul says in Ephesians 6:18 *praying with all prayer and supplications in the spirit.* Why Paul?

According to Paul, Paul let us know that we wrestle not against flesh and blood, but we are wrestling against these spiritual dimensions that are out there. Political attacks are coming from all angles. And Paul is saying these are the things that we are in spiritual warfare against. And that's why we got to pray because we are in warfare. The secret to praying always is having an attitude of prayer. Even in midst of an immediate crisis like we are going through. In the midst of a pandemic like we are going through, we shouldn't be panicking. We should be praying. *But prayer* ought to be the number one thing on list. *But prayer* was made without ceasing. They were stretched out. And I just believe if the churches, and the reason I say churches is because we have many different affiliations out there, but we all make up one church. We all make up one church. I just believe that the church, the one church that Christ said He builds upon the Rock_ I believe if the church but pray without ceasing before God, God will deliver us all over the country, all over the world. I don't know how God will do it. He'll do it on His own terms and in His own way, sending healing and deliverance.

I just see God and science working together. The Bible doesn't just talk about science, but science is all over the Bible. I just believe that God and science can come up with a remedy, a Balm in Gilead, a Balm in America, and a balm all over the world. *But prayer*! Somebody's got to pray. He will send deliverance.

And as I get ready to leave you this morning, my last few words, if there is one weapon that the Church has in its arsenal that is powerful and potent, it is prayer. We can be rest assured that God's Word can be trusted. We can get our prayer answered. We can get our prayers answered when we truly pray from the depths of our heart. Circumstances will change. Crisis will calm down. Conflict will stand still. And when all these things calm down, change, and stand still we all can shout as the body of Christ, we can shout the victory because our victory today is in Jesus. As I quoted to you earlier, Andre Crouch penned the song way back, Jesus is the answer to the world's problems today. He is the answer this morning.

CALL TO DISCIPLESHIP

My brothers and sisters this is my message to you today. I pray it has been a help, a benefit, an encouragement. And if anyone out there who is listening to me who is lost and not saved, I would that you would pray today. But prayer can save the lost. But prayer can change sinners from sinners to saints. But prayer. And if you this morning are a sinner out there wanting Christ as your Savior and Lord, I beg you, I pray you that you will ask Him in your heart right now. Just pray and say, "Lord I'm a sinner and I need saving. Save me now. Save me from my sins. Save me from myself. Save me from the enemy." And I believe that if you pray that God will come instantaneously, spontaneously. He said the day you hear my voice harden not your heart, He'll come in right then and change and save your life. Pray that prayer and ask God to save you.

And as soon as this pandemic is over and we get back into our church houses, we would go to God that you will go to somebody's church and make a public profession of faith and say, "I have accepted Him as my personal Savior and as my Lord and I want to unite with a church and fellowship with a church that will help me to become stronger, better, and wiser." I would encourage you to do that. If you can confess the Lord Jesus with your mouth, believe in your heart that He died for your sins and was raised from the dead you're saved just that easy, just that quick. God bless you. Thank you. I hope this Word has been a blessing.

And now I'm going to ask Rose to come back and share another selection. And we will come back and close this day out. In the meantime, just enjoy this beautiful day that the Lord has given you, cherish this word, and feast on this word. Amen.

SELECTION

Because of Who You Are **by Vicki Yohe**

CLOSING REMARKS

Thank you so much for participating with us in worship on today. Oh, I feel so much better now. I just feel *good*, and I hope you feel just as good as I feel about now. And let me just say to St. Mark this morning, thank you. We love you. We love you to death. And I just can't wait until we all get back together again. I believe in that old hymn that we use to sing at the church years and years ago, when all of God's children get together, what a time it's going to be. We're going to be glad to get back up in there. Amen. So, I just thank God for the way that the Lord has allowed us to come across by way of Facebook and some on Zoom, some on YouTube. God has fixed it so we can get the Word out. And I believe through this a lot of people have been touched and reached, because just about everybody now has Facebook and so forth and so on. I think I need to cut this off right about now because I think time is just about up.

But let me just make mention this quickly. St. Mark, you know what today would have been if we had all been at church. This is our sacrificial efforts day. So, don't forget your sacrificial gift and effort to the Church. Thank you for those of you who have already done you part. Those who have not, we encourage you to do so, and the Lord will bless you.

This coming week would have been spring revival, but I just believe that revival is taking place even in our homes in America today. I just believe that the Word is getting around. So, we are having revival, whether we are at our individual churches or not.

I hope that we will be back in Church in the future. I don't know when or how soon. We will be getting together. We will be talking about it. I love you. I thank God for you. Good to see you one more time. Praise the Lord. As we close this thing out, we ask that you bow right where you are as we give the benediction.

CLOSING PRAYER

God, we thank you for this day, we thank you for this worship experience. We thank you oh God for every member, every friend, and every neighbor who has tuned in today. We pray that they will be stronger, better, and wiser throughout the rest of this week and their lives. And now may the Grace of God, the Love of God, and the fellowship of the Holy Spirit, may He now rest, rule, and abide in the hearts of this thine people now and forever, let every person out there say Amen.

They Have the Word
Sunday, May 3, 2020

OPENING REMARKS

Good morning, Saints of God, Church Community, friends and family far and near. It is a blessing to be here on this first Sunday of a new month, the month of May. Our year is moving quite fast. This season is a great time to be alive and to know it. Well, welcome to another worship celebration. I come today to celebrate our Christ, the Lamb of God. I want to thank Him for awakening me this morning. I want to thank Him for awakening you this morning, and that you can tune in with us on this great day of celebration. I want to thank God for His new mercy. His mercy is renewed morning by morning. You know I am glad He did not consume me. Amen. You need to take a moment and just tell the Lord; thank you, you didn't consume me, but you kept me alive. And I am here to say I'm alive because of His good grace and mercy. Somebody just ought to shout Amen!

WORDS OF ENCOURAGEMENT

Well, I've got a word of encouragement today. There is a verse of scripture that is found in the Old Testament. The book of Isaiah 66:2. Listen to this verse. This is the quote of God Himself saying,

These are the ones I looked on with favor; and those who are humble and contrite in spirit, and tremble at thy word (NIV).

My brothers and sisters there are two words in that verse of scripture I want to lift to encourage you right where you are this morning. The first one is *humility*. Humility may bring *favor*. Listen to that word favor, that's the second word I want to lift. Humility and favor, humility brings favor. But envy, selfishness and ambitious ways hinder it. Confess and ask God to help you overcome if you are envious and if you are selfish.

Now look at the word favor. Favor means something done or given out of good will, rather than justice or reward or pay. Favor is a kind act. It is to ask favor, that is favor from God. Favor is from God. And when He does something for us, when He does kindness and shows us good will, it is not because we deserve it, but because He is a loving God. God said through the prophet Isaiah, *these are the ones I looked on with favor.* Amen. I thank God that He has shown me favor in another day. He has shown me an act of kindness. This is a kindness that comes from God. That is just who God is. He's always doing something for us, showing us kindness. That is His Will. He wants to show favor. He wants to bestow this upon all of His children. This is my word of encouragement to you this morning. Amen.

CALL TO WORSHIP

Let us prepare for worship now. I look forward to today's worship because this is the Lord's Day, and I'm going to rejoice in it just because He's shown me kindness and great favor. Well, *the Lord is in His Holy Temple; let the Earth be silent before Him.*

Now as we prepare to go forward, I'm going to ask Sis. Rose to come at this time and lead us with a song. We'll come back with a word of prayer. We want to have intercession. We want to invoke the Lord to move in our favor today. Move in favor of our nation. Move in favor of our world and do something great. Do something marvelous. Do something magnanimous for our world. We need the Lord. We need favor in this world today. So, we'll come back and petition the Throne of Grace after this beautiful selection coming from Rose. Amen.

SELECTION

***Oh, How I Love Jesus* – Verses by Frederick Whitfield, Refrain – Anonymous**

Oh, how I love Jesus because He first loved me. He loved me before I knew how to even love myself. Amen. It is prayer time, and I pray that you will pray with me as we now come to the Throne of God boldly, as we come to petition Him in prayer and supplication. The Bible tells us to make our petitions, or our requests made known unto God. It is not that God doesn't know us and our plighted situations, he already knows, but He just inhabits the praise and the worship and the invoking of His children to come to Him. He just wants us to get up in His face. God wants us to look in His face. Just to behold His face is beauty. It's mesmerizing just to know that God will allow us to come into His presence. So, let us now go to the Throne of Grace.

PRAYER

Our Father and Our God, we are your children by creation. We are your children by the new birth. We come into your presence now, to offer up to you, thanksgiving. As we think back over our lives, we see all the wonderful things you have done for us, and they are so many. First on our list, you saved us. You redeemed us. You forgave us when we sinned. You fed us when we were hungry. You healed us when we were sick. We just want to tell you this morning, thank you.

Thank You for loving us when we didn't know how or what love was about. But thank you, for you have demonstrated love at its best. Even when we were sinners and weren't fit to live, you died for us, I want to say thank you. Thank you even right now. Lord, I thank you for my Church family, my Church Community. Thank you for the whole household of faith all over your land and country. Lord we just pray that you keep them as the apple of your eye. And as men and women believers, keep us Oh God after your own heart. We know you can. We believe you will. You have never let us down. And we don't ever have to worry of you letting us down. God, we have let you down so many times. We have broken your heart. But we ask now that you forgive every one of our sins.

Touch us now, in the Name of Jesus. Touch the old. Touch the young. Lord we even ask that you touch the careless and the unconcerned. Cover us, Oh God, with your blood even now. Bless every need your people have. And Lord there are so many special needs out there: food for the body, shelter over our heads. Someone needs you right now Lord. And we know that you have medicine in the hems of your garments for a wounded and a sick body. Touch the lonely. Touch someone who is ready to give up and want to throw in the towel on life. But God we say to you this morning, speak in their souls, even right now. There is someone Lord who fears what the future may hold. Let them know God that you've got the future under control. Show them how to lift up their eyes to the hills from whence cometh our help. All our help comes from the Lord who made the heavens and the Earth.

Lord, we pray for the leaders of our nation and cities. We pray for all medical and critical workers. Don't forget, we know you won't. Bless the pastors of our Churches, keep them encouraged as they minister while away from their flock.

And Oh God we just come to bless you this morning. And we will always bless you, for your praise shall continually be in our mouth. Oh, we magnify you today. We lift you up. In the precious Name of Jesus, we do pray with a heart of thanksgiving. And let all the people of God who hear this prayer say Amen, Amen, and Amen.

God bless you and thank you for participating with us in that prayer. We know that God will hear us. He's going to answer in a readily and right time. Let us now prepare our hearts for the Word of the Lord. And I pray that today's Word will be a blessing to you as it has already blessed me just in the preparation of the lesson it blessed me. And I pray that as I impart it to you, that it will bring you the same blessing that I have received.

SERMON

There is a passage that is found in the New Testament, a familiar parable, or narrative as you may refer to it. It is found in the Gospel of Luke, Chapter 16. There are eleven verses I want to lift from that passage starting at Verse 19. The passage reads:

> 19. *There was a certain rich man, which was clothed in purple and fine linen, and fared sumptuously every day:*
>
> 20. *And there was a certain beggar named Lazarus, which was laid at his gate, full of sores,*
>
> 21. *And desiring to be fed with the crumbs which fell from the rich man's table: moreover the dogs came and licked his sores.*
>
> 22. *And it came to pass, that the beggar died, and was carried by the angels into Abraham's bosom: the rich man also died, and was buried;*
>
> 23. *And in hell he lift up his eyes, being in torments, and seeth Abraham afar off, and Lazarus in his bosom.*
>
> 24. *And he cried and said, Father Abraham, have mercy on me, and send Lazarus that he may dip the tip of his finger in water, and cool my tongue; for I am tormented in this flame.*
>
> 25. *But Abraham said, Son, remember that thou in thy lifetime receivedst thy good things, and likewise Lazarus evil things: but now he is comforted, and thou art tormented.*

26. And beside all this, between us and you there is a great gulf fixed: so that they which would pass from hence to you cannot; neither can they pass to us, that would come from thence.

27. Then he said, I pray thee therefore, father, that thou wouldest send him to my father's house:

28. For I have five brethren; that they may testify unto them, lest they also come into this place of torment.

29. Abraham saith unto him, They have Moses and the prophets, let them hear them.

30. And he said, Nay, father Abraham: but if one went unto them from the dead, they will repent.

31. And he said unto him, If they hear not Moses and the prophets, neither will they be persuade, though one rose from the dead.

Thus, ends the reading of God's Word. This morning I want to lift this thought, and it is coming out of Verse 29. And I'm going to paraphrase it a little bit. I am going to talk about **They Have the Word.** It's coming out of Verse 29 when Abraham says, *they have Moses and the prophets, let them hear them.* In other words, they got the Word with them. All they have to do is to hear him or them. That's what I want to lift this morning. **They Have the Word.**

Today's narrative speaks loudly once again no Christ's concern because He's telling this narrative. He's telling this story, and He was concerned. He's concerned today about those who are the least, left out, and the overlooked people in society. And we're going to see in the text today an overlooked man. Men and women alike are being overlooked in society. But it also challenges those whom society deemed to take responsibility to help those who are not well off. And they got it going on.

Even today as we are living amid a pandemic, a crisis that is happening in our society, statistics as we know it, or have heard over the past weeks show that over 30 million people have lost jobs. And out of the 30 million people, many need food. I've watched in some of our major cities around the country. People are lining up to get a helping hand, hoping that things will get better sooner or later. But I learned just listening at statistics and data this week, while focusing on myself and those whom I live around, it says to me in my spirit it's them today, grant it maybe you tomorrow.

The pandemic is no fault of ours, but it's here, and we've got to deal with it until it is over. In the meantime, we've got to stay prayed up. Pray that no one goes without for a long period of time, we've got to pray that God will meet every challenge that His people suffer. It's a challenge, and we will see in the text today. We'll see a challenge that takes place. And what must we be made to understand clearly in this narrative? This narrative is not a criticism of being rich. There's nothing wrong with being rich. But you see in this story, the topic of conversation is a rich man and a poor man who was a beggar named Lazarus. The rich man did not find himself in a place of torment for being wealthy any more than Lazarus found himself at Abraham's side because he was poor. You see, wealth and riches do not guarantee anyone the privilege of getting into Heaven. Being poor does not guarantee you will have a place in Heaven either. It's what we do and what the Word of God says that gets us to Heaven.

We've got to know what the Word of God says as to how to get to Heaven. We are to accept Jesus Christ as our Savior. The rich man did not go to hell because of his riches. Nor did Lazarus go to Heaven because he was poor. The reason why the rich man went to hell is because he did not have a relationship with Jesus. And the poor man went to Heaven because he had a relationship with God. I wish I had a couple of hours because this is a big topic. This is a big text to preach from this morning. So, I've got it condensed so I can get a point across this morning. Jesus does the saving of men's souls.

Paul tells us in Ephesians 2:8, *You are saved by grace through faith and not of yourselves lest any man should boast.* See, in order, to be saved, you've got to have faith in the grace and favor of God. So, Paul is telling us this is how one becomes saved. You're saved by grace through faith and not of yourself. You can't do it yourself because if you could do it yourself then you would have reason to boast. You could pat yourself on the back and say look what I did. But it's not what you did. It is the grace of God that worked out favor through faith in you. The rich man did not go to hell because he was rich. He went to hell because he did not have a relationship with God. Paul says you don't work to get salvation, you must work it out. He says work out your salvation. Work it out. You've got to work out your salvation. You don't work to get salvation. Christ did that work on the cross. All you have to do is just believe the works of Christ.

You must have faith. You see, faith without works is dead, and works without faith is also dead. You also must work out your faith. By no means am I criticizing this morning the rich man of our text. I'm not criticizing him for his wealth, but I'm trying to convey this morning that he had to have a relationship to get to Heaven. Listen, you don't have to do *nothing* to go to hell. Did you hear what I said. You don't have to do *nothing* to go to hell. You don't have to believe *nothing*. You don't have to love anyone. You don't have to give *nothing*. You can do *nothing* and go to hell. But if you're going to go to Heaven, you've got to know Jesus. You can love Jesus. Do I have any help, out there this morning? I feel a little preach coming on. Yeah. The rich man did nothing. Because he did nothing, his nothingness sent him to hell. The rich man did nothing.

He saw Lazarus every day lay in his bed. And not only that, but Lazarus was also full of sores. All Lazarus desired, all Lazarus wanted was the crumbs that fell from his table. He didn't ask him for the whole loaf of bread. He didn't ask him for the whole piece of meat. He just needed someone to just give him a bite to eat. You know what? The rich man did nothing. And I'm sure that as the rich man would come home daily from his chores or from his business practice, he would see the poor beggar lying at his gate. He would just step over him and go on into the gate into the house without doing anything. Without probably saying 'excuse me sir.' He didn't even ask him 'why are you lying here?' No questions were asked.

Moreover, the Bible says the dogs came, and the dogs licked his sores. The rich man did nothing. The dogs did more for Lazarus than the rich man. An animal versus a human; the animal licked his sores. He did something. The rich man did nothing. Can you see that doing *nothing* can send you to hell? As I have already fore stated, you don't have to believe *nothing*, you don't have to love anybody, you don't have to give to anybody, and you can go to hell. I don't know why I'm preaching this, this morning, but this is what the Lord gave me. I told you I've already preached it to myself.

But listen to the story. Listen to both men. Guess what happened? Both men died, which says to me the rich die and the poor die. Lazarus died, but he went to heaven carried by angels into Abraham's bosom. But guess what? The rich man died. He was buried, and he went to hell. But he saw Lazarus in Abraham's bosom. Isn't it ironic that it takes you to die before you can really recognize a man? He saw Lazarus in Abraham's bosom but when he was living and on Earth, he walked over the man. He gave him no attention. He paid him no mind, didn't ask him, "How are you feeling today? What can I do for you?" But he died. They both died.

I've got three more things I want to lift out of this passage, and then we are going to look at the characters in the text as the narrative portrays to us. We want to look at the rich man's plight. Then we want to look at Lazarus's bliss. Finally, we want to look at Abraham's reply to the rich man's request.

First, let's look at the rich man's plight. You see, the rich man was condemned. He was condemned to a place because of his lack of faith or no faith. The Bible talks about a whole lot of different kinds of faith: little faith, no faith, great faith, lack of faith. This man evidently did not have faith in God. He had no room in his heart for God. Yes, he was rich. He was prestigious. He has all the qualities working in his life. But he had no room for God in his life. He had his resources. Evidently, he was a talented man, in order, for him to have gained the benefits that he now possesses. He's rich. He's wealthy. He's got all these resources, a business he didn't work for but inherited it from his family. I noticed something else about this man, he surrounded himself with the best things of life. When I read the text, he wore the best clothes. The text says he dressed in purple and fine linen. He dressed to kill every day. He had a different suit, or a different piece of garment on him. That's the kind of man he was. The Bible says he ate the best food. He went to the best restaurants and ate the best food. How you know Reverend? The Bible says *he fared sumptuously every day* meaning that he had everything he needed or wanted. He ate three meals a day, but he couldn't give a man the crumbs that fell from his table.

My Brothers and Sisters, Lazarus didn't ask for it all. Sometimes we just want the crumbs. And sometimes there is just as much substance in the crumbs as there is in the whole piece. Is there anybody out there that has lived your life on the crumbs? On the meager things, the small things, the little stuff? You didn't have the best? You didn't wear the best clothes, but you had some clothes on? You didn't eat the best food, but you had food on your table because the Lord prepared a table for you every day? It may not have been what you wanted, but you had food to eat. Maybe it was a molasses sandwich, but it was something to eat. The rich man fared sumptuously every day, but he did nothing, in regards, for God and his fellowman. He did not have God in his heart. Because he did not have God in his heart, he had no heart for humanity to help a brother along the way.

Can't *you* hear the conversation that is going on now in heaven? Listen to the rich man. He's talking upward. He's talking to heaven now. Listen to him. He's asking heaven to show him some mercy. Not only is he asking heaven to send mercy, but he's asking heaven to send Lazarus to help him out. Isn't it strange that the shoe is on the other foot now? You couldn't help a man just asking in a whisper, "Can you give me a crumb from your table?" But now he is crying out with a loud voice saying, "Send Lazarus to me that he may dip his finger in water and cool my tongue!" I don't know all together what Abraham said to him, but I can imagine he said, "I'm not going to send Lazarus down there because Lazarus is not a bell hop. Lazarus is not an errand boy. He can't leave heaven and come down there because there is a gulf between you and us. You can't pass here, and we can't pass to where you are." That's his plight. That's the rich man's plight.

Let me take you to my second point. Look at Lazarus's bliss. Look at Lazarus's comfort. Look at Lazarus's happiness. Look at Lazarus's joy that is going on in Heaven right now, a man that did not have earthly riches. He did not have a royal status on Earth. As a matter of fact, while he was on Earth, he had a sick body. He had sores all over him. And while he was in this devastating condition and circumstance, nobody gave him time of the day. People walked away from him because he had sores on his body. He was looked on or seen as nobody to be close to because he's full of sores. He had no friends to give him a helping hand. The only friends that he seemed to have had were dogs. You know there's an old saying that a dog is sometimes a man's best friend. Do I have any help in here?

Being poor does not give you a guarantee and a ticket to Heaven. I think I need to say that right about now. Apparently, the poor man Lazarus trusted God. He had a relationship with Him, in- spite of his financial and physical condition. Anybody out there this morning you don't have the world's riches, the wealth; but you have a relationship with God. Can I just go on and tell you that all that really counts is that knowing you have a relationship with the Christ who saved you? Yes. I don't have all the world's riches, but I can tell you this morning one thing I got, I got the Lord. And if I got the Lord, I got His word. Not only do I have His word, but I have His Spirit in me. Anybody out there got the Word this morning? But look at this man. Look where he is. He's in Heaven. He's enjoying the presence of God. You see to be absent from the body is to be present with the Lord. Because Lazarus died, he's present with the Lord. And in the presence of the Lord, there is strength. There is joy in His presence. He's enjoying the bliss of Heaven. You don't want to miss Heaven shooting for the stars. Don't miss Heaven, shooting for the stars. And let me look at this word *star;* metaphorically or symbolically *shooting for the stars.* See, we can spend our days shooting for riches, for cars, and for clothes, jewelry, and power, but those things won't get you to Heaven. Rich or poor, it won't get you to Heaven. But what will get you to Heaven is knowing Jesus as your personal Savior is what gets you to Heaven.

Jesus doesn't condemn a man for having riches. There are going to be some rich folks in Heaven. You know they know Jesus. They love the Lord. They don't mind doing the Lord's work in the Earth. But what gets us to Heaven first and foremost is having a relationship with Jesus as your Savior. That's my ticket to Heaven. Jesus says, *"I'm the way, the truth and the life. No man cometh to the Father but by me".* I tell you He's your ticket today. Can I get a witness out there this morning? He's your ticket to Heaven. So, don't miss Heaven, my brothers and sisters, shooting for the stars. Don't miss Heaven shooting for all the creature comforts of this life and miss the essence of what God has already planned for your life. He wants us all to go to Heaven. He doesn't want any of us to die and be separated from Him.

Here is the last thing I'm going to lift, and I'm going to bid you farewell for the day. Listen at Abraham's reply to the rich man's request. Abraham's reply to the request of the rich man for Lazarus's sake, he says to the rich man, "Lazarus can't come and dip his finger in water. That's a no-no. He can't come to you." But then Abraham had to remind him of his lifetime. Abraham says to him, "Do you remember in your lifetime?" I don't want God to say do you remember when. I don't want to hear God say that to me. That will be sort of insulting to me knowing that I didn't do anything. I didn't do *nothing.* I didn't believe *nothing*. I didn't love *nothing* or anybody. I didn't give *nothing* so I could be in Heaven. But Abraham had to remind him, "Do you remember?"

That suggests to me that Heaven's got a record on us. I said Heaven's got a record on us. Heaven is watching us. Heaven knows what we do. Heaven knows when we are doing the best that we can. Heaven knows when we are doing nothing. Abraham says to him, "Do you remember in your lifetime? In your lifetime…you know what, you received good things. Man, you had it going on. You were getting all the good stuff, the good food, the best clothes, the best house. You had the best friends. You had the big friends. You had the good things in your lifetime."

Abraham says to him further, "But Lazarus received evil things. He got overlooked. He was cursed out. He was told to move, 'get out of my way with all your sores on you.' He got insults. He got the criticism, the ostracism. He got all those evil things, said, and done to him." God had to remind the rich man. My brothers and sisters, the rich man had one more request. He says, "I *ain't* through yet. You can't send Lazarus, but I got one more request. If you can't send him to me, send him to my father's house, because I got five brothers down there. Can you just allow him to testify to them that they don't need to come to where I am? I'm in a place of torment. Can you send him quickly that he might go and tell them don't come to this place?"

But I do want us to visit Verse 29 because that's where my text, my subject came from. Abraham's last reply to the rich man's request in Verse 29; *"They have Moses and the prophets; let them hear them."* In other words, they've got the Word there because the preachers are there telling them to get it right. They have the Word, so I can't send him back to your house, back to your dad's house to give a fair warning not to come to where you are. I can't send them there. But they got the Word. The Word is being spoken. The Word is being declared. The Word is getting out. Do they have an ear to hear what thus saith the Lord?

My brothers and sisters, as I prepare to wrap this thing up, you see the Word of God is the remedy for man's sins. The Word of God the remedy for every situation. What does the Word do for us? The Word guides us. The Word strengthens us. The Word encourages us. The Word points us to Jesus, and the Word points us to eternal life through Jesus Christ. Anybody out there got the Word this morning? Are you being guided by the Word? Are you being strengthened by the Word? Are you being encouraged by the Word? Is the Word consistently pointing you to Christ? Is the Word of God assuring you this morning, "I got Him? I got His salvation. I got His Word. I got His hope."

David says this, The Word *is a light unto my path*. Your Word *is a lamp unto my feet*. Anybody got the light of His Word? When things get dark, I get in the Word. The Word will lighten up my pathway. It allows me to see further than I'm seeing, because right now all I see is darkness. All I see is shadows. But I know that the Word has power. The Word can move me, guide me, and strengthen me to where I need to go. Anybody got His Word out there? The Word is a light. Not only is it a light, but it is a lamp. It's my lamp. It's right there at my feet. When I walk up on something the Word won't let me stumble. The Word won't let me fall because the Word is my lamp. It guides me. Oh, have mercy today. Do you have His Word? Do you have His Word this morning?

When I read John 1:1-4, there is the other Word. You see we have the Living Word, and then we've got the Word Himself. Do you know who the Word Himself is? The Word Himself is Jesus. Listen to John Chapter 1, Verses 1 through 4: *In the beginning was the Word, and the Word was with God, and the Word was God. The same was in the beginning with God.* Anybody got the Word this morning? I got Jesus. And there's a song that we use to sing at Church: I got Jesus and I don't need nothing else. I got Jesus. I don't need nobody else. I don't need another savior. I've got the Savior. I'm not looking for another blesser. I have the Blesser. His Name is Jesus. I've got the Word. And this is what the Word continues to tell us in John 1:1-4. He says, *"All things were made by him; and without him was not anything made that was made. In him was life; and the life was the light of men"*.

This morning can I just testify for a moment and tell you I've got life because Jesus came that I might have life. John 10:10 says, *"The thief cometh not, but to steal, and to kill, and to destroy; I am come that they might have life, and that they might have it more abundantly"*. I've life. He is the life of men. I got life, but I've also got light. And when you got life and light, oh, I tell you you've got a combination. I don't worry…I don't have to worry about where I'm going when I die. I'm going up yonder. Somebody might ask the question, "Reverend where is up yonder?" Well can I go on and tell you up yonder is in Heaven. I'm going to Heaven and when I get there, I'm gonna sing and shout and nobody will be able to put me out. That's where I'm going. And the reason why is because that's where my possessions lie. That's where my possessions lie. That's where my Savior is. That's where my eternal abode is, eternal with Him. Having things, the riches of this world, doesn't send us to hell. And being poor doesn't send us to Heaven. It's all about Christ, and knowing Christ, and having Christ in your life. That determines whether you go to Heaven or not. He makes the difference.

You were created a free moral agent. And being a free moral agent, you can choose whatever you want. You can choose Him, or not choose Him. But I would encourage you to choose Him, because if you choose Him, you choose life eternal forever. You choose not Him, you have not life, and you won't have the light of Him in you.

This is my message to you today. It was to me earlier this week. So, I just came to dump what the Lord dumped on me. And I pray that it was a good dump to encourage us that are saved, and to plea to those who are not saved. To let them know you've got a choice. You can choose Christ and live and cannot choose Christ and not live. I choose to live. And the Bible says, in Proverbs, *"there is life and death in the tongue"*. You can speak life, or you can speak death over you. I speak life over me. I speak life into you through the Word. Listen if you want to have that personal relationship with Christ.

CALL TO DISCIPLESHIP

Is there anyone out there today that has not met this Blessed Savior? I want you to know He lives, and He has life. He will impart life to you if you ask Him. Ask Him to come into your heart and save you from sin and self. Ask Him to change you and to transform you into this new creature. Just ask Him to forgive your sins and you accept Him as your Savior, and guess what? You are saved. It's your choice. You choose! You choose the way you want to live. But there's a good consequence, and then there's a bad consequence. Whichever you choose, you will reap the consequence.

So, this is my word to you today, and my invitation to anyone that's out there. You can accept Christ right where you are. You don't have to be in a Church building. Ask Him right there to come into your heart, save you and He will come in. But then as soon as we can get back into a Church structure find that Church, go to that Church, and let them know that you have received Jesus Christ as your Savior and get in Church. Do not just be in the Church but work out your soul's salvation. Work it out. You're not working to get saved, but you are saved to work. That was in the message. You're saved to work. God Bless you and thank you. Hope this has been a blessed message for you today.

We're going to ask Sis. Jarrett to come back and give us a closing song after this invitation. Then we will come back and just look forward to a great day.

SELECTION

The Blood Will Never Lose Its Power **by Andre E. Crouch**

CLOSING REMARKS

Anybody know anything about that Blood? That Blood of Jesus which never, ever loses its power. It has reaching power even into the heights and depths. Thank you for sharing that beautiful selection with us this morning. Well, my brothers and sisters this is bringing us down to the closing of this morning's worship experience.

Well let me say this before I sign off. Next Sunday is Mother's Day. Normally when we are at our Church house on Mother's Day it is a joyful and great time of celebrating mothers and selecting a mother of the Year. Of course, by not being in "the house", I'm working on something; trying to use my technological skills. I was working on something, and I hope that I can get this project up and working between now and next Sunday. If so, I'm going to tell you Wednesday night after Bible Study. I'm working on something, and I think you'll be excited. I'm hoping it will work. I'm trying to use my technological skills, and I don't have very good technological skills. But I'm working on something reflective. Amen.

Thank you so much and do tune in on Wednesday night for Bible Study. We hope that many of you will chime in and do Bible Study with us. We pray that it will be a blessing to you. And let me say to the rest of you, Happy Rest of Your Sunday! We hope you have a happy rest of your day.

I want to remind you that there is testing for the Coronavirus today from 12pm until 3pm at the Ripley Elementary School. For those of you who want to know if you have the symptoms or have had the symptoms, it's free of charge. Just go on down there and do it. I'm thinking about doing it. I'm kind of on the edge because I don't like that thing, however, I think I'm going to go if the line isn't long.

So have a good day my brothers and sisters. I love you. I love you with a passion. Guess what? You can't do one thing about it. I love you. I love you. I love you with a Jesus love. If you will, let's bow and give the benediction.

CLOSING PRAYER

The Lord blesses you and keep you. The Lord make His face to shine upon you and be gracious unto you. The Lord lifts the light of His countenance upon you and give you peace both now and forever. Amen.

A Mother's Faith in the Time of Crisis
Mothers' Day Sunday, May 10, 2020

OPENING REMARKS

Good morning! Good morning, St. Mark Family, my Faith Community, and friends around the country. First, let me say Happy Mothers' Day to all the mothers out there. Let me say this to our mothers. You are a jewel. You are a prized commodity to the human-race. You are just like God. You are a giver of life. So, this morning we ought to just take our hats off. We ought to just bow and thank God for mothers. Whether she is with you today, or she has made her abode in Heaven with the Lord, we still ought to thank God for mothers. And I just want to say to every mother out there this morning and Happy Mothers' Day. Enjoy your day. Enjoy motherhood. Enjoy the festivities that you will be engaged in today.

Let me just say to God be the Glory for the things He has done. He has done great things. Let us give God Glory today. You ought to, right where you are, just clap your hands Oh ye people. And if you're happy and you know it you ought to just clap your hands. Go ahead! You might as well clap your hands. In-spite of, we ought to be able to just give God the Glory today.

WORDS OF ENCOURAGEMENT

Well, I have a word of encouragement for you before we proceed into today's proceedings. My words of encouragement will come from Philippians Chapter 3:14, a very familiar passage. These words are the words of Apostle Paul. Listen to what Paul says, "*I press toward the mark for the prize of the high calling of God in Christ Jesus*". Let's look at this passage.

Paul says *I press*. The verb *press* is translated, *I follow after*; and it carries the idea of an intense endeavor. It's an intense endeavor. Now the Greeks use this word to describe a hunter. This is what a hunter does. A hunter eagerly pursues his prey. My brothers and sisters, a person cannot press or follow-after if he or she does not have what I call determination. You got to have determination.

Again, Paul says *I press toward the mark*. Well, what is the mark? The mark is the goal that you are determined to reach. You are pursuing. You are intensely endeavoring to pursue whatever you are after. The goal is your aim. Now, you're determined to reach the goal just like a runner who runs to reach the finishing line in the race he or she is running. Well, you must aim. You must aim at the goal. You must strive. You must endeavor. You must pursue. Now, let me tell you this. If you aim at nothing, you will hit it every time.

Paul says *press toward the mark of the high calling of God in Christ Jesus*. Therefore, we must look for the goal. What does look or looking mean? It means fixing your eyes on, and you are looking attentively. What is that saying to us? It speaks of our need to consistently focus on Christ regardless of our circumstance or our condition. My brothers and sisters, in the words of the Apostle Paul, press on, follow Christ. And I believe if you press on, and if you follow Christ, you will reach your goal. God bless you. These are my words of encouragement. We need encouraging words these days in which we live. Paul helped us this morning just telling us to *press toward the mark for the prize of the high calling which is of God in Christ Jesus.* Press on. Reach your goal. Pursue. Endeavor. Be determined. Aim. I said aim this morning. Focus your aim. Shoot high. Don't shoot low. Shoot high. God Bless you.

CALL TO WORSHIP

At this time, I'm going to prepare us now for worship on this beautiful sunny Mothers' Day. And as we prepare for worship, let me just say The Lord is in His Holy Temple, let the Earth be silent before Him. My lovely wife Sister Rose will come and lead us in a selection, after which I will come back and lead us in a word of prayer; intercessory prayer for mothers, for our country, and for our world in which we live and for so many other reasons. We have a multiplicity of things we need to be praying for in these days of uncertainty.

SELECTION

Oh, Give Thanks by Alvin Fruga

The Lord is good. He is so good. Anybody out there know that the Lord is good! If you know that the Lord is good give Him some praise. Give Him a hand clap of praise right where you are because He is good. God is good and He's good all the time.

Thank you, Sister Jarrett for sharing that beautiful selection with us. We know that we are blessed by her music. Let me just give her praise today for being such a wonderful source of help. Without her I couldn't really give you music. She has been gifted by God, and we just thank God for her willingness to be here by my side and to help me bring worship to you every Sunday morning while we're under quarantine. Amen. Amen. So, I just want to say to her, thank you from the depths of our hearts.

Let me just say Happy Mother's Day one more time to all those wonderful mothers out there, my mother as well. Amen. She doesn't have Facebook, but we've got her on the phone so she can hear. She can hear us as we speak. Amen.

Now let us proceed to the Throne of Grace at this moment. We're going to ask that you will bow with me right where you are. We know that prayer is always in order. Man ought to always pray and not faint. The fervent prayer, the warm prayer is what he is saying. The fervent means the warm and the hot prayers are so relevant for such a time because *the fervent prayers of the righteous availeth much*. So, let us go before God's Throne at this time.

PRAYER

Our Father which art in Heaven, hallowed be thy name, thy Kingdom come, thy will be done, in Earth as it is done in Heaven. We come now into thy very presence. We pray that now you will consecrate each of us to Thy service by the power of Grace Divine. Allow our hearts and souls to look up to thee with a steadfast hope. We pray that our wills be lost in thine. On this day which we come to celebrate, a day that has been set aside to honor mothers, we take this time to say to them thank you for the gift of life through Jesus Christ. Not only through birth did our mothers give us, but they went through agony and pain to give life. And even after birth, they continued to give us protection, love, and hope. So, therefore our mothers are worthy of praise. For we read in Proverbs 31, it says the virtuous woman's children rise-up to give her praise. They praise her for her household duties and motherly wit. She teaches. She trains. She taught us even our names. Thank You for mothers that prayed for us that we would come to know You, Oh God, as our Savior.

And as we pray today, Lord we pray for the sick, we pray for the shut-in, Lord, heal today. Heal those who are recovering from whatever the situation that was in their lives. Whether it was surgery, whether it was Covid, heart issues, Lord we just pray now that you will heal in the

Name of Jesus. And Oh God those who are bound by strongholds of Satan we pray you will break every chain. Set the captives free.

Lord, I pray a special blessing on our Church family this morning. We've been apart for more than six weeks. Lord thank You that tragedy has not come, nothing ill. Lord we just pray that you keep them covered. Keep them comforted. Lord it's just not our Church family only, but we pray for the Church Community. We pray for all our Pastors. Bless them as they lead their flocks by virtual communications. Keep them safe. Keep them sound. Lord, bless every ministry that is reaching out and touching lives even in difficult times.

Lord, we continue to pray for our nation. Bless America and bless the world. And Lord we know that businesses are starting to open. And I pray for the safety of those who are going and patronizing businesses and may be susceptible or exposed to the virus. Lord we just say that you will let it be a safe opening. Keep us! Lord! Shield us from these unseen viable diseases. And Lord, we want to say today we thank you. We love you. We bless you. We praise you. For it's in the name of Jesus we pray with a heart of thanksgiving. Amen, Amen, and Amen.

SERMON

As we prepare now to share a miniature message with you this morning, we pray that it will be a blessing and pray that it will be an encouragement this morning. And again, this is Mothers' Day, and I thought I would say something about a mother, a mother from scripture and a personality that I love. And this story is found in the book of Exodus. Exodus Chapter 2, Verses 1 through 10. I think that will be enough to kind of give us a gist of this beautiful mother. Exodus 2:1-10. Let's read:

> 1. *And their went a man of the house of Levi and took to wife a daughter of Levi.*

2. *And the woman conceived, and bare a son: and when she saw him that he was a goodly goodly child, she hid him three months.*

3. *And when she could not longer hide him, she took for him an ark of bulrushes, and daubed it with slime and with pitch, and put the child therein; and she laid it in the flags by the river's brink.*

4. *And his sister stood afar off, to wit what would be done to him.*

5. *And the daughter of Pharaoh came down to wash herself at the river; and her maidens walked along by the river's side; and when she saw the ark among the flags, she sent her maid to fetch it.*

6. *And when she had opened it, she saw the child: and, behold, the babe wept. And she had compassion on him, and said, This is one of the Hebrews' children.*

7. *Then said his sister to Pharaoh's daughter, Shall I go and call to thee a nurse of the Hebrew women, that she may nurse the child for thee?*

8. *And Pharaoh's daughter said to her, Go. And the maid went and call the child's mother.*

9. *And Pharoah's daughter said unto her, Take this child away, and nurse it for me. And I will give thee thy wages. And the woman took the child and nursed it.*

10. *And the child grew, and she brought him unto Pharaoh's daughter, and he became her son. And she called his name Moses: and she said, Because I drew him out of the water.*

From that passage this morning I want to talk about **A Mother's Faith in the Time of a Crisis.** Let me begin this sermon by giving us a biblical definition of faith. Now the Bible definition of faith it says in Hebrews 11:1: *Now faith is the substance of things hoped for, the evidence of things not seen.* In today's world it appears that seeing is believing rather than faith. Now biblical faith is believing when you don't see it, but you know it's out there. It's out there somewhere because God has it in reserve. God has it under control. So, Biblical faith is believing when you don't see it. When you know that you know, but no one else seems to know what you know because they can't see it and because you have the faith of God in you.

Again, the Bible says that *faith comes by hearing, and hearing by the Word of God.* I hear people say all the time, I need more faith. But can I tell us parenthetically this morning that if you want faith, get in the Word of God. The Bible says that *faith comes by hearing, and hearing by the Word of God.* God's Word is all the faith that you need. God has heard us, but the God that we serve is heard through our Bibles, through scripture, speaking to every heart that is open to hear and believe His every Word. That's what faith is. And that's what I saw in Moses's mother, Jochebed. That was her name, Jochebed.

Jochebed had faith amid her crises. She knew what she was believing God for amid uncertain times and even threats. She knew that everything was going to be alright in her life and in the lives of her family. Those of us who are saved and fellowship with God daily, live by faith. We don't live like the world lives. The world lives in seeing, and they say seeing is believing. Faith in God says I'm believing, even though I don't see it. That's why Paul, the writer of the text and in other passages he says *the just shall live by faith.* That's how I live. That's the way God says for us to live. We are to live by faith. The just live by faith even amid a crisis. I don't care what's happening. I don't care what's going on. We must live by faith even in crisis. That's what the mother of Moses did. That's my subject this morning, **A Mother's Faith in the Time of Crisis**. We've looked at the mother's faith. But let's look at the crisis.

What is a crisis? According to the **American Heritage Collegiate Dictionary**, it says that a crisis is *a crucial or a decisive point or situation* – or a turning point if you will. It's a turning point. Things have turned around. You were going along, and things were just going great. Things were fine. All the bills were paid. No debt. Then, suddenly, a crucial, decisive point and or a situation came and turned things in a bad way.

The second thing I want to say about a crisis is, *it's an unstable condition*. Can't you see that we are living in unstable times? Even the economy has become unstable. At one time it was flourishing. Yes, the Dow Jones was up, but now we are in a crisis. The Stock Market is down. People are looking for ways to get by, to get through this crisis that we find ourselves in. Yes, something has impended or imputed into our circumstance. It has become abrupt. We got an abrupt change now.

The other thing I want to say about a crisis; It *is a sudden change in the course of a disease or fever*. Last year this time we were going along happy as a lark. But here we are in 2020, with a sudden change in the course of life. A disease has come among the races or people, countries…a disease. And it has caused emotional stress. It has caused a change in people's lives. Things are not what they use to be. It's not normal. We're wondering if we'll get back to a life of normalcy. Everybody is hoping and praying that we can get back. That's a crisis. We find ourselves in a crisis. But let me hurry up to my text. I had to set us up for what's about to come.

In our text this morning, a mother's faith and a crisis are not an unusual combination. Let's look at Moses' mother Jochebed. She encountered a crisis, an unstable condition involving an impending abrupt of decisive change. Pharaoh, the king of Egypt, one day decided to kill all the male babies. Can't you see the crisis coming on? He just abruptly decided, "I'm going to take out all the male babies because I see growth among the Israelite people. And they may one day rise-up and fight against us and take our nation away from us. They are multiplying, and I am going to kill all the male babies. Here Jochebed, as the scripture says, she was of the house of Levi. She was the daughter of a Levite. She had conceived a child. She bore a son. Jochebed knew that her baby was to be taken out to be killed. So, Jochebed had to grab hold of her most holy faith. She had to hold on to her faith in the time of a crisis. Did you hear what I said? Jochebed, what did she do in the midst of her crisis? She grabbed her faith, her most holy faith. She held onto her faith in the time of a crisis. And that's what we've got to do in this time in which we live. We've got to grab our most holy faith.

She was a woman of faith. The reason why I know she was a woman of faith is because when I read Hebrews 11:23, she is placed in the Hall of Fame of Faith. She's there with great giants like Abraham and Sarah, Joseph, Isaac. She's there among the heroes, and she's a "she-roe" of faith. It is said by faith Moses when he was born was hidden three months by his parents...why? They saw he was a beautiful child. And you know every mother thinks that her child is beautiful. I don't care how ugly he is. And what others say about him, if a mother has a child, that's my baby, and he looks just as good as anybody else's baby. They saw him as a beautiful child. But that verse also said something else. Verse 23 says, *and she says they were not afraid of the king's command.* They were not afraid of the king's command. A diligent faith counteracts fear. Moses' mother, she lived by faith, believing that God would take care of her child in the midst of a crisis. Can't you see diligent faith counteract fear? "I don't care what Pharaoh says, he ain't going to take my child." And I believe mothers that have young children ought to rise-up today and say, "I'm not going to let the Pharaohs of our day take my child." We see senseless stuff going on around our country where our children are being murdered in the streets like animals. Mothers need to rise-up, live by faith, and trust God that He will take care of our children amid a crisis. But we've got to teach our children how to be good children. God will protect them.

You know what? I just believe Jochebed believed God would have His angel to keep watch over her baby if he would live. She believed a way would be made, and God would make that way for her son. She believed that God would protect him from harm. My brothers and sisters, we've got to pray. We've got to have faith even in the crisis that we are going through. We've got the unseen virus that is threatening, and not just old folks, but even young folks. And then we've got the violence and the ignorance that's in the streets. We've got to pray that God will protect our children, our seed, our young men, and young women alike. Protect them from harm. I just believe Jochebed lived with courage deep in her heart. She kept the courage deep down in her heart. She waited. She watched. And she prayed. That's what we've got to do. We've got to wait. We've got to watch. And we've got to pray.

When Jochebed discovered that she could no longer keep her son in hiding, what did she do? She devised a way that she was going to spare her son, even if it meant taking him down to the Nile River, build this little bulrush, pitch it with lime, and then place flags and lay it along the riverbanks. She just believed that if I just prepare a way to save my son's life, God is going to watch over him. God is going to take care of him. She did what she had to do. We must do what we've got to do. God will do what God has to do. She could no longer hide him, but she could hide him in God.

And then what was so ironic about it, she dispatched her daughter, Moses' sister. She dispatched her, and Moses' sister stood afar off to watch to see what would be done to Moses, if he would just float on down the Nile River or float on out of the area. She watched him. She waited. She prayed. But I need for us to watch God. Watch God work. She was trusting in the providence of God, and God didn't fail her. God never fails us when we pray, when we wait, and when we watch. All you got to do is stand still and see God at work.

Now watch God start putting things in perspective. When the king's daughter decided that it was time to take a bath, guess where she comes? But it's the hand of God, the unseen hand of God that is working. I'm sure God has a way of getting into our spirits and says to

Pharaoh's daughter, "It's time to go take a bath. And take you maids on down there with you." So, she goes to the Nile and takes a bath, and when she got there, she saw the basket, the ark. And she discovered that there was a baby there. She heard the cry. I don't think she had any children at that time, but I just believe in reading the text that a maternal instinct told her to rescue the baby. Take care of him. See God. Watch God. God used the baby's cry. God used the baby's tears to control the heart of Pharaoh's daughter, who was a princess.

And He used Miriam's, Moses' sister words to arrange for the baby's mother to raise the boy. She says to Pharaoh's daughter, "Would you care that I go get one of the Hebrew women…" Look at God. "…to raise this child. …to nurse this child?" Don't tell me that God is not in the miracle working business. He's working a miracle every day. I'm a living miracle this morning. When I woke up this morning about 5 o'clock, it was a miracle. When you woke up whatever time this morning you were a miracle. God is working miracles every day, even amid crises. Don't underestimate God in the middle of a crisis. If you got the faith, trust God. You know what Pharaoh's daughter says to Miriam? "Yes, go get me one of those Hebrew mothers to nurse this baby for me", but not only that, "I'll pay the expense for the raising of the child." Tell me God won't work things out in your favor if you just trust Him and if you got faith. He made the enemy's daughter pay for it, wow. Look at God, won't He do it! It's all because Moses had a praying momma. Moses had a mother of faith amid a crisis.

God can use the weakest things to defeat the mighty enemy. Won't He do it! He will use the weakest things. Stuff that we think is strong, more powerful, God says, "I don't need that. Let me just take the little things, the minute things and work a miracle." He will work things out in your favor. The daughter of Pharaoh adopted Moses. Look at God further working this thing out, bringing favor to Jochebed's house. She adopts Moses as her own son, which means Moses had favor. Moses had a position in the land. Look at God. This is God's set up because God is looking at the future. This man will become Israel's liberator. He's going to be like a Christ, Jesus Christ who would come to liberate us from the tyranny of sin. Moses liberated Israel through the hands of God and brought them to Promise. Yes, this young boy grew up in Pharaoh's house, ate at Pharaoh's table, slept in Pharaoh's bed, and was educated in Pharaoh's school. Look at God. God worked things out. If you got faith even amid a crisis God can still bless you.

This boy became a mighty man who did God's work. God can bless you amid a crisis. If you got the faith, God's got the power. He can work things out in your favor. I just believe through this era, this crisis that we're going through God is going to work out some favor in the crisis. We just got to have faith, trust God, and give Him time. He's got to have time. He's got to work on some stuff. He's got to work on some people. He's got to work on some hearts. And when He gets through working on the hearts, He's going to work it all out. We just got to have faith.

You can't hurry God. Don't push Him. Just trust Him. "Trust Me when you can't trace Me. Trust Me when you don't see which way I went. Trust Me." I feel good right now. I'm about to shout in my own seat. I've got to trust Him. You've got to trust Him. We all got to trust Him. The whole world has got to trust Him. We've got to lean hard on Him.

Mothers I just come by to say to you this morning, when you're going through something, don't let anything or anyone get in the way of you and God. You know what people will tell you, "I wouldn't do that. I wouldn't go that way." Well, you ain't me. I'm talking to God. I'm trusting God. This is the way God is leading me. They will question why you are doing the things you do, and the way you are going. "I wouldn't go that way. I'd do it this way." That ain't the way God told me to do it. Moses' mother knew where to take him to get his best help. And this was God working behind the scenes. Can I tell us this morning?

God is working behind the scenes. You don't see Him working, but His hands are moving all the time. God is working even in the midnight hour. He's working while we're asleep. He's working it out.

Let me use another character in the Bible. You remember the story of the woman who had the issue of blood for 12 long years. This woman had gone through this process of losing blood. She spent all. She went to this doctor. She went to that doctor. She went to this specialist. She went to that specialist. Guess what? They could not do her any good. She had this crisis. This was a crisis in her life. How do you know it was a crisis? She couldn't get well. She has spent all she had. She had nothing left. She *had* but one other alternative, and that's Jesus.

The doctors couldn't heal her. They couldn't get her back. She's stressed and depressed, going through crises. But you know what, she heard about Jesus, and now she had to get up from where she was and seek Jesus. And when she sought Him, she discovered that there was a crowd all around Him. She had to buck her way. She had to push her way. She had to press her way. Press through pride. Press through the crowd. Press through her sickness. Push through the crowd to get to Jesus. Somebody ought to be pushing this morning. Somebody ought to be pressing like Paul. That's why I told you this morning you got to press toward your mark of your high calling. You've got to see where you are going. You've got to aim. You've got to be determined. She pressed her way through the crowd.

My question for mothers today is what does it take for you to get to Jesus? People may ask you why you raise your hand in praise all the time. Why are you always shouting? Why are you always talking about this and that? Well, some may want to know why you always yelling, saying hallelujah and praise the Lord. See you know where you been. You know you have been brought through a crisis. This is a crisis after every crisis. Looks like when you get over one thing something else comes along. You take two steps forward. Then you take five backwards. Crises come; crises go.

And people are wondering why you're throwing up your hands. You don't know what I been through. You got to shout. That's why I lift holy hands. That's why I give the Lord praise. Because I know if it had not been for the Lord who was on my side, I never would have made it. Men this message is for you too. It isn't just for women or mothers. We men have our crises. We go through it too. But when we get through our crises, we ought to shout. We ought to throw up holy hands and just tell Him thank You. Praise Your Name.

Tell them the reason I praise the Lord is because when I went through my crisis, crisis after crisis, I had nobody to help me but the Lord. And that's why I make all this crazy noise. That's why you see me wringing my hand. That's why you see tears fall from my eyes. That's why you see me do what I do. He's been good to me. He was good in the time of a crisis. You just hold on, and don't let go. Keep the faith. I just believe that good mothers have found that when you trust in the Lord, He will turn your hard times into good times. Your setbacks become leap forwards. Thank you, Jesus. He will turn your defeats into success. He'll turn your failures into victories.

Is there a mother out there this morning that knows He'll do it? He'll do it. What He's done for others, He'll do the same for you. I know He'll do it. This mother, she's one who has learned that weeping may endure for a night. But guess what? Joy will come in the morning. Yes, it will. Anybody out there knows that joy will come! Is there a mother out there who can declare right now, "I know the Lord will answer prayer? The reason why I know He will answer prayer, I tried Him for myself, and I know He will."

And as I close, I just want to say to the mothers, hold on. Just hold on. Hold to your faith in this time of crisis and in this time of a pandemic. In this time just maintain the faith. God has got you. God will hear you. He's hearing you right now. He's just waiting for His time. And when He says enough is enough, it's over then. I don't care what nobody says. I don't care who says it. When He says enough, it's over. That's the way God works. He said put your trust in Him. You live by the faith that you have, and God will reward you for your faithfulness.

Thank you, this morning. God bless you mothers. God bless you. Have a great rest of your day. We pray that your families be blessed. We pray that your children will be a blessing to you. Oh Lord, I tell you I feel good right now. I hate to close it, but I know I've got to close. There's nobody like Him, I say this all the time. He's in a class all by Himself. He has no equals. Nobody can measure up to Him. He has a standard that no one else can mimic or emulate. He has a standard, and He's trying to bring us to it in our faith's level. Grab faith! If you don't know what faith is, get your Bible and read what faith is. It is *the substance of things hoped for, the evidence of things not seen.* Yes sir. *The just shall live by faith. Faith comes by hearing, and hearing by the word of God.* Get in the Word, and let faith have its way.

CALL TO DISCIPLESHIP

I'm going to open the doors of the Church right here. I'm going to say to any person out there this morning that doesn't know Jesus as his or her personal Savior, you have a chance right now, right where you are to just ask the Lord in your life. Just tell Him, "Lord, come into my heart. I'm a sinner, and I need saving grace. Save me." And if you can believe that Jesus Christ is the Savior of sinners, and that He died for your sins…if you can trust Him, if you can just put your faith in Him, you can be saved right where you are. You don't have to be in the Church house. You can be in your house. You can be in the back yard. Wherever you are, you can be saved. Just ask Him in your heart. Ask Him into your life, and He will come in. And He will set up residence. He will make that radical change in your life. If you can believe it, receive it today.

And when this thing is ended, go to somebody's Church, and let the Church know that you are a part of God's body. You are a part of the family. And some Church will receive you and take you in as a member of the Church family. God bless you. Thank you so much. We want you to just give God Glory today. Sis. Jarrett is going to come back now and give us a selection.

SELECTION

Take My Hand, Precious Lord **by Thomas A. Dorsey**

CLOSING REMARKS

Precious Lord, take my hand; Lead me on, let me stand. I know we get tired sometimes. We're going through storms, through nights. We need the Lord to take our hand and lead us on. And when the ways grow drear, you want the Lord to linger. When life is almost gone, we want Him to hear our cry. Hear our call. Hold your hand because we're subject to fall. Take my hand Precious Lord. Lead me home. Thank you so much. This is going to bring us to the close of today's message, today's moment of worship.

I have something special for you guys at 5 o'clock this evening. When you have finished your Mother's Day dinner, and you're not too busy, this is something I believe will be blessing to you as you go into tonight. The Lord put it on my heart and for some reason I just put my hands on it. I said you know this will be great to share Mother's Day afternoon. It's like coming back to Church. Come on back at 5 o'clock. We're going to enjoy this and you're going to love it.

I was blessed this week to hear from my oldest Church member, our oldest mother Sis. Harriet Barbee. She called me and said, "Pastor I just want to hear your voice." We talked about 15 minutes. She's 102 years of age. She'll be celebrating another birthday come this August. And with the power invested in me as the Pastor of St. Mark

Missionary Baptist Church, I want to declare her right now as "Mother of the Year". Do I have that right? She's one hundred two years old, and she's worthy of recognition. She has lived through some crises, and able to look back and talk about it with a smile. So, we want to say to Sis. Harriet Barbee I am selecting you as the "Mother of the Year". Enjoy this day Sweetheart, and just keep on doing what you do. Press on my sister. God Bless you.

Happy Mothers' Day again.
Well, let me give the benediction and let me go.

CLOSING PRAYER

Now the Lord bless you and keep you. The Lord make His face to shine upon you and be gracious unto you. The Lord lifts the light of His countenance on you and give you peace both now and forever. And all the people of God said Amen.

Thank you everybody for worshiping with us all over the place.

The Battle Is the Lord's
Sunday, May 17, 2020

OPENING REMARKS

What a beautiful selection this morning. I woke up this morning. I felt like shouting. I felt the Holy Spirit. Oh, what a great morning it is to be alive. First and foremost, let me say good morning to our Church family. Good morning, Faith Community! Good morning, everybody that is listening to me right now. Anybody out there hasn't told the Lord good morning? If you haven't, you need to tell Him right now, good morning, God! Isn't it wonderful to wake up in the morning and stir about your house; and you see everybody is well and doing good? You say good morning mom, good morning dad, good morning son, and good morning daughter. You know God feels the same way when we wake up in the morning and breathing His fresh air, we ought to just tell the Lord "Good morning, God! He needs to hear from you this morning if you've not already told him good morning. So, you might as well go on right now and just tell Him good morning if you have not told Him good morning, God!

You see if it had not been for the Lord who was on our side where would we be right now. So, why don't you just go on and give Him some praise because God inhabits the praise of His people. Did you not hear what I said? God inhabits the praise of His people. If you've just got one more praise in you, why don't you just let it out right now, right where you are? It doesn't matter where you are just let it out. Just give God some praise. The Bible says *let the redeemed of the Lord say so*. If anybody got the right to say so, you know what, it is the redeemed. Who are the redeemed? The redeemed are those who have been purchased by the precious blood of Jesus Christ. In other words, Christ bought you back. We were sold out to Satan, and we had no means of being redeemed other than through Jesus Christ Our Lord. So, He's, our redeemer. So therefore, He is worthy of our praise. Amen. So, if you got one more praise, give it to Him. Give it to Him. He deserves your praise.

WORDS OF ENCOURAGEMENT

Well, first and foremost let me get started here. I've got a word of encouragement for you. We all need encouragement along the way. Things come our way and sometimes it takes our spirit from us. It just takes our joy away from us. Oh, but let me take this morning, God's word has so much encouragement. It doesn't matter where you go in your Bible to read, there is encouragement in God's word. I want to encourage you this morning from Psalms 136 Verse 1 through 5. Listen to these verses. They are almost repetitious, but there's so much information there. Listen to Psalms 136 Verses 1 through 5. Listen:

1. *O give thanks unto the Lord; for he is good: for his mercy endureth forever.*
2. *O give thanks unto the God of gods: for his mercy endureth forever.*
3. *O give thanks to the Lord of lords: for his mercy endureth forever.*
4. *To him who alone doeth great wonders: for his mercy endureth forever.*
5. *To him that by wisdom made the heavens: for his mercy endureth forever.*

How often do you thank God for what He has done in your life? Do you ever tell God thank you? If you don't, it's a good time right now to just tell God thank you for as many times as you call on Him in the times of trouble and for your needs. Tell Him thank you. Understand this truth of God and how He deals with us according to His mercy. That's how God deals with us according to His mercy. And know this about God; God has plenty of mercy. Did y'all hear that? God has plenty of mercy. He never runs out because the Bible says *He is rich in mercy*. So, you don't ever have to worry about where you are going to get your mercy from. It is from the Lord. He giveth mercy because He is rich in mercy.

Psalm 136 is a Psalm that calls the Church to praise. It is a Psalm that calls the Church to praise with a reason to praise. Also, it calls us to give thanks to God for his mercy. Did you hear him in verse 1, 2 and 3? Each verse starts off by saying *O give thanks unto the Lord. O give thanks to the God of gods. O give thanks to the Lord of lords.* It calls the Church to praise with a reason to praise for his mercy. He never runs out of it. So, we need to give Him thanks for His mercy.

Now he tells us there's another reason or cause that we should do this, the cause for His wonderful and marvelous works. Oh, I tell you God has done great things, marvelous things and He's yet doing great things. He will continue to do great and marvelous things. Why? *Because His mercy endureth forever.* What is mercy? I know we've heard it said and expressed in so many ways: it's favor, it's this, it's that, it's the other. But I looked at this verse and it shows me another extension or meaning to God's mercy. What is His mercy?

Let's look at it from this perspective; his mercy is simply the expression of His love which *endureth forever*. That's His expression of His love, and that love *endureth forever*. God loveth us at all times, and He will continue to love us. There's nothing we can do that will cause God not to love us. He loves us in-spite of… in-spite of our bad situations…in-spite of our bad ways. If we don't even look at Him, He still loves us. Oh, bless His Name. That's greater love or unconditional love in-spite of. Amen. So, He's telling us this morning that His mercy, His grace and His love is a continual process.

God's mercy was present in creation. God's mercy was present in our redemption when we got saved. His mercy is present with us right now, just go on and claim His mercy because His mercy is present right now for you. Not only that but His mercy will present us even in the future of His glory. Listen to David in Psalm 23:6 - the last phrase of it. He said *surely goodness and mercy shall* what, *follow me all the days of my life.* You are never without God's mercy, and that's why the psalmist is telling us "*O give thanks unto the Lord for he is good and his mercy endureth for ever…forever ever…forever.* How long is forever? There is no limit. It's unlimited. That's what God's mercy is all about. Yes, His compassion, His expression is always love to us.

These is my word of encouragement to you this day. I hope you take this Word and allow it to sync itself in your hearts and produce a fruit that will be always ripened. God bless you.

CALL TO WORSHIP

As we prepare for worship now, The Lord is in his holy temple let the earth be silent before Him. It is time for worship. Are you ready for worship out there this morning? It's been a long week. It's been a troublesome week. But you know what, we going to still worship God in-spite of, because *God's mercy endureth forever.*

So, Sister Rose is going to come now and bless us with a selection. After which we will come back with a prayer, an intercessory prayer for the many needs the minute things that is encumbered upon us. We need God's mercy. That same mercy is still available today. It endureth how long? *Forever,* amen.

Come on Sis. Rose.

SELECTION

God Has Smiled On Me by Isaiah Jones

How many out there today know that God has been good to you, and God has smiled upon you one more time? Thank You, God for Your amazing and truly wondrous love. He does smile on us. And every now and then we must look up, you know, just see that big old' smile that God grants us. You just look in the sky, just look at nature. Just even look at yourself and discover that God has smiled on you one more time.

My Brothers and Sisters it is time for prayer. We need prayer in these difficult and evil days in which we now live. I just believe that prayer is the key. Prayer is the answer to the world's situation today. When we pray in faith believing that the God we serve will intervene, He will do something for us in times like these. He will. If we've got the faith, God's got the power. Faith unlocks the door to God's blessing my brothers and sisters. Hebrews 11:6 bears that out to us. It says *he that cometh to God must believe that He is to rewarder of them that diligently seek Him.* If we seek God and if we are diligent with Him, then God rewards what we are seeking diligently for. You've got to want it. You've got to believe. So, let us now petition and plea at the throne of Grace, even right now. Shall we bow.

PRAYER

Most Holy and All Wise God, *How Excellent is Thy Name in all of the Earth, i*t is at Your Name that *every knee shall bow, and every tongue shall confess,* whether it's in Earth or beneath the Earth, *it will confess that You are Lord.* So, we come now humble with a submissive spirit. Lord, we ask you to forgive us for unknown and known sins that are in our lives. And we confess them as we come into your presence. Lord, we just want to thank you for another day's journey. Thank you for your mercy which endures forever. Thank you for peaceful night of sleep and slumber. Thank you for your special graces and your choice blessings you have bestowed upon us. Lord, we thank you for the gift of Salvation. Without you we would yet be in our sins groping and moping in the dark crevices of this world. But thank you Lord that you gave us life through your Son, Jesus.

And now God we pray for the sick, those in hospitals and convalescent homes. Lord, we come with a special prayer and pray your choice blessings and your special graces be upon all. Even now Lord, touch their bodies. Heal like only you can. And Lord, we know you can because you said with you all things are possible if we only believe. So, Lord we believe today that you going to touch them. You are going to heal them. Lord, bless the families that are by their sides. Be with doctors and nursing staff. Lord, we heard you saying in your Word *there is a balm in Gilead to heal the sick*. There is a Balm to make the wounded whole. So, we say to you this morning, have your way Lord even now. And we believe you're going to work it all out.

And Lord we pray for those families, again the passing of loved ones, be with them as they travel to and fro, for Lord it seems as though when you get over one thing another comes. But we know that you've got them all, keep them in the hallow of your hand. We ask Lord to keep your hedge of protection around our Church family and Churches in this community and around this country. Lord, we lift our Pastors. Keep your hands upon them, Oh God, as they feed the flock that you have made them overseers of.

Keep your hands on America as we reel and rock through corona virus. We pray for our scientists. Lord, we know you will in your own good time show them a method. You will give them a discovery of a vaccine to combat this virus. We believe you will. So, Lord we are just going to trust you. And we ask you, oh God, to keep your hands on our leaders. Touch them in your own special way. And as we close this prayer today God, we just want to say thank you. We want to say Lord continue to allow your mercy to endure. We praise you now. We ask it all in your precious, your promising, and your powerful name, Jesus the Christ our Lord, Amen, and Amen, and Amen.

SERMON

Thank you for sharing in that prayer this morning. We believe that God is going to hear and answer every petition that has been spoken in his presence today. Amen. Now let's get into the Word. It's time for a Word from the Lord. I pray that it will be a blessing to you this morning as the Lord put on my heart to share this with you today. Let me gather yours minds to an Old Testament book. The book of 1Samuel 17.This is a familiar story, and we're going to look at Verse 38 through about Verse 47 because my subject matter will come from Verse 47. But the previous verses will set you up for what's to come in verse 47.Let's start in Verse 38:

> 38. And Saul armed David with his armour, and he put a helmet of brass upon his head; also he armed him with a coat of mail.
>
> 39. And David girded his sword upon his armour, and he assayed to go; for he had not proved it. And David said unto Saul, I cannot go with these; for I have not proved them. and David put them off him.
>
> 40. And he took his staff in his hand and chose him five smooth stones out of the brook and put them in a shepherd's bag which he had, even in a scrip; and his sling was in his hand: and he drew near to the Philistine.
>
> 41. And the Philistine came and drew near unto David; and the man that bare the shield went before him.
>
> 42. And when the Philistine looked about, and saw David, he disdained him: for he was but a youth, and ruddy, and of fair countenance.
>
> 43. And the Philistine said unto David, Am I a dog that thou comest to me with staves? And the Philistine cursed David by his gods.

44. And the Philistine said to David, come to me, and I will give thy flesh unto the fowls of the air, and to the beasts of the field.

45. Then said David to the Philistine, Thou comest to me with a sword, and with a spear, and with a shield: but I come to thee in the name of the Lord of hosts, the God of the armies of Israel, whom thou has defied.

46. This day will the Lord deliver thee into mine hand; and I will smite thee, and take thine head from thee; and I will give the carcases of the host of the Philistines this day unto the fowls of the air, and the wild beasts of the earth; that all the earth may know that there is a God in Israel.

47. And all this assembly shall know that the Lord saveth not with sword and spear: for the battle is the Lord's, and he will give you into our hands.

From these series of verses this morning I want to talk from the subject, and it's coming from verse 47 midways the verse, **The Battle is the Lord's.** Can you just say that with me right where you are **The Battle is the Lord's? The Battle is the Lord's.** Amen. Amen. Amen.

As I began this message this morning by stating this: What truth there is to receive. What truth there is to receive? What lesson to be learned from this text and this subject? **The Battle is the Lord's.** All too often as believers in Christ we try to fight our own battles by ourselves. We try to fight our own battles by our own strengths. But listen at the text this morning it says *the battle belongs to the Lord.* He's the one that gives the strength. He may use us in the battle, but the battle truly belongs to the Lord. It belongs to the Lord. So, we need to stop trying to fight our battles by ourselves, because too many times we try to move our mountains with our own feeble strengths. My Brothers and Sisters we even try to solve our own problems through our own abilities. And all too often we endeavor to run our race many times without God's help, and we end up in devastating situations. Sometimes we end up in discouragement; we are despaired and even defeated because, guess what, we tried to do it through our own strengths. **The Battle is the Lord's.** After all our battles, and some of our battles that we find ourselves battling in, they are fierce and they're dangerous. So, as Christians we don't have, or we don't possess the strength. We don't possess the ability, the experience to deal with some things that come our way or into our lives. It is not for us to try to fight because they're too difficult. We need somebody bigger than our problem.

My brothers and sisters it is no wonder that so many of us surrender. We give into the enemy. We as Christians, we need to realize that without God we'll never overcome a battle or overcome a problem or situation that arises. Don't misunderstand me. We need to apply ourselves to the fullest. We need to be determined to do our best. We need to abide by the rules, abide by God's Word. But also, we must realize that when we have reached our limitations, when we have reached our limitations, when we have done all that we know how to do or can do then it's no longer ours. It becomes God's because we realize that God has no limitations. See when we have reached our extremities, then it becomes God's opportunity to deal with it. You and I may not know what to do at any given point in our life, but God knows what to do. You may feel like you're losing the battle, but can I tell you, you're not losing. You're not losing because when the battle is the Lord's, the Lord can't lose. He never loses.

I remember years ago our youth use to sing a song *He Always Comes out a Winner at the Finishing Line*. God always comes out at the finishing line. It looks like whatever is coming at us is winning, and it looks like God is nowhere in the picture. But my brothers and sisters God is working from behind the scenes, and God is working this thing out. He can't lose. He never loses. He's always a winner at the finishing line.

My brothers and sisters if the battle is the Lord's, He can also use us in the battle as we submit to Him. Can't you see David in the text? David submitted to the Lord, and God used him in the battle, but the battle was the Lord's. David submitted to the Lord. Once upon his submission to God, then he could win over this big giant. Yes, David and Goliath, as we know this story, is the best-known story in the Old Testament. It is an historical account that illustrates the battle. Let's describe this battle. Yes, we're looking at a giant, but listen to what is happening behind the scenes in this process. It is an historical account that illustrates a battle between what? Right and wrong. Who's right? God is right but Satan is wrong. It's a battle between good and bad. Who's the good in this? God is the good. The devil is the bad. It's a battle between what God can do versus what the enemy can do. It's a battle. It's a story about a boy and a giant.

The Bible says this little boy was ruddy, he was pretty, a little boy as the text would tell us, but he knew God. This giant in the text, was 9 feet tall plus 9 inches. This is a battle between a boy and a giant but behind the scenes there is a conquering God. Yes, it's a story about how humility overcomes pride. Can't you hear the giant saying "*Y'all* come out here. I'm gonna take your flesh and I'm gonna feed it to the birds." He's blurting out. He's doing all his bragging about what he's going to do. Look at pride. David just came in humility trusting his God was going to give him victory over the giant.

I see something else in this text this morning. I can see weakness conquering strength so to speak now. I can see weakness because here is a boy and a giant. This man was huge. He had strength. David is a little boy looked upon as a weakling, but Goliath couldn't see the strength behind the little boy that his strength was in God. When you got a giant in your life you need to rely on your unseen strength, God. Our unseen strength is God. He's always there for us when we need Him the most. He uses us in the process. In order to see the underlying principle, to this showdown, that is about to take place between a boy and a giant, I need to take us back to Chapter 16 and Verse 13. See this uncircumcised, oversize giant was relying on the physicality of his own body and strength to overcome this boy and the people of Israel.

But this giant did not see what David had on him. Then something happened in Chapter 16. What happened Reverend? Well God sent Samuel down to Jesse's house to anoint a boy who would become the next King in Israel. You know what? Samuel gets his horn of oil. He proceeds down to Jesse's house. When he gets there, he greets Jesse. Jesse greets Samuel. As they dialog, as they talk for a moment, I could just hear old man Jesse saying to Samuel, "Why are you here today?" Samuel's reply to Jesse is, "I've come to your house because the Lord has sent me to anoint one of your boys." I could hear Jesse say, "OK. Well, you know I've got seven of them here at the house right now. Alright, let's start the process."

They started the process, and these boys of Jesse started to walk underneath the horn of oil. But as they walked underneath the horn of oil, no oil poured on their heads. And it was from one to seven that nothing happened. And Jesse, I'm sure, now is wondering well nothing happened. Did the Lord really send him? So, Samuel says to Jesse, "Do you have one more boy…do you have another boy at the house?" Jesse says, "Well yes, I got one. He's out there in the field. He's young. He's attending the sheep." "Well, you need to send him to the house." When little David came to the house, Samuel raised up the horn of oil, and oil start the flow upon David. Samuel says, "He's the one." You see, what I'm trying to say this morning in this text entitled **The Battle Is the Lord's** you see the underlining principle to the showdown that was between this boy and this giant is David had the anointing of God on his life. This is what helps us in the time we are going through in fighting battles.

We need the anointing on our lives because the anointing of the Holy Spirit is what makes the difference in the life of a child of God. That's what makes the difference in the life of a child of God, it is the anointing. It is having the Holy Spirit, the Holy Power working in your life. Without the anointing that comes from God, guess what, we are weak to defend even ourselves against the enemy of our souls. Without the anointing we are too easily distracted from the responsibilities one faces when we are without the anointing. We need the anointing. David did not do anything until he was anointed of God. So, it is with us. We should not attempt to do anything until we have been anointed by God. As a matter fact, whatever you put your hands to, if it's not anointed of God it won't amount to nothing. It won't make anything grand or great happen. You've got to have the anointing. If you're going to do ministry, you've got to have the anointing. Whatever you do that's in the Name of the Lord, you need the anointing.

We've got the anointing in our lives, but we don't know how to access Him. See when you got saved it was the Holy Spirit, the Holy Ghost that brought about your Salvation. It bothers me when people try to make themselves have more of the Holy Spirit than others. If you're saved, you got Him. Now the only people that don't have the Holy presence of God and the anointing of God is the unsaved folks that's in the world. If you got the Holy Spirit, you got power to defeat whatever is in your life. You just got to access Him. You've got to let Him operate in your life. He has a privilege. He should be given the privilege in your life to operate. You can quench the Spirit. You can hold the Spirit back by not allowing Him to take free course in your life. And when you insult Him by not allowing Him to do what He's supposed to do, He steps back. That's when we make a mess of things when we don't let the Holy Spirit have free course and operation in our lives. He's been given to you to operate in your life. That's what made the difference with David and this nine-foot nine giant.

My brothers and sisters, we've got activate Him this morning. If we don't have Him working freely, we've got to activate Him. Don't insult Him this morning. Don't insult the Holy Spirit. Without the anointing we are so easily distracted from our responsibilities that we are facing. But David did not do anything until he realized that the anointing was upon His life.

On this morning, we see David and Goliath standing down there in Elam. Elam was this place where there were hills on both sides. The

Philistines were up on one hill, and the Israelites on another hill. And here is a valley between them. And here this giant has come down and he's blurting out send me somebody that can fight me. And a nation of soldiers was afraid of this huge nine-foot nine giant. This went on for days. I said that went on for days, threats after threats. The nation felt like this was a losing battle. Nothing was going to become this army of Philistines. But one morning the father of David told this young boy, "I'm concerned about my elder boys out there in that battle. I need you to take them some food. And while you there bring me a report back as to how they're faring in this unholy war." David took the vittles and the food, down to the army. When he got there, he could hear this giant making his accusations. He was defying the God of Israel. David heard him. So, David goes to his brothers and while they're there in there fighting positions, he asks his brothers, "Who is this giant? What are his accusations against Israel? Why do I hear him defying the God of Israel?" Every time he would make these accusations, it would just cause David's spirit to sink. I can hear David saying, "I'll fight him. I'll fight him." But then David's brother says, "You don't need to be here. You're too young. You need to go on back home. Get out the way. Go on back home." But there was something rising-up in this little boy every time they would tell him "You can't. You don't need to be here. Go home." But the anointing is on his life, and he cannot take it. See when you're anointed of God, there are some things you just can't leave alone. But if you're not anointed, then there are some things you best not take on.

Every time Goliath would show up and make his threats, Saul who was the King would hide in the tent. Why? Because he had not the anointing on his life! He was hiding from responsibility' How do you know Reverend? How do you know he was not anointed? Well, he had the anointing on his life, but because he never took responsibility as King, and he always made various types of excuses for not doing things, God took the anointing off him. But God has anointed David. And what David was hearing disturbed him. He was concerned why nobody was doing anything to stop the blaspheming of the God of Israel. You see if nobody else has the nerve or the courage to face the giant, then he did. And what was the difference? The difference was he had a life with God and with Christ. He had the anointing. And as David chose to fight, he could have ended up in a fight with his own brothers because they're telling him, "Go home! Go home!" But he wouldn't fight with his own family. You know sometimes we want to fight our family. We *ain't* got time to be fighting against each other. David realized, "I *ain't* got time to be fighting with y'all."

We can't fight with each other in our own domestic family, our church family, our community family, our nation family. We can't fight against each other. If we fight against each other, we destroy ourselves from within. We need to be fighting against the common enemy against us all, and that's the devil himself. We can't afford to fight against each other through in-house fighting. We destroy ourselves from within, and that's what the enemy wants. He wants to destroy us from within. David says, "I can't fight from within. I can't fight my own family members because there's a giant over here that's big. I've got to get rid of him."

Eventually, somebody brought David to the King's attention. Saul sent for David. You see that in verse 31. Saul sent for David, and David told Saul that there was no reason for the people to be afraid of Goliath, for he would go out and fight him himself. Saul's response was, "You can't go out and fight against the giant. You're too young. You're too inexperienced." That's verse 33. "And you are not trained and equipped for battle." Listen to what David said, "You don't know my history. You know as I would tend my father's sheep, and as I would lie in the nighttime looking up in the sky, I would hear the bears and the lions roaring and coming after the sheep. Oh King, I took these little bare hands by the strength of God, and I would slay the bear by these little hands. I even killed the lions. So, I got a historical record behind me. If I can kill a bear, if I can kill a lion, the king of the beast, what is a big nine-foot giant against me?" Tell me God won't do it. I'm about to get happy here. Saul gave into David's credentials of him fighting the bear, fighting the lion.

I just wonder ... how many of you here today have some credentials under your belt? Is there anything that you have defeated…some giants that's been in your life have you defeated them? They may not have been a nine-foot giant standing on two legs with a mouth to talk. It may have been a giant of sickness, a giant of cancer or heart issues, or whatever the case might have been. But you didn't fight it. You put it in the hands of the Lord because you knew that it was a battle for the Lord to take care of. The Lord fixed it. You are cancer free this morning. He's a heart fixer. Won't He, do it? Somebody ought to say He'll do it for you. Now today you can stand and say I'm free. I'm cancer free.

Maybe you had a giant debt that gave you some setbacks. But one day God came through for you, now you can stand boldly and say, "You know what, the Lord came through for me. I don't have any debt anymore. I'm debt free. God has cancelled my debt." Won't God, do it? I just wonder anybody else out there got some battles that you've been through, and now you can look back and say, "I thought it was big, but it was just right for God." Oh yes, I just believe that it's extremely important that you have some victories in your life and under your belt before you try to take on a giant. You need some victories already under your belt. David had some victories under his belt. He knew if the Lord did it then, He can do it now. Yeah, Lord, have mercy!

Look at verse 38, *And Saul armed David with his armour, and he put on his helmet of bronze upon his head; also, he armed it with a coat of mail.* He says now, "Here's my sword. Go on out there David." David says, "Wait a minute. Let me test this stuff." You know Saul was a tall gentleman. He stood head and shoulder above most the men of the nation. Can you imagine this little boy trying to put on this tall man's armor? David said, "I tried to test it here. No, I can't wear your armor, King. It's too large for me. I can't bear your sword, King because it's dragging the ground. I'll just take what I've already got. I'll just take this little sheep sack I've got, the one that I put the oats in and feed the little lambs when they come up to me. I don't need that. All I got is a slingshot. I just believe if I use what the Lord has given me, what is in my possession, God can take what I already got. I ain't got to go looking for nothing. It's already here." Many times, our answer is right where we are. You don't have to go anywhere looking for anything to fight with because God has given you what you need.

Yeah, can't you hear this giant saying, "Little boy where are you coming from? I'm going to take your flesh and I'm going to feed it to the birds." David says, "That's what you think." David goes down to the brook and he gets five smooth stones. Somebody asks, "Why did David go and get five smooth stones?" Can I tell you this morning that Goliath had four more brothers just as big as he was. And David said if I kill one, you know how it is when you're fighting against a family; if you do something to one, the rest of the clan come. David said then I'll be prepared for them too. So, you've got to be prepared for whatever might come. You've got to prepare yourself. Even though you know God got you, you've got to be prepared for whatever comes.

David came back and this giant continued to defy God, to defy Israel, and to degrade little David. All David had was a slingshot and five smooth stones. The Bible says as they engaged eyeball to eyeball, little David just reached in his sheep sack and pulled out a stone. I like the way the old preachers said it years and years ago. They'd say David took the smooth stone out of his sheep sack, put it in a slingshot, and wound the sling up, one for the Father, and one for the Son, and one for the Holy Ghost. He used it to sling the stone, the stone hit the giant in the forehead, and he fell dead. Tell me God won't come out a winner at the finishing line. That's some of the lyrics in the song; *He always comes out a winner at the finishing line.* See the battle is the Lord's. The battle is the Lord's, and that's what we got trust in today. The battle is the Lord's.

We're going through some stuff in 2020 like never in our history. In most of our lifetime, our living history, we've never lived through

The Battle Is The Lord's

anything. But you know what? The battle is the Lord's. The Lord is going to win over this thing. We've just got to be prepared for the Lord when He starts moving in our direction. Oh, I wish I could hoop right here. But I just want to let you know just how good and awesome God is. Anybody out there ever had some battles that you were in, and you didn't see how you were going to get out of them? You were hemmed in? Your back was up against the wall? You'd go forward, but you are still hemmed in? You go backwards, you're hemmed in? You go to your left, hemmed in? You go to your right, and you're still hemmed in? And then suddenly God just opened away for you. And you said now if it had not been for the Lord who was on my side, I never could have made it. I never would've made it. But thank You Lord. Thank You for the battle.

Somebody ought to just go on and thank God for the battle right now. I'm going to do it in advance. Thank you, Lord. Thank you for the battle. Thank you for the battle. Thank you for the battle. See if you had never had a battle, you would never know that you could through God have victory over the stuff that you're facing. Sometimes when we get through our battles, we can take the stuff that we've been through and use it as trophies. Oh yes. See after David had hit that giant in the forehead and he fell dead, David cut his head off, and brought the head to the tent of the King. David said, "Look here, I got his head, not only do I have his head, but I've got his sword." They kept that sword in Israel to show that God through David was victorious over a big giant. I want to know this morning does anybody out there have any trophies to show that you've been in the battle. You've got something to show for it. Thank You Lord for my battles, I got some trophies.

Maybe somebody out there says I've been in this fight. I stayed in the fight. I got my battlefield scars. Have you been wounded? Have you been through some conditions or circumstances that put some stuff on you? Now you are able to live to talk about it - the scars. Now you are seasoned soldier. You're seasoned soldier. Now you can tell somebody else that's coming on, some buck private or Pfc, or a little sergeant.

You have graduated. You're a colonel now. You have been through. You can tell a private how to get through. You can tell a sergeant how to get through because you're a colonel now. And you're working on becoming a general. You don't just get promoted. You got to go through some stuff. You've got to have been through the struggles, through the training, and through the unbearable conditions. You have blazed some trails. Now you can look back and say, "Thank God for my battles."

Thank you so much this morning. My heart is overly rejoiced. Thank you, this morning for just sharing that with me. It's been on my heart all week, and I just been waiting to dump it. Now I've dumped. I feel better now.

CALL TO DISCIPLESHIP

I want to just, right here, open the door to the Kingdom of God. There may be somebody out there this morning that have been in a fight, been in the battle. You have gone through some stuff. You have gone through some unbearable conditions and circumstances. And now you don't know which way to turn. But let me tell you, turn it over to the Lord. Whatever it is, put it in the Lord's hands. Let Him work it out. You've been trying too long. You have tried everything and everybody else, and it has failed you. You only got one other option, and that option is God. I guarantee if you release it and put it in His hands, He'll work it out for you. So, my Brothers Sisters if you are unsaved, and you don't know the Lord today, this is a fine time to get to know Him because He will help you through this battle that we're experiencing right now. Let me encourage you, whatever it is turn it over to the Lord. Let Him work it out for you. If you're unsaved, ask Him into your heart. Say, "Lord, save me now. I'm a sinner. I need Salvation." And if you can believe that Jesus Christ died, and that Jesus Christ was raised third day; if you can confess it with your mouth, believe it in your heart, He can and He will save you right now. After this pandemic and when the church doors swing open again, you go in get involved in somebody's

Church. Well, let me say it this way, the Lord's Church. Let the church know that during this pandemic, "I received Christ as my Savior." Start a fellowship right there wherever you are.

God, bless you thank you. I hope there are some that are doing this, and I looked here after this thing is over how many people in our area and around the world have come to Christ during this crisis.

CLOSING PRAYER

God, we thank you for another fellowship. We thank You God for the listening ears out there. We pray that this message has been a source of strength even hope in the midst of a pandemic. Lord, we thank you, Lord, we praise you and we bless your Name. Lord we just ask now that you cover us with your choice blessings and your special graces, even right now continue to bless. Bless us in our spirits. Bless us in our bodies. Bless us even in our domestic area. Whatever those needs are God, we heard you say you able to supply according to your riches in glory. So, we just even praise you and thank you even in advance, in Jesus' name, Amen.

Sister Jarrett is going to come with another song. We hope you enjoy this one. We'll be back with closing words.

SELECTION

Jesus, I Love Calling Your Name **by Shirley Caesar**

CLOSING REMARKS

Sweet Jesus, oh how I love calling Your Name. Amen. There's no name like the name of Jesus, sweet Jesus. Amen. Thank you for that beautiful song. Again, we want to thank everyone out there for sharing with us this morning. We pray that this message has been a blessing to you and for you. We pray that you will take it with love and with great concern. I pray that God will just give me what they say to His people during such a time as this in our land in our world. I know that we all from time to time just need to hear from the Lord through his Word, and through each other. As a matter of fact, we are a source of strength to each other. But most of all, we all need the Lord to be strength to all of us. So, I just encourage you just be strong and keep faith. God is going to see us through what we're going through.

And let me just say this quickly. I have another throwback I would like to share this afternoon. Let's say about 5 o'clock if that's okay. And you know what? I got so many congratulatory remarks from last Sunday's throwback that went all the way back to 1992. It was just a blessing to experience '92 even in 2020. So, I have another one. This one is about twenty years old. We hope that you will enjoy this one, and guess what? It speaks to the very times in which we live. Would you believe that? You know I was talking about this kind of stuff twenty plus, thirty years ago. I've been out here for over forty years now. So, I got some age under my belt just watching time. As time has come and as time has gone, you see the signs of the times, the way the times are changing, the people, the situations, and the circumstances. So, you know this message this afternoon if you will come back and share that with me, you will see this is where we are in the 21st Century that was spoken at the beginning of the century. Amen.

Thank you so kindly. See you back at 5 o'clock. Come on back and join me at 5 o'clock if you're not doing anything. If you're busy, I understand. But for those who have the time, it's just like going to the movies in a sense. So, we'll give you something to look back to. It will spark up your remembrance of those who were with us at that time but are no longer with us. It just did so much for many of us. God bless you and thank you. If you love the Lord, thumbs up.

Consider Our Challenge
Sunday, May 24, 2020

OPENING REMARKS

It is your season to be blessed. It is your season. Why don't you just go on and claim your season. Today is your season to be blessed of the Lord. Good morning! Good morning, saints and family, Christian family around the globe. So glad you could join me this morning in fellowship and in worship. Thank the Lord, He has kept us another day. Oh, I tell you this is your season. Go on and claim your blessing. Go on and claim your season.

This is the Lord's Day. It's Sunday. It is the first day of the week, and we want to start the week with worship. I just come by to say this morning worship is what I do. I believe it is what you do. This is a great atmosphere for worship, real worship. This is a wonderful atmosphere. Can't you feel the presence of the Lord right now? The Lord's presence is with us wherever we are because the God that we serve is omnipresent. That means He's everywhere at the same time. He's at my house. He's at your house. I don't care where you go the Lord's presence is there.

David says it so greatly in Psalm 139. He said, *where shall I flee from the presence of the Lord if I took the wings of the morning and fly to the uttermost parts of the earth he's there.* He said, *even if I made my bed in hell, guess what, the Lord is there.* His presence is everywhere at the same time.

Can't you just feel His presence right now? You know what, in his presence I feel protected. In His presence I never feel disconnected or alone. I'd rather be in His presence at any time, all the time. Yes, when you're in the Lord's presence, it's a pleasant feeling my brothers and sisters. Amen.

WORDS OF ENCOURAGEMENT

I have a word of encouragement for you this morning. The Lord gives me these little encouraging moments each time we come together on Sundays. He's giving me another one for today. I want to call your attention to Matthew 7:24 & 25. I just want to cover those two verses. It says:

> *24. Therefore whosoever heareth these sayings of mine, and doeth them, I will liken him unto a wise man, which built his house upon a rock:*
>
> *25. And the rain descended, and the floods came, and the winds blew, and beat upon that house, and it fell not: for it was founded upon a rock.*

Let me just share this quick scripture to lead into this The Bible says *God sends the rain upon the just as well as the unjust.* You've heard this scripture. Our God sends rain upon the just and the unjust. Well, being a man or a person of faith doesn't exempt you from difficulties. Did you hear that? Being a person or a man or woman of faith doesn't exempt you from difficulties. But Jesus told this little parable about a wise man who had built his house on a rock. And I believe the man honored God by building upon a rock because the rock is symbolic of Jesus Christ, the Solid Rock. He is a Solid Rock. Well, the wise man did just that. He built his house on solid rock.

But then he goes on in the text, he talks about another man he considered as a foolish man. What did he do? He built his house on sand which suggests to me he did not honor God. He did not receive God as The Rock of his Salvation, the rock that holds all things together. Well, something happened to both men. The rain descended. The floods came the scriptures says. The wind blew and beat up on the houses of both men. This is the kicker. After the storm was over, the house that was built on the rock was still standing. It was still standing because that house was built on a foundation. It was built on a rock. It was built on Jesus Christ. Yes, the house that was built on the sand was destroyed. What it is trying to say to us, we need to learn how to build our houses. This house is considered symbolic or a typology of you as a person as to how you build your life. I rather build my life on Jesus Christ and his righteousness than to build it upon sand, sinking sand.

Well, I don't care what difficulties come or go. You may knock me down. I may go through some dark, stormy times, but just as a part of my life I realize that it rains on everybody. It rains on the wise. It rains on the just. None of us are exempt from trouble. But the key to it all is how your life is built. I believe the difference is that when you honor God, when you keep the faith, you have the promise. You have this promise that when the storms are over or when the storms pass, you won't be a victim. You'll be a victor. So, keep on standing on the rock. *On Christ the solid rock I stand, all other ground is nothing but sinking sands.* These are my words of encouragement to you today. I hope and pray that this little, short synopsis of this particular parable be a blessing to you today and tomorrow and forever is my prayer.

CALL TO WORSHIP

Let us continue now in this great worship celebration. As we prepare for worship let me just say *the Lord is in his holy temple let the whole earth be silent before him.*

Well, my lovely wife Sister Rose, my helper in this pandemic moment as we've been going through these series of services, she's been there to share from her music and her music talents. Amen. So, we are going to allow her to come and give us a selection. And I will come back and lead us further into today's service.

SELECTION

Falling In Love with Jesus by Jonathan Butler

Thank you so much. Thank you so much for that beautiful rendition. What is the greatest thing you've ever done? I know we've done a lot of things in life, but I just believe the greatest of all things that you've ever done, if you know the Lord Jesus Christ, is to fall in love with Him. Falling in love with Him is the greatest thing that you can do. Can I just go on and tell you God has fallen in love with you, and He has given us a great love! Greater love He says no man has than this that a man will lay down his life for a friend. God was obsessed with us. When I think about John 3:16 where He says *for God so love the world that he gave his only begotten son, n*ow that's obsession. That's all out. You know God went all out to show us that He loved us so greatly. Then I look at Romans 5:8 *but God commended his love toward us, in that, while we were yet sinners, Christ died for* our sins. Oh, it doesn't any greater, it gets no better than that. Thank you, Sister Jarrett. Thank you so much.

Now we're going to ask that you would bow in prayer with us as we now get ready to petition the very Throne of God. We seek His mercy. We seek His grace. We seek him for His unconditional love. Shall we pray.

PRAYER

Dear Heavenly Father, the *God of our weary years, the God of on silent tears, God who has brought us thus far*. We come now into your presence

Consider Our Challenge

this morning realizing you are a kind and loving Father who worketh your will for our total good. And you have done this for all of mankind down through the generations. For we heard you say in your Word that you have been our dwelling place in all generations. Before the mountains were brought forth forever now has formed the earth and world even from everlasting to everlasting you are our God. So, Lord we ask now for your power, the power of the Holy Spirit, to be with us as we seek to worship you in spirit and truth.

Open our hearts and make us receptive to the Word, to the song, to the prayer. Lord, I feel like David when he says *my heart panteth after you as the young heart or the young deer.* So, we say to you this morning feed our hungry spirits. Revive our souls that we may live to praise you and love you as the good and kind Father that you are. You alone deserve our praise.

And Lord as we embarked upon another Memorial Day weekend, a national holiday, Lord we want to remember those who lived among us, those who sacrificed their lives for the joy and the freedom that we might live. Thank you for those who have lived and labored among us even in the Christian warfare. Thank you for those great soldiers of faith that champion for the Kingdom of God. We thank you for their unselfish lives and sacrifice that they made that our churches would remain strong and vibrant even right now. More so Lord, we thank you for Jesus who died that we might live and have life more abundantly.

And while we pray Lord, we lift the sick and the shut in this morning. God, we want to thank you that you heard our prayers. Thank you, Lord. And today we pray that you will look upon those who are known to us and have been part of our church community for many years. We pray that you will lift them today, and the many that are in the nursing home that we don't know and in the hospitals. And Lord we lift the bereaved families to you. So, Lord we pray this morning lift them today we pray. And God we pray and ask that you keep your hands upon our Church family and Church community. As many are contemplating reopening I pray for safety and common sense through this process.

And Lord, we ask you now for forgiveness of any and all sins we have committed whether they be of omission or commission. We pray that you keep now as only you can our pastors and leaders, and Lord as they lead as you lead them in Jesus' name. Lord, we thank you now. We thank you in advance that all of this we pray and ask in His Matchless, Marvelous, and Magnificent Name, we pray with a heart of thanksgiving. Amen, Amen, and Amen.

SERMON

Thank you for sharing in that beautiful devotional period of prayer. It is time for a Word. I pray that the word that is about to come forth will be a blessing to you. It will be a source of strength and encouragement and maybe it will be a conviction. I don't know. Just however the Lord leads me.

There is a passage that I want to lift this morning in one of my favorite Psalms. I've got many. This one perhaps maybe top the list, or maybe it's somewhere in the top 10. It is a familiar Psalm, and every time I have approached this Psalm God gives me just a little bit more of His Word from the Psalm. I've come to learn that God's word is inexhaustible. You can read it today and get one thing. You could come back and read it a day or week later and God will give you something else. You can read it all your Christian life and God still speaks volumes through this particular Psalm.

But there is one verse in that 23rd Psalms. One verse in that particular Psalms, Psalms 23 verse 4. Verse 4 is what I want to lift. Verse 4 says,

> *4. Yea, though I walk through the valley of the shadow of death, I will fear no evil:*

From that one verse this morning I want to talk from this thought or this subject: **Consider Our Challenge.** In other words, pay attention to our challenge. Pay attention. Be attentive. So, **Consider Our Challenge.**

Let me begin by stating this morning that life is certainly unpredictable. One never knows what may be just around the next bend or the next corner. One situation and circumstance can change rather quickly without ever warning us. You can be minding your own business, taking six months to mind your own business, and taking six months to stay out of other folks' business. Your life can be peaceful with the sun shining. The birds can be singing. The flowers are blossoming, but yet there's no guarantee that it will be that way when the sun hides behind the western clouds.

How quickly your health can be good and then suddenly it turns to sickness. How quickly how happiness can turn to sadness and your blessings that you are enjoying and can turn to burdens. Oh, how quickly. Unless you are firmly grounded in your faith and trusting in the everlasting God that we serve they will become deeply depressed. My brothers and sisters, all of us have valleys through which we must pass through from time to time. I wish that we didn't have to, but we do. There is a little chance that we can ever avoid going through some valley moments in our lives.

Oh, I wish, as I say often, I wish it was always up and never down. I wish for those things. I wish there was all bills paid and no debt. I wish it was always health and wellness and never sickness. I wish it was always joy and jubilation and never sadness. I wish. However, I'm afraid to tell us this morning it's not that way in the kind of world that we live in right now.

There are valleys of disappointment when things do not go as we planned or hoped to. There are valleys of loneliness when it seems that nobody understands or even cares for us or what we may be going through. Oh, I tell you sometimes it's just that way. But I've come to learn this morning that none of us can avoid valleys as of such. We must learn them and make the best of them so that we can benefit from our valley experiences. We must remember that it is in the valley where we realize that God's grace is sufficient for whatever we're going through. But we can trust His Word because His word is trustworthy, and His power is overwhelming. God is able to help us even in our challenges.

It is in the valley of life we discover that the Lord is the Shepherd of our life even in the shadow of death. You see is not on the mountaintop of rejoicing and singing and shouting when we learn these things in the valley. Did you hear what I said this morning? It's not on the mountaintop of rejoicing and singing and shouting that we learn some things about life. And we learn some things about our God. Yes, now here are some practical truths which I have discovered that will help us to go through our valley, because we're going to go through the valley. Well let me just take a little moment here and backup Verse 3 and Verse 2, to Verse 1 of our text and show you something.

You see Davis starts out in Psalm 23, Verse 1 he's talking about *the Lord IS, the Lord IS my Shepherd, and I shall not want.* Oh, I tell you in Verse 1 the sun is shining. In Verse 1 David is exclaiming how great his God is, his Shepherd, and how he has no need or want because the Shepherd is making his provisions and He's meeting everyone. *The Lord is my Shepherd, and I shall not want.* David is just being personal. *The Lord is my Shepherd I shall not want he makes me to lie down.* Yeah, the sun is shining in his life. He's on his mountain top. He's rejoicing. He's shouting.

Then he goes to Verse 2. He says *he leadeth me beside the still waters.* David is still shouting *he leads me beside the still waters.* I'm drinking from the still waters of life. Things are quiet and things are peaceful in my life right now. Somebody ought to say Amen. He's, my Shepherd. He's taking care of all my wants, but He's also leading me beside some still waters. I'm able to drink from the still waters. Not from the running waters but from still waters. Then he moves on and he says now *he leadeth me in the path of righteousness for his namesake*. He's leading me in paths. He's taking care of all my wants. He's taking care of my thirsty needs, and He's leading me in right paths. So, everything is going good for me right now. All my needs are met. I don't have any wants. I'm not thirsty. I'm not hungry, but I'm being led now in paths of righteousness. I'm looking to do the right thing because God is doing all the right things for me. I have no reason but to praise Him.

Oh, but when we get to Verse 4, **consider the challenge**. Something else is in the picture. David is not being led now by still waters. He's not now being led into paths of goodness and righteousness. Now he's walking through the valley of the shadow of death. It seems like God was doing the leading in Verse 2 and Verse 3, but in Verse 4 now David sees himself walking alone. *Yea, though I walk through the valley of the shadow of death*. He's in a valley. He's in a low place. He's among the muck and the mire. He's down.

I just believe David is saying Yea, though I **walk** through this valley. He said walk. He didn't say run. He didn't say skip. He didn't say trot through it, but he said Yea, though I walk…Yea, though walk through the valley. I'm not running. My Brothers and Sisters, we often attempt to run through, to hurry up and get through this thing. Oh Lord, have mercy. Sometimes in life when challenges come, when challenges get in our way, when challenges put us in low places, when challenges seem like they're overwhelming us and there is no way out, but there is, my favorite word, there is some hope in every situation. Most valleys are not pleasant, but I come to tell us this morning, but you still got to walk. You can't run. You can't skip through it. You've just got to walk through it.

You see when you're run through some things, it's easy to make some mistakes. When you run through some stuff sometimes you can trip over stuff. You become regrettable because of the perspective by which you were going through what you're going through. You walk through it. It gives you time to pray. It gives you time to think things over. It gives you time to put things into right perspective when you walk through and not run through.

Oh, I tell you this morning we need to learn how to slow down when we're going through the valley. You need to slow down. You need to put the foot on the brake. You need to get off the accelerator. Slow down, don't speed through because you might miss something along the way. See in order that we might have a sure and solid footing as we go through, we should walk. One of the advantages of walking instead of running through a valley is that you would miss many of the nice important messages that God has for you if you were to run. So, when you're going through you've got to be patient, because all which God want us to learn, He wants us to learn it through patience.

Notice that David used the word **through**. *Yea, though I walk through the valley.* Can I tell you, this morning, that the Lord will not leave you standing in the valley! He will see you through whatever you're going through. David says now *Yea, though I walk through the valley of the shadow of death.* Let me fast forward to this word **shadow** because to have a shadow that means that some light is somewhere. You just can't phantom the idea we're going through this dark place and not being able to see.

When I go back to Verse 1, David says now *the Lord is my Shepherd I shall not want; he leadeth me beside the still waters; he leadeth me in the path of righteousness for his namesake.* Now God is in front. God is doing all the leading. God is making all the provisions. God is making all the right decisions for David's life. Then God just kind of flipped the script. He says now I'm going to get out of the forefront. I'm going to get in the back things. Now David you've got to walk by yourself. I just believe that as David was walking through his dark valley, the Light of the World, Jesus Christ which is the light was in the background. He was shining enough light to give David a picture of a shadow as he was going through the valley. That's the way God does us sometimes.

Consider Our Challenge

He leads us, and then God says, "now let me get in the background and give you a little spotlight, a shadow, that you can go through. Does anybody hear me out there this morning?

Yes, the Lord won't leave you stranded. He won't leave you by yourself. He will shine a little light to give you a shadow even amid your valley experience. David says, "Yes, I'm going through this valley of shadow. I'm going through this valley shadow of even death." You've got to trust Him. You've got to trust Him. You see if you are child of God, if you've been redeemed from your sins, if you know Him personally, then you know without a doubt that He will see you through. He didn't bring you this far to leave you. He didn't bring you this far to throw you out. He's still with you. He's putting some light. He's giving some shadow. He's letting you know my presence is still here. I'm not in the front, but I got your back. How many you know that God's got your back? He's got your back. He's watching you. He's not going to let you fall. But you've just got to have the faith that *I'm going through*. I'm going through. Well let me share a few things and then I'm going to leave you alone for the morning.

Without a doubt He will see you through. Can I tell us this morning He saw Noah through the universal flood? Even when nobody else believed that God was in charge and that God had given Noah a vision of what was that a place, many around Noah didn't believe the vision that he was telling them about. He told them it's going to rain. God has told me to build an ark. Others laughed and others scorned and said, "You've got to be crazy. You're going to build an ark, having it rain on Earth. This sound foolish to us." Maybe my brothers and sister, maybe there's a lot of folks out here today that feels like that is foolishness to believe God and believe His Word. But I thank God for Noah. Noah went down in the list of the Heroes of Faith. By faith Noah built God in ark. He saw Noah through what Noah's day was encountering. If He brought Noah through, then He will bring others through. I'm just trying to show us our challenges. That was Noah's challenge.

He saw Joseph through his Egyptian imprisonment. Yes, he was lied about. He was put in prison. He was forgotten about in prison. Yes, but God saw him through his valleys…through his shadows of death. Then one day word came that Joseph was a dreamer. The king brought Joseph to his Palace and said, "Tell me in my dream." God through Joseph gave the king of vision of what was going to take place. Can I tell you, God brought him through, and then the king promoted Joseph? He made him the Prime Minister of Egyptian agriculture. Sometimes you've got to go through, in order, to come up. Sometimes you've got to go through to come out on the other side. I wish I had some help!

These stories, these events in history are put in the Bible as Paul said as *examples,* which we get the word example. These are examples for us when we're going through our valleys and through our difficulties. Look back at what God has done for others because the songwriter says *what He has done for others he will do the same thing for you.* He's going do it for us!

God saw the Hebrew children, them saw him through the fiery furnace. Yes, that was their valley. It was their challenge. But you know what? God saw them through the fiery furnace. They had their valley, but they had faith. You know what they said? They said, "If God don't deliver us, that doesn't mean that He's not able." My brothers and sisters if God does not deliver you, guess what He'll do? He'll see you through it. He saw the Hebrew children through the fiery furnace. He'll see you through too.

He saw Daniel through the lions' den. Yes, Daniel was placed in a lions' den to be eaten up by the lions. But you know what? When you're a child of God, God won't let anything eat you up. He can keep you in the midst of whatever is eating at you. Lord, help me today. I got a few more things and I'm going to let you go this morning because I'm about to get happy here.

He saw Paul through a Philippian jail even in the midnight hour. When everything was quiet all Paul and Silas did was prayed and sang and praised God. Sometimes you just got to praise your way through whatever you're going through. One songwriter said, "Praise is what I do." Sometimes you just *gotta* praise as you go through your valley and your shadow. Not only did Paul go through a Philippian jail, but he went through a thorn in his flesh. Paul didn't like this thorn in his flesh, he went to God three times and said, Lord, remove it. Take it out. Take it away." But every time Paul went to the Lord and asked for relief, he didn't get any relief. Finally, God answered Paul and said, "My grace is sufficient."

Even in your weakness, when you think you're weak, that's when you're strong. When you think you're strong that's when you're weak! My grace is sufficient even in your weakness, even in your valley, just knowing that God will see you through. Paul goes on to tell you that I had my many valley experiences. I was shipwrecked at sea. And no lives that were on the ship were lost. We all got to safety. We got to the other side of the wreck. God was there. All he told me to do was as I was in the midst of my valley, in the midst of my toil, to hold on to my little broken pieces. I just held on to the broken pieces. Sometimes my brothers and sisters, all you got to hold onto is just broken pieces. Whatever the broken piece is just hold onto it. God will see you through even on broken pieces. Not only that but David would tell us like the Apostle Paul, "I'm just gonna be content with whatever I find myself in. I'm just gonna stay on course. I'm going through this thing." I God believe he will see us through COVID-19 if we just wait on Him. He's going to see us through it. Yes, we're in it now, it is a valley for lot of us. But He's going to see us through this valley, this shadow of death.

We've got to be like David. I can't let it get me down. I can't let that keep me back. See I got one more piece on this verse. There is one more thing David said. David says *I will fear no evil.* I believe what David is saying that regardless of his plight, he will not allow fear to control his life, or influence any decision, or to disturb his peace of mind. We can't let anything steal or disturbed our peace of mind. We just got to keep trusting, keep having faith, because when I look at Verse 4 faith is all in it. What's there, Reverend? *Yea though I walk through the valley.* I know I'm walking, and I'm going through. *I will fear no evil,* he goes on in the next verse to say because *I know that Thou art with me. Thy rod and your staff they comfort me.* We need the rod of God, the staff of God to comfort us even in this time. Go on through your valley. We're going to have to go through our valley because nothing much has changed in midst of this process.

We going to go through and we're going to learn as we go through. And I believe when we go through, we go come out better on the other side of going through. We're going to know more about the power of God. We are going to know more about His keeping grace. And we're going to know a whole lot of more stuff about this old world. We're going to see a lot of things about people. This is a learning period. This is a growing period as we go through this valley. I wish you would hear me this morning. I've learned so much already in these 8 to 10 weeks that we've been through, and there is yet more to learn. There's more to learn about life. There's more learn about God. There's more to learn about what people think, how people think, how people care, and how people don't care. We're going to be wiser when we come out of this. Just going through the valley is going to make us wiser.

As I get ready to close, there are so many who don't have relationships with God. Fear has had a tremendous influence on so many of those people's lives. Fear has stolen many of the people's joy. Fear has killed a lot of people's spirits. But listen, David said, "I *ain't* got no reason to fear," because he knew that the Lord was with him. And I stopped by to say God does not want us to live our lives in fear, but we ought to be concerned. Did you hear me? He doesn't want us to fear to the point then we fall out, we faint, give up, or throw in the towel. There's no reason to be afraid because God's got this thing. He's got it, and I'm glad He's got it. Now if we know that the Lord our God is our Shepherd as David did, we have absolutely no reason fear what may come. We know that our God is in control of whatever is causing us to fear. Don't fear, but be concerned, put it in God's hands. I put it all in the Lord's Hand. A song used to be sung around the Church, *I put this in His hand. I put that in His hand. I put everything in His hand. In His hand. In His hand.* God worked it out. He worked it out. Thank God we do not have to fear. Yes, the challenges we face may be great, but God is greater. Let me say this again; don't be fearful but be concerned. Yes, God wants us to be concerned. You're not human if you don't have any concerns; be concerned, but don't fear.

Let me leave you this morning with a song. You all know the song. I love it because it has so much truth. The title of the song is *God Will Take Care of You.* Anybody out there believes that God will take care of you. He will take care of you. He will take care of you. The songwriter says,

> *Be not dismayed whate'er betide, God will take care of you.*
> How is He going to protect me and take care of me Reverend?
> *Beneath His wings of love abide, God will take care of you.*
> What is He going to take care of me with?
> *Through days of toil when the heart does fail, God will take care of you.*
> *When danger fierce your path assails…*

When dangers get all up in your matters, all up in your path, let God take care of you. All your needs; I need you to know today He will supply. He will provide. Nothing you ask of Him will He deny if you ask Him by faith.

No matter what the test may be, no matter what's coming your way, no matter what you're going through, it could be your valley, it could be whatever, *God we'll take care of you.* What do I need to do during this process? The song says, *Lean weary one upon His breast.* Lean upon God, you have lean hard. You got lean strong because *God will take care of you through every day o'er all the way.* Through every day. Every day I get up God is taking care of me. When I lay down, he is watching over me all night long. He's taking care of me. *God will take care of you through every day over all the way. Yes, He will take care of you. God will take care of you.* Anybody believe He will? Just think back over your life. The stuff you've been through already from childhood to manhood and to womanhood, or from a child to a teenager because some of our children have been through some stuff. You're still here. The reason why you're here is because the Lord has taken care of you. *Be not dismayed whate'er be tide, God we take care of you.*

This is my message to you this morning. God bless you .**Consider your Challenge**. Consider our challenge. Just remember God will see you through. Just go on and walk through. Walk through it. You don't need to fear but be concerned. Don't fear. The Lord is going to get you to the other side. You just *gotta* walk through it. Take your time. Go on and walk through it. Thank you, this morning. God bless you.

CALL TO DISCIPLESHIP

I want to appeal to anyone out there that doesn't know the Lord as your personal Savior this morning. I admonish you to consider calling upon the name of the Lord and asking Him in your life. Say, "Lord, save me. I'm a sinner. I need your saving grace." And the Lord will come in and save you right where you are. All you've got to do is just confess with your mouth, believe in your heart that God has raised Him from the dead, thou shall be saved. Just tell the Lord, "Lord, I'm a sinner. I need saving. Lord, I want to be saved. I want to live my life eternally with you. "If you can believe it and confess it, God will come in your heart. He will change, He will transform you from an old man into a new man or old woman into a new woman. And behold all things will become new in your life. It's simple. Just acknowledge, believe, and confess. ABC, Acknowledge, believe, and confess and you're saved. If you can believe that today, do it right now. He will save you.

And when this too shall pass, when we get back into corporate fellowship, go to somebody's Church and make a public profession of faith that you were saved by God through hearing the word preached. *How can you hear without a preacher; and how can he preach except he be sent?* Somebody must share that Word, and I hope through this sharing this morning that it has made a radical change in your life even right now. Amen. God Bless.

Sister Rose is going to come and close us with a song. And I will be back with several announcements. Amen.

SELECTION

***I Won't Complain* written by Rev. Don Johnson & recorded by Rev. Paul Jones**

CLOSING REMARKS

God bless you. Thank you, Sister Rose for letting us know that we won't complain. The reason why we won't complain is because the Lord has truly been good. Not just me, but He's been good to all of us and for that we are just so grateful and thankful.

God bless you. Thank you. I hope you had a great day today, a great time. I hope the Word was a blessing to you as you go forward this week. I want to say this has been a good day. This has been a lovely day. This has been a marvelous day. So, enjoy the rest of your day. Be safe. Do mask up. Keep your distance 6 feet apart. Wash those hands. Let's be safe. Let's keep each other healthy. Let's try and keep each other alive. Amen. God Bless. Have a great rest of the day and eat well.

God Is Able

Sunday, May 31, 2020

OPENING REMARKS

Good morning! Good morning, Church Family, and my Church Community. I am so happy to greet you today with joy of Jesus the Christ which is my strength, and He is your strength as well. *This is the day that the Lord has made, I will rejoice and be glad in it.* I thank God that He has allowed us to connect this morning, and it's always good to connect to people that we love, people that we share a fellowship with, and we just thank God for today's connection. We can all give Him praise and give Him worship. You ought to just give Him a hand clap of praise right where you are, and just thank Him for the connection this morning. Thank God that we're connected to Heaven. We can reach God right where He is because the in song, we just listened to says I don't believe that God has brought me, He has brought us this far to leave us. We have come too far from where we started from for Him to leave us now. I just don't believe God will leave us. God is not a deserter. He doesn't desert His people. He doesn't desert those whom He loves. I know sometimes we feel it in our spirit perhaps He has deserted us. He's left us. But I come to serve notice on you this morning, that's not the kind of God that I serve. My God promised that He would never ever leave me, nor would He forsake me. Amen. So, we thank God this morning for the connection. We thank Him for the connection. This is a great time to connect because we know that we're living in some very turbulent and troublesome times. But I don't believe that my God has brought me, nor us, this far to turn around on us now. No. That's not the God that I serve.

Well, thank you for tuning in. I see some are yet coming in, and we are grateful for your participation this morning.

WORDS OF ENCOURAGEMENT

I've got a word of encouragement for you this morning. My words of encouragement this morning will come to you from a passage of scripture that is I think a great piece of information for us. Galatians 6:9. You've read it. You know it perhaps by heart. Let me quote that verse to you and say a few things about it. It says,

> *And let us not be weary in well doing: for in due season, we shall reap, if we faint not.*

Now, let me try to make some sense of this verse for us this morning. God knew that we all would face one challenge. God knew that we all would face one challenge or challenges. And that challenge is weariness. You know, trying to live this life and to maintain, it is easy to get tired. It's easy to become overwhelmed. Weariness means to lose your sense of pleasure; to feel or not to feel enjoyment that you wish for. You see you are doing all the right things, but not getting the right results and we feel weary. Sometimes it feels like the battle is taking too long. We think. So, you become weary. You become tiresome. But let me encourage you. Your season, your time is on its way. It's on its way. Don't be discouraged. You've got to hold on to your faith. Don't let discouragement convince you to give up or settle for the lesser. Amen. You may be dealing with battlefield fatigue today. That's a soldier's thing.

You know when you're in the military and you're out on the battlefield, you're engaged in the battle, it becomes wearisome, tiresome, because you're going day and night, sometimes with and sometimes without. And you become fatigued. The battlefield fatigue today, my brothers and sisters, you're tired of fighting, and don't think you can go on. But you don't have to do it on your own. You don't have to do it on your own. God says let Him take hold of your strength and my strength because it's available. But you must hold on to it. You must take hold of it. When your thoughts tell you things are not going to change, things are not going to get better. Just say, "No. My time is coming." Anybody believe today that your time is coming? God will give you strength for this battle. He will give you the strength that you need to fight this battle. Paul says it best. *I can do all things through Christ which strengthens me.* I can do all things, all things…How? Through Christ which strengthens me. It is the Christ who gives us strength for our weariness. If we hold on, if we don't give up, your season will come. You will reap if you faint not. Don't pass out. Don't give up. Don't throw in the towel. You can. You can…How? Through Christ who gives us the strength. My strength, your strength, lies in the One who says I have all Power in My Hand. That's my word of encouragement for you today. I hope you will take this this week and let it just marinate within the confines of our heart and mind. God Bless You.

CALL TO WORSHIP

We're just so delighted to have you in worship with us this morning. I'm still talking about being connected. God has allowed us to connect one more time. I don't take this time for granted. This is God given. Amen. So, we're going to prepare now for praise and for worship. As we prepare for worship let me just say to you today, *the Lord is in his holy temple let the whole earth be silent before him.* Where is His Holy Temple? It is in you. Amen.

We're going to ask my lovely wife Rose to come and she's going to render us a selection. And then I will come back to you with prayer because our country, our cities, our towns, our community, our little mole hills need prayer this day. Amen. So, come Rose.

SELECTION

Victory Is Mine by Alvin Darling & Dorothy Norwood

Amen. Anybody out there know that victory is yours today? Victory is mine. Go on and claim your victory today because we know that we have Victory in Christ. Jesus Christ has never been a loser. Even though there were many times it looked like Christ was losing, even in His death, even His Crucifixion itself when He was being crucified, they were saying this is it. He's over. Jesus is out of here. We don't have to put up with Him. They forgot what Jesus said, "You'll kill me and in three days I'll get up again." They forgot that Jesus was the Victor over sin, death, hell, and the grave. We've got Victory today my brothers and sisters. We've got it. Go on and claim your Victory. Satan's got nothing on you. You've got everything on Satan. If you've got Christ on your side, you've already got the Victory. You're walking in Victory. So, just go on and claim what you rightfully own, victory in Jesus. Amen. Thank you. God Bless you.

Let us now proceed to the Throne of Grace because we need the Lord in our times in which we live. We need Him more than ever in our lives. But we've got the Victory. Sometimes we don't see it with our optical eye. We must see it with our eye of faith, faith in the Lord Jesus Christ Himself. If you don't mind, just bowing right where you are and let us petition God's Throne.

PRAYER

Eternal God Our Heavenly Father, we come now to give you thanks for your tender mercies and your loving kindness that you have demonstrated toward us not just today, but daily. We ask you to forgive us of our sins and restore us to a right relationship with you. And help us to learn how to forgive one another and move forward with renewed sense of trust and hope. But also, God teach us how to love one another. And to love not with lip service, but to love with action and demonstration, in the manner and the way that you demonstrated to us in that while we were sinners you gave your life for us.

We thank you for the comfort of your Word, and, the comfort of the Holy Spirit Whom you said you would send a Comforter, and this Comforter would function in or lives. He would teach us. He would lead us. He would guide us. He would bring all things to our remembrance. Thank you for your Holy Spirit. And Lord we, we just want to tell you today that we love you. And we praise you today for all you do for us, even when we don't deserve the things you do. But thank you anyway. Thank You for saving us when we were lost and had no mind of you. We didn't think of you. We didn't even know who you were.

So, God we just come today to tell you that you are our Mighty King. You are our Lord. You are our Ruler. You sit on the Throne, and you reign. Thank You Lord for being on the Throne, because if you were not, we don't know where we would be this morning. We would be like the songwriter who said, "Father I stretch my hands to Thee, no other help do I know; but if Thou would withdraw thyself from us, oh tell us where we shall go?" Thank You Lord.

And we come before you today to lift-up all families. Lord, we pray that you touch today. Touch where doctors can't touch. Build up where they are torn down. Keep your hands upon them as they plead and seek your Divine intervention. Lord, we lift them up. And God our country is reeling and rocking at the hands of the death of George Floyd. We lift his family, friends, and neighborhoods before you today. And we know as a result, cities around our country are protesting. There are properties being destroyed. There is looting of businesses. Lord, we pray for a peaceful end, and bring calm to our cities and communities.

Lord, we see that there is so much pain and suffering in our land. We pray for spiritual healing and deliverance. And we know today that you and you alone can help us in times like these. Lord, we got protests, suffering, and pain on one side and then on the other side, Lord, we are confronted with Covid-19. We need a Word from you. And you alone can solve this grand issue that we are confronting and bombarded with every day seemingly, even around the clock. Lord, we just invoke that you come, come, and meet our needs. And God we pray that you keep your hand upon our Church Family. Bless their every need. Keep our leaders. Help them in the midst of what looks like a hopeless and helpless situation.

And God we pray that you hear our prayer today, and not just hear it, but answer. Do something. Speak Lord. And when it's all said and done, we'll bless your Name. We'll give you Glory. We'll give Glory to the only Wise God and Father. And we pray this morning this prayer with Thanksgiving. Amen.

Thank you all for sharing in this prayer with us and I hope and pray that you prayed with us, prayed mightily for spiritual healing for our land and for our country.

SERMON

Well, let me share what the Lord told me to say today. There is a passage of scripture this morning that is found in the book of Jude, Chapter 1. There is only one Chapter in the book. And let me share from Verses 24 and 25. Here's how the passage will read:

> *24. Now unto him that is able to keep you from falling, and to present you faultless before the presence of his glory with exceeding joy,*
>
> *25. To the only wise God our Saviour, be glory and majesty, dominion and power, both now and forever. Amen.*

This morning I want to talk about, **God Is Able**. **God is Able**. That's my subject for today, **God Is Able**. Anybody out there today know that **God Is Able**. Allow me to begin this message by saying when we look at the world in which we live, our world is filled with hatred and violence. We are battling a pandemic. We see economic disparity and despair all at the same time. We are also experiencing a cultural warfare. We're in the midst of a cultural war. And this cultural war is dividing the masses. It is dividing people is what I am trying to say. People are edgy. They're frustrated. Some are scared. And many are in despair. When we see society has lost its vibrancy, lost its vibrancy and respect for human life, that's the kind of world we're living in today. It appears that our young people have lost respect for authority. Whereas they look to authority, they trust authority, but authority has let them down. They seem to believe that they have been lied to. So, they have lost all respect for authority. And in times like these we need a prophetic word. We need a prophetic Word in an angry world.

It comes to mind to me now as I reflect upon the prophet Ezekiel, who prophesized in a time when Israel was in disarray. They had been deported. They were in seemingly a strange land. There was pain. There was hurt. There was suffering because when Ezekiel went out into that massive valley, the scripture says in Ezekiel 3:15 *and he sat where they sat*. And he assessed what was going on among his people. He analyzed the pain and suffering, the degradation. But what was really going on in Ezekiel through the presence and power of the Holy Spirit, Ezekiel had a prophetic voice for the people of Israel during the dark period in her life. A prophetic voice speaks to disjointed and disconnected masses and situations. That's what a prophetic voice does. It speaks to that which is dead and disjointed.

Because what Ezekiel saw as he sat where they sat and as he began to take an analytical view of the situation all he could see was dry bones - disjointed and disconnected masses of people. And God gave him a prophetic voice, because God came to Ezekiel and said *son of man can these bones live?* And Ezekiel says back to God *Lord Thou knows*. And then I hear God say to the prophet who would use the prophetic voice and says, "Speak to these bones and tell these bones to live…to live…to live!" And my brothers and sisters that is what a prophetic voice does. It speaks to that which is dead, which is disjointed. It raises the possibility of new existence and hope. It tries to bring them out of pain and places of injustice to a place of hope. That's what a prophetic voice does.

One would be inclined to believe that there is no solution to the problems of the world today. But I beg to differ. I don't have a brilliant mind, but I listen to the Lord. My brothers and sisters one of the greatest truths of our faith is that it teaches us that **God is Able** to overcome every situation that human life faces. I hear it in the text today. Verse 24 of Chapter 1 says *Now unto him who is able to keep you from falling*. Our faith teaches us that **God is Able** to help us to overcome every situation that we face. And I wonder how many of you trust God to bring you out of your dark night of your soul? And this is where we are in our world. Somebody just needs to know this morning that **God Is Able**.

One of the central truths of our faith is that we serve a God who *is able to do that which is exceedingly, abundantly above any and all things that we can even ask or think*. Our **God Is Able**. How do you know He's able Reverend? Because God has a track record. His track record eclipses all that the scripture gives us of His goodness and of His Greatness, His awesome power to deliver us. He's delivered us seemingly in every generation. We've lived through some stuff. Our fore parents lived through some stuff. But we're still here because of His goodness, because of His greatness, and because of His great power to deliver. And He's delivered in every generation. I don't know what will come out of all of this that is happening right now, but I do know when something bad happens, there is always another side. There is some good that can come out of every bad situation because **God Is Able** to make it happen. God has track record. Anybody out there that believes that God's got a track record?

Have you watched God over the courses of the years that you've been living? I know I've got some youth out there who haven't lived through very much. Maybe this is the first major event in their lives that they've seen this kind of stuff that is going on. But even in my lifetime and some of you who are listening to me, in your lifetime, you've seen the track record of God. Oh how, He has brought good out of the bad and the ugly. But I am sure you agree with me that God is unlimited in power to accomplish in us and through us His Divine Purpose. God Is Able. Through His power He can accomplish His purpose through us.

Yet there are times when it looks like we are living in defeat and despair, feeling as though God has deserted us. But did you hear me in my words of encouragement this morning where the Apostle Paul said *be not weary in well doing for you shall reap in due season*. I know there are times when it looks like there's no hope. It looks like God is not saying anything. *He won't say nothing.* We feel like we've been deserted. But I come by to tell you this morning God has not deserted us.

I recall Job in his day of trials and tribulations. In his day of trouble, he felt that God had deserted him and said, "Oh if I could find God and plead my case before Him, I would tell God some things." But you know what? God waited on His own timing. While Job was sitting in his ash pile, God just showed up in a whirlwind and rolled up to Job and said, "Now you been questioning my whereabouts. You've been questioning what I have been up to. But Job here I come to you today, Job I have a few questions I want to ask you. Job where were you when I put everything in perspective? Where were you when I carpeted the grass? Where were you when I put the moon and the stars and the sun in the sky? Where were you when the sons of the morning sang? Where were you? Answer my question." Job couldn't answer it. My Brothers and Sisters I know we question some things about God. It's alright to ask questions. But Job discovered that his Redeemer yet lived.

Listen to Jude, the writer of this book, it's a powerful little letter. It reminded the saints of his day that they faced no difficulty from which God could not deliver His people. The same power and presence to them is available to us. But my brothers and sisters the question that I want to raise today is, "What is God able to do?" Jude said, *"Now unto him that is able to keep you from falling, and to present you faultless before the presence of his glory with exceeding joy."* What is God able to do?

Well, Paul in another passage can help us also to further understand this. In Romans 16, verses 25 through 26, Paul says there *Now to him that is of power to establish you according to my gospel, and the preaching of Jesus Christ, according to the revelation of the mystery, which was kept secret since the world began.* Now to him that is of power to establish you according to His *gospel, and the preaching of Jesus Christ.*

If you want to be fixated, if you want to be established, then it is the Word of God, the gospel Paul says is what fixates us. The preaching of Jesus Christ, according to the revelation of the mystery which was kept in secret is what keeps us. God had this thing in mind in the Old Testament. He kept it a secret. It was a mystery. You see you have to learn something about the Old and New Testament. You see the Old Testament concealed things, but the New Testament reveals stuff. God already had in mind what He was going to do with the mysteries of The Gospel. The Gospel is about Jesus Christ, His Life His Ministry, His Death, His Resurrection and His Power.

So, this mystery that Paul talks about, that was of old has now been revealed since the beginning of the world. It's no longer a secret. It's out in the open, because Verse 26 says, *But now it is made manifest,* meaning that it's no longer a mystery. It's no longer a secret. It's nothing hidden any more. God has put it out in the open, and everybody ought to know. *And by the scriptures of the prophets, according to the commandment of the everlasting God, made known to all nations for the obedience of the faith...*it's been made known to all of us, all people, all nations for the obedience of faith. Now tell me that God isn't able through His manifestations and by the Word of God. The good news of Jesus Christ has been made known. All God wants is for somebody to believe it and be obedient to the faith. Let me say three things about this text, and then I will bid you good morning.

The first point I want to make is that *God is able to keep you*. He's able to keep us from falling. That's the first thing He says in Verse 24. He is able. God is able to keep you or me from falling. God is able to keep you because He has the power. There are two key words that illuminate this text. The first word is *able*, the same word that is used in the New Testament for *dunamis* or *power* or *dynamite*, whichever one you want to call it. That's power. You see God has more power than a locomotive. He has all power. He has the power to keep us from falling. He's able. Now a second word is "*keep*", which *means to guard or put a garrison around something or fortify something*. God has the power to build around us a garrison to prevent us from falling into harmful and troublesome situations. God can keep you in the midst of turbulence. He's able to keep you in the midst of a pandemic. He's able to keep you when the enemy is trying to take you out. He can keep you from falling into sin. And He is able to keep us in many other ways, destructive situations and even the temptations that come. Paul says in another passage when we fall into temptation, He gives us a way of escape. But when God gives us the way of escape, don't hang out and try to figure it out. Just move on out of the way. God is able to keep us from falling.

There is another side to this. God is not only able to keep us from some things, a lot of times He keeps us in things. He can not only just keep us from it, but He keeps us in it. What can He keep me in? Well, Paul says *He can keep us in His perfect peace.* Don't you know that God can give you peace in the midst of your trials and tribulations and bring you out on the other side, but we must trust in His power, His keeping power, knowing that God is able. How many of you out there this morning … God has kept you in some stuff? You didn't want to be in it. You wanted to get out of it quickly.

You remember last Sunday's lesson we talked about going through the valley. We can have our high points, but then there are times we can come to our low points. Just like He led David in the path of righteousness, He led him by the still waters, and after all that good leading into the watery places, and places of goodness and righteousness, then David had to end up going through the valley. Guess what? He kept him in the valley, just like He kept him on the path of righteousness. He can keep you in some things that are uncomfortable to you. Yes, He can. We all, if you are of age, we know we've been kept through some things. And if God had not kept us, oh, we couldn't have made it. We wouldn't be here today to talk about it. Thank God that He can keep us even in the midst of our troubles, and certainly in His perfect peace.

The second thing I want to lift out of the text this morning that I want to share is that *He is able to present us faultless*. Faultless. That's what Jude is telling us this morning. God is able to present us. That is to cause us to stand firm in whatever we're in and we won't fall down. He's able to keep us from falling and to present us faultless. Paul says something in Ephesians Chapter 6, Verse 1. Paul says to the saints there is some stuff you've got to put on. He says *Put on the whole armour of God, that ye may be able to stand against the wiles of the devil…* the tricks of the devil. The devil is tricky. He's of no good to himself and to no one. We are fighting against this devil, this enemy that lurks in the unseen, unknown, or unlikely places. And he comes out. But we've got to be ready to defend ourselves by putting on our armour so that we are able to stand against his tricks, his schemes, and all of the things that he has in his bag. And he'll come out of his bag on you if you're not careful.

Paul says in verse 13, *Wherefore take unto you the whole armour of God, that ye may be able to withstand in the evil day, and having done all, to stand*. My brothers and sisters we're living in some evil days, and we have an evil enemy. So, therefore we must be prepared, ready for the evil day and the evil enemy. And we need to start learning now how to defend ourselves and defeat the enemy. He's already defeated, but he's wreaking havoc on people. And God says, "I'll keep you." Are you listening to me this morning? God says, "I'm able to keep you from falling when he comes." It doesn't mean that sometimes we can't fall. God says, "I can keep you from falling. And I can present you faultless." That's what God says He can do.

But let me tell you, after you put on your armour, there are some things you must do also. You must *stand; therefore,* you've got to have your loins girded *about with truth* and have on your *breastplate of righteousness.* You've got to gird up yourself. You can't fight this fight of faith and you've got all this looseness on you, these loose garments. So, he says gird up your loins, and you've got to do it with truth. Let truth prevail. Who is truth? God is truth. His word is truth. We are to stand on the truth. Truth sometimes seems like it gets to your destination slow, and a lie gets to a place fast. But the truth will always stand. It will always outstand a lie. God says that faultless means that we will stand before Him without blemish and without spot. We will stand before Him in truth, as the Christian transformed life will be complete in Him. There is no believer who needs to feel overcome by the forces of evil and the awfulness of sin. God has given us the power to overcome sin and its dominion. I don't care where it comes from or who it comes from. We've got to depend on the power of God which can help us overcome its dominion, because it (sin) wants to dominate you. We got what it takes. We've got the enabling power of God.

My last point, the third thing I want to share with you. *God is able to keep us because He is our Savior.* How do you know Reverend? Verse 25 says, *To the only wise God our Savior.* Jude in the text refers to God as our *Savior.* Often in the scripture the *Savior* is used of Jesus, Our Lord and Savior Jesus Christ. Well, we know that God and Christ are the same person, but in different manifestations. So, here we see God is the source. *To the only wise God our Savior,* He is the source. God is the source of our salvation. He's the Savior of our salvation. How do you know Reverend? John 3:16 says *For God so loved the world, that he gave his only begotten Son, that whosoever believeth in him should not perish, but have everlasting life. God so loved the world* that those who believe in Him *should not perish but have everlasting life.* I want to show us today that God is the source of our salvation. *God so loved the world.* And then he says that he *gave his only begotten Son.* What is that saying? That is saying to me that Jesus Christ is the sacrifice of our salvation. And then he says that we *should not perish.* That is the security of our salvation. God is the source. Jesus is the sacrifice. And we have put our trust and belief in what God did for us. It secures us. We'll not perish but we'll *have everlasting life. To the only wise God our Savior.* Aren't you glad this morning that you have security in Jesus Christ and God? My brothers and sisters that's why Paul could stand firmly declare *I am not ashamed of the gospel of Christ for it is the power of God unto salvation, to everyone that believeth, to the Jews first and then to the Gentiles.* Don't be ashamed of what you got. I'm not ashamed of what I've got. I've got salvation. I'm secure. Are you secure this morning? If you're not sure, I want you to know God is able. I say God is able.

And as I move toward my close, I want us to know that God is the One that brings us out of every one of our tests and trials. He saves us from our sins. We're going through some testing. We're going through some trials in our land and in our world, what we can hold on to in these testing and trying times is the hinge, and to cling to the heartbeat of the gospel of Jesus Christ, because that is our faith in the One who made it all possible for us. That's all we can hold on to. Put not your trust in man. If you put your trust in man, he'll let you down every time. I'm not talking about fixing your automobile, and you going and buying his goods. I'm talking about trusting him with your faith and trusting him with your life. Trust God for everything that you need.

There is something else that God is able to do, and I shared this with you a few Sundays ago. God will fight your battles. Remember I told you in a sermon the battle is not yours, but it's the Lord's. Have you been keeping up with me? God can fight your battles for you. But you know what you must do. Sometimes, not all the time, but sometimes you've got to keep still because God is able to deliver you from some things. And some things He keeps us in, He keeps us through some things if we trust Him, but in these troubled times keep in mind that God is able. And I want to say to any of our young folks out there listening to me today, trust God. Learn now at an early age to trust God. So, as you grow older you start to see the evil of the day, because Paul says the evil days are here. Solomon says it best in Ecclesiastes Chapter 1, Verse 1. He says, *"Remember now thy Creator in the days of thy youth, while the evil days come not.* Young folk, evil days are coming but you better remember, you've got to remember God. God can bring you through because He's able to do it. So, you better build a foundation, and build it strong on His Word. Build it faith. Build it on trust. Build it on love. You can make it. You can make it in these troubled times.

As I get ready to go now, we must leave here with this message. These things you need to take with you as you leave with this message today. There is some work to be done. Jesus says work while it is day because when night comes no man can work. There is some work to be done. Second, there are some testimonies that must be shared. We've got to share our testimonies. See, you cannot have testimony unless you had some testing or tests. We've got a story to tell. We've got to get the message out. The message has got to be told. And the next thing is there will have to be some prayers prayed. There's got to be some praying going on. And then lastly, we've got duties to perform. All of us have duties to perform. We've got a duty to pray. We've got a duty to get the message out. We've got a duty to tell our testimony. We've got a duty to work to get it done. God bless you. That's what the Lord told me to say to the Church, to the community, and to whomever this message reach. We've just got to trust that God Is Able. Yes, we are living in a world that is filled with violence, with hatred, with a whole lot of stuff. But we've got to get the Word out. We've to get the message out. We've to pray. We've duties to perform. God bless you. Thank you.

CALL TO DISCIPLESHIP

If anyone out there heard this message today, and you don't know Jesus as your Savior, I quoted it in the sermon John 3:16. It says, *For God so loved the world, that he gave his only begotten Son, that whosoever believeth in him should not perish, but have everlasting life.* I tried to make it so simple and simplistic when I said that God is the source of our salvation. Jesus is the sacrifice for our salvation. And we have eternal security if we accept the source and the sacrifice. You can be saved. All you have to do is just believe. It's as simple as ABC. You've got to acknowledge you are a sinner. You've got to believe in Jesus the Christ. And you got to confess with your mouth. It's so simple. "A"- Acknowledge, "B"- Believe, "C"- Confess, and He will come into your heart and save you right now.

God, we thank you for this day, for this time, for this fellowship. We ask that you touch somebody's soul, somebody's mind, and let them know that they need You even in this dark hour in which we live. Lord, we pray that somebody will be blessed, changed, transformed, made into a new creature by just hearing Your Word today. We thank You in Jesus Name. Amen.

Alright, Sister Jarrett is going to come and share a selection with us, and I'll come back and close us out for today. Will you come now.

SELECTION

He's Sweet I Know by **Mahalia Jackson & A. Jackson**

CLOSING REMARKS

He is sweet I know. We've just got to tell the world wherever we go that He is sweet, I know. God bless you and thank you for participating with us this morning. As we started off this morning, we talked about being connected. Let me say it this way, we have connected today through worship of Our Lord and Savior Jesus Christ. Thank you for connecting with us and we hope that the message has been an encourager and a source of strength in these dismal, and dreadful, and dark times. We know that we serve a Mighty and Able God. So, He's going to get us through this. And I just have the belief that this too shall pass. I pray that out of all that has transpired, some good will come out of this. There are a whole lot of things I could say, but I won't say this morning. God has a unique way of doing things, and sometimes we don't understand. I just feel, I just believe that some great and some good things will come out of all that is happening around the country and around this world. Amen.

CLOSING PRAYER

May the Lord be with you, and bless and keep you in love, causing you to bound in the Grace of God, be filled with knowledge of Him. May you walk in His ways that will be pleasing to Him. Walk in love, walk in the Spirit being led by the Spirit. For it is in Jesus' Name we do pray. Amen.

Living the Abundant Life
Sunday, June 7, 2020

OPENING REMARKS

Anybody out there this morning got something to thank the Lord for? Certainly, He is continuing to bless us repeatedly, and for that we're so grateful and thankful. First and foremost, let me say good morning. Good morning to my Church Family, and certainly, to our Faith Community, good morning to you also. It is another day that the Lord has kept me. It's another day that the Lord has kept you. He has kept all of us. He has kept us from harm. He has kept us from danger. He has provided. He has given us covering; given us shield from all that could have overwhelmed us. For that, we are just so grateful. We ought to just tell the God Thank You even right now.

To God be the Glory for the things that He has done. And He has done so much. I just can't begin to name all the things that He has done. The list is so long, and I wouldn't have the time or the breath to even just tell God how much He has done for us. And we're so grateful and thankful that you have tuned in with us this morning. I can see you tuning in and getting online for this time for worship.

Let me just say welcome to another worship service, worship experience. Why don't you just give the Lord a big hand clap of praise right on your living room couch, wherever you are watching us live this morning. Yes, give Him a big hand of praise. I can't hear it, but I believe I can just feel it in my spirit, Amen, that you've got praise in you. If you got praise in you, you ought to just let it out right about now. Amen, because God deserves it. He deserves our praise. Yes, He does. Yes, He does. All the praise that we can give Him, we ought to just give it to Him because the Bible says He inhabits the praise of His people. If anybody has praise, it ought to be the redeemed of the Lord. And the redeemed of the Lord ought to say so. Amen. We ought to say so.

WORDS OF ENCOURAGEMENT

Well, the first thing this morning is I have a word of encouragement for you. I don't know why the Lord has given me this word of encouragement each Sunday as we come together live streaming. It's for a reason. God has His unique way of dealing with each one of His ministers, pastors, evangelists, whatever your title is. God uses all of us for His unique purpose. Amen.

My word of encouragement for you this morning will be coming from Romans, Chapter 12, Verse 2. You know this verse. It is a familiar verse. But God gave me a little bit more insight into this verse again this week. Let me read that verse in your hearing this morning. And it says, *And be not conformed to this world; but be ye transformed by the renewing of your mind, that you may prove what is that good and acceptable, and perfect will of God.* Amen.

Let me say this. There is a unique person in all of us. I don't care who you are. There is a unique person in all of us. This new, unique person in us is gifted, talented. Just because this person is in you does not mean he or she is automatically going to come out. This unique person is in you, but it doesn't mean that this unique person will automatically come out. This person that's in you has to be released. He has to be released.

Now, the Apostle Paul gives us the key that will allow this person, this unique, talented, and gifted person to be released. Paul tells us in this verse, *be ye*...which means you...*be ye transformed by the renewing of your mind*. Now, the word transformed or **metamorphosed** is where we get our word metamorphosis. We know how caterpillars metamorphose into a butterfly. Paul is saying that if you get your thoughts going in the right direction, if you get your mind transformed and not dwell on the phrase *not able to(not able to thoughts)*, and program you mind with what God says about you, then you can have a transformation. A unique transformation will take place. Then that unique person that is in you will be released. He will come out.

Now, here's the key. It's not up to God, but it's up to you or it is up to us. The only way to release your butterfly, your uniqueness, is to get your thinking in line with God and with the Word of God. Then you will see a talented, gifted, and unique person metamorphose or birth out. Amen. This is my word of encouragement to you this morning. Amen.

CALL TO WORSHIP

As we prepare for worship this morning, let me call us to worship, to fellowship. The Lord is in His Holy Temple. Let the whole Earth, the whole Earth be silent before Him. Amen. And as we now prepare to move into the next phase of this worship experience, I'm going to call upon my wife, Sister Rose, to come and lead us in a selection. After the selection, I will be back for further instructions. Amen.

SELECTION

Emmanuel by Norman Hutchins

Emmanuel. And we all know what that title is...Emmanuel, which means God with us. Thank God that He is with us. I'm glad He's with me. And not only is He with me, but I believe He's in me. And that is close. That is communal. We worship the Lord. We come to worship Him. We get our minds off ourselves. We get our minds off our problems. We get our minds off anything that may be besetting us at this time and focus on Him in the act of worship. Amen.

As we move into this service this morning, we're going to ask that you bow right where you are. Let's petition the Throne of Grace right now because Our God will hear our prayer. He answers sincere and earnest prayers that are prayed to Him. And we want to ask Him this morning for healing. We want to ask Him for blessings. We want to ask Him for protection this morning around our land and country. We know that prayer is the key to the Kingdom, and faith unlocks the door. We've got to turn the key if we expect to trip the lock. So, at this time, we're going to ask that you bow with me and proceed to the Throne of Grace.

PRAYER

Oh God, in whom we live, move, and have our being, we pray now that you keep us in this hour of prayer. Protect us by your unseen hand that guides us in paths of righteousness and right living. Forgive us our sins, and willful neglects of the way that leads to life. We pray today that you will give strength to the week, peace to the troubled hearts, hope to the hopeless, courage to those that are afraid. Give light to those who walk and grope in darkness and after the course of this unfriendly world. Lord, we pray today that you will heal our land. Heal the sick. Heal the diseased. Heal the fainted. Lord, just heal our sick world.

And God I pray and thank you today for your Son Jesus who came and died that we all could experience the gift of salvation. He came that we all could have a right to the tree of life. We lift every need to you, and we know that some of us need one thing and others need another. But whatever the need is, you alone are able to supply. And so, God we pray now that you will meet every need, every challenge that your people are experiencing. Lord, we trust your power. We trust your judgment because we know that you know all things. Nothing escapes you. Nothing surprises you because you're all knowing, all powerful. You're everywhere at the same time. Thank you for being our Awesome God even in a weary land. Thank you for being shelter in the time of a storm. Thank you for being water in dry places. Just Thank you for being our Master, our Lord, Our Savior. You're just everything to us.

And God, we thank you today that you have heard our prayer. Bless the bereaved all over our country. For those who have lost family members due to brutality, through protests, those who were injured, those who were battered, Lord we pray and ask you to touch these families. And may all those who have quit this walk of life and gone to their eternal abode, Lord we pray that you allow their souls to rest in you. Lest we forget we pray for the leaders of our country, and our cities, our towns, our communities. Lord there is pain. There is fear. And we know you know all about it. Watch over the protesters. We pray that our streets stay safe, and no more life be lost. Lord, keep as you see fit. Lord this is our prayer today. And as we prepare to worship, Lord we pray for a worshiping spirit for you see true and spiritual worship. Hear our prayer. And we pray it in the Name of Jesus, Our Elder Brother, Amen and Amen.

God bless you. Thank you so much. Prayer works. I just believe in prayer. Anybody out there this morning know that prayer works. It has worked in our past. It works in our present. And I just believe it will work in our future. Jesus said man ought to always pray and not faint. God bless you as we now prepare for a Word. I don't have an awful long word for you today.

SERMON

This is what the Lord gave me to share with you today. There is a verse of scripture that is found in the gospel recorded by John. John 10:10. But I'm going to be emphasizing the *b* part of that verse today. And the verse reads,

> 10. *The thief cometh not, but to steal, and to kill, and to destroy:* ***I am come that they might have life, and that they might have it more abundantly.***

And from this verse this morning I want to use for our theme **Living the Abundant Life**. The book of Ecclesiastes Chapter 3, Verse 1 says this: *To everything there is a season and a time to every purpose under the heaven.* We also have heard this old saying, history does repeat itself. And I concur, I agree with King Solomon's assessment that everything has a season and a time. And time and season have purpose under heaven. In the times in which we are living seems to remind me of just a few decades ago and it appears that history is repeating itself of the things we are witnessing in the 21st Century. We see hate. We see crime. We see marching in our streets. We see burned infrastructure, police brutality. We see it all that's happening in our nation and around the world. And as I pondered this week on what I would speak about today after both seeing and hearing all that has transpired over the past week. As a result of the death of George Floyd, my mind carried me back to my youthful days during the height of the Civil Rights Movement, and the civil unrest that was taking place during that era. Dr. Martin Luther King, Jr. was leading marches and protests of injustice, inequality, and the things that were facing the poor, the least, and the left out. During that era much of our secular music was centered around the themes that many were suffering and going through during the time. Music was a way of expressing how people really felt. And I remember very vividly a song that was played over the radio by the late Marvin Gaye. The song's title was *What's Going On*. The lyrics of the song went like this:

> *Mother, Mother, there's too many of you crying,*
>
> *Brother, Brother, Brother, there are far too many of you dying.*
>
> *You know we've got to find a way to bring some lovin' here today, ,*
> *Father, Father, We don't need to escalate,*

You see, war is not the answer, For only love can conquer hate,

You know we've got to find a way to bring some lovin' here today,

Picket lines and picket signs, Don't push me with brutality, Talk to me so you can see

Oh, what's going on, Yeah, what's going on.

Oh, what's going on, Simply, because our hair is long.

Oh, you know we've got to find a way,

To bring some understanding here today.

My Brothers and Sisters I remember that song as a teenager. There were so many others that addressed the issues of that day. And it seems as if we have to revisit some of our old historic music and information to understand what they went through then and what people are going through now. But as I come to my text this morning, Jesus says these words, *I come that you might have life, and that you might have it more abundantly.* Jesus came that we might live and not have to die. He came that we could have life that is worth living, life more abundantly. My question is, "Is it possible to live the abundant life? Can man really be happy? Can one be content in a world like ours?" Oh, I have a series of questions this morning. The question is, "What is the status of your life today? How is life serving you? Are you really living? Is it well with your soul?"

Time's greatest challenge and humanity's biggest problem is in the realm of living a livable life. It is a fact today, even now that for humanity most of the life of humanity is lived in a dilemma. We're in a dilemma. Many of you are in the throws or in the horn of life's painful dilemma even right now. You see our world is confused. Our times are turbulent. Our generation is so bewildered that man is afraid to live, and man is afraid to die. That's where we are. He's afraid to live. He's afraid to die. And I can just hear Jesus saying, *I come that you might have life and that you might have it more abundantly. I came that you might live.* Man is afraid to live because of the known realities. It's sad when man is afraid to walk with himself in the daytime. It's sad that man is afraid to sleep with himself at night. That's bad. **Our society is so *denied*,** and our generation is so frustrated. Our times are so uncertain that for many, life has become a curse instead of a blessing. Yet, I hear the Lord saying, *I come that you might have life, and that you might have it more abundantly.*

Jesus was counteracting what He said in the *a-part* of the verse. He says, "Now I know what the thief comes to do. He comes to steal. He comes to kill and to destroy. But I come that you might have life." **Our society is so *denied*.** Our generation is so frustrated. Our times are uncertain. For many, life has become a curse instead of a blessing. For many, life is a miserable failure instead of glorious success. You see, for many, life is literally hell instead of a hopeful heaven. The reason being in the first place this age and generation is filled with *not enough*. Jesus said I want you to have the abundance. But this generation says that it is filled with *not enough*.

So, what is it called? It is called in our times marginal living. Marginal living is living on the border line. Marginal living is like a man in a business. He's making a marginal profit and is barely staying in business because he's on the border line. They find that their today looks bad, but their tomorrow looks worse. And it's bad when people feel, "I'm living in a bad time, but my tomorrow looks worse than my right now." Marginal living in midst of a world of trouble. Marginal living in midst of a pandemic even at the same time. Marginal living in midst of confusion. But I can hear the Lord. I hear the voice of understanding speaking. I can hear the voice of peace speaking. I can hear, in midst of death, I hear life speaking. In midst of sadness, I can hear the voice of joy speaking.

What can you hear Reverend? I can hear the voice saying, *I am come that they might have life, that you might have it more abundantly.* In midst of hate, I hear the voice of love speaking. And the reason I can hear these things is because I hear the Lord saying, and He keeps saying it over and over in my head, *I am come that they might have life, and that they might have it more abundantly.*

And as I move to a close, I can hear Jesus saying in this verse also. That's why Jesus broke ranks in eternity and took up ranks in time that they might have life. He knew that the devil would want to take life. That's why I can hear Jesus saying, "That's why I died a vicarious death on Calvary." Why? That they might have life. That's why Jesus took hell's keys, and death's sting, and the grave's victory because he wanted us to have life. That's why Jesus rose from the grave that you might have life, I might have life. That's why Jesus authorized the Church to preach the gospel that they might have life and have it more abundantly. That's why Jesus said, *I come that you might have life, and that you might have it more abundantly.* He wants you to have the abundant life today.

He wants you to live, and to move, and to have your being because it is in Him that we live, we move and have our being. So, my brothers and sisters hold on to what you have. Don't let the enemy, the thief steal, kill, and destroy. Remember what Jesus said, "I want you to have life, the abundant life." How do you describe abundant life? It's almost indescribable; but the only perceived idea I have to explain what abundant life is like is that you can take a teacup and go to the Atlantic Ocean, dip out a cup, look back at the ocean, and you will have more yet in the ocean than you have in the cup. That's abundance. I believe that that's the kind of life that Jesus wants for us…more than enough. God bless you. This is what the Lord put on my heart, and I am sharing what He place in me.

CALL TO DISCIPLESHIP

If anyone out there this morning that has heard this little, short sermonette and believe the Word, and you want life…the abundant life…you can have it because Jesus came that you might have abundant life. He wants to hook up with you. He wants to unite with you so that He can impart to you this life…abundant life with Him. If you can confess it with your mouth, believe that the Jesus we talked about who took death, hell, and the grave and defeated it…If you can believe Jesus died, was buried and raised the third day…if you can confess that in your heart and in your mind, and you right now can be saved right where you are. You can't get it *no better* than that. It's free. *It don't cost you nothing.* All He wants you to do is just have faith in Him. It's as simple as ABC. Acknowledge (admit). Believe. Confess. Just say it. Say it with your mouth. I Believe. And He will save you. God bless you and thank you.

Sister Rose is going to come back and bless us one more time, and I'll be back.

SELECTION

You Deserve It by David Bloom

Come on now let's give the Lord what He deserves. Somebody ought to just give Him a Hallelujah right where you are. Go on and do it right now. Go on and give Him what He deserves. He deserves all the Glory, all the Honor, all the praise. What a wonderful, beautiful, magnificent, magnanimous song – just giving God the praise, the hallelujah, and the glory. Amen. He deserves it all. I don't have anything that God wants other than my Hallelujah, my praise because whatever I have it's the Lord's anyway. It's His anyway. What I know, He taught me. What I have, He gave it to me. He's already the owner of it. I belong to Him. So, all I owe to the Lord is a Hallelujah and a great praise. Thank you so much Sister Jarrett for blessing us in music ministry. Thank you for being here to help me out in that area. Amen. God bless you.

CLOSING REMARKS

Oh, what a wonderful Sunday morning this has been. Amen. It's been great. I really feel good in spite of all that has transpired around the world this week. God has just shown up in magnanimous ways, and He deserves the praise. I'm just so glad to see peace about to be made. We don't see any more violence in our streets, maybe just a tad bit. But we see God moving in methodical ways. Amen.

Let's keep each and every one lifted in prayer. Let's keep each and every one lifted to the Highest of the High so that we can get through this. I am missing Church so badly…the House. The Church is in us, but the Church house where we congregate and have dialog and face to face fellowship. And I just pray that God will move through this pandemic so that our Churches can come back into fellowship. I know some are going back kind of early I believe.

I don't want to move too fast and get anyone infected with this disease because it's still here. It's still happening in our own county, in our state, and yet around the world. But I am praying that the Lord will give me a time and a day. And probably after next week, I'm going to meet with our brethren so that we can have the proper plan in place. So, when we go back, we won't go back half together. We want to be together on this going back to worship on Sunday. We're going to have to implement some things. I know many of you have been asking, "When, When, When?" I pray that the Lord is going to give me an answer. And I pray that when He gives me an answer it will be feasible, it will be proper, it will be right for us to move back in and not expect the worst.

So, I want to say thank you today for participating with me my friends and Church family from far and near. Thank you for tuning in today. I pray that the Word was a blessing. Thank God for this fellowship again.

CLOSING PRAYER

So, let me say so long. God Bless, and may He forever keep you is our prayer, in Jesus's name. Amen.

Unity
Sunday, June 14, 2020

OPENING REMARKS

Anybody out there, know you are blessed this morning, better Than Blessed. If you are blessed, then you ought to thank the Lord even right now. That was the late Cassietta Baker George that blessed us with that beautiful rendition, the daughter of our late pastor, Pastor P.H. Baker. I just so happened to stumble upon some of her music from back in the day when she sang with the Caravans, Dorothy Norwood and all that group. That song still sounds good today.

I'm blessed. I'm better than blessed. If anybody out there know you're blessed this morning just give me a thumbs up or give me a heart to let me know that you are blessed and grateful to be here another Sunday morning.

Good morning! Good morning! Amen! Good morning Church Family and friends far and near. It's just good to be here today. We thank the Lord for another day's journey, and I'm glad about it. He has kept me alive. He has kept you alive. He has kept us alive. I have learned we can't keep ourselves. I'm too weak. I don't know enough. I'm not big enough to keep myself. But thanks be to God who keeps all of us. We are kept by His divine power.

Thanks for tuning in with us today. We pray you will be blessed by what the Lord has in store for us in His Word. We know that He has a Word for us on today. We pray that when we have finished this worship today you will be better off than when you tuned in to today's worship. So, why don't you just pause for a moment and give the Lord a wave praise. Just give Him a wave praise right now. You can do it with one hand. You can do it with both of your hands. Just give Him a wave praise. Why? Because He deserves it. He deserves it all. And all to Him I owe. I owe Him too much for the things He has done. I owe Him too much. I couldn't have done it like the Lord has already done it. So, that why I owe Him all the praise. I owe Him all the Glory. Amen. We are grateful and thankful that you chose to share this hour with us.eH

WORDS OF ENCOURAGEMENT

Well, I have a word of encouragement for you this morning. Another word of encouragement. Our word of encouragement will come from Daniel, Chapter 6, Verse 23. Listen to it. It says,

> *Then was the king exceeding glad for him, and commanded that they should take Daniel up out of the den. So Daniel was taken up out of the den, and no manner of hurt was found upon him, because he believed in his God.*

That's what that verse says. Amen. Well, in Daniel, Chapter 6 it is a story of how the enemies of Daniel conspired to get him arrested. They knew that Daniel could get arrested because he was a praying man. The king sent out a decree that anyone that was seen praying would be destroyed. So, Daniel did not cease to pray. He prayed three times a day with his face toward Jerusalem. That was his character. That was his personality. He believed in God. He believed in the power of prayer. But his enemies conspired against him to have him arrested and thrown into the den of lions for refusing not to stop praying and worshiping his God. Daniel's attitude was God's got me. He's got me in the palm of His hand. And my brothers and sisters I want you to know today that God's got you too. He's got you in the palm of His hand.

He controls the lions that were in the den with Daniel. He stayed the lions in peace. And everyone thought that the lions would devour him. But we serve a God that has supernatural powers. God used that supernatural power and closed the mouths of the lions. God never promised that we wouldn't have difficulties. But He promised that He would give us strength for every challenge and take whatever was meant for harm and use it to our advantage. You may have a good reason to worry about some things, but there is a simple phrase you have got to get down in your spirit. *God got this.* That's what we got to put down in our heart and let it sync. Let it marinate in us no matter what we are surrounded by or what we are surrounded with. You've got to have a spirit deep down in you saying *God got this*. He's got the solution. He's got the solution whatever the circumstance. So, live out of a place of peace and trust. It's just a matter of time before you see things in your life begin to turn around in your favor. That's what Daniel did. We need to adopt the same vernacular, the same attitude that Daniel had when he was placed in the den of hungry lions. God through supernatural divine intervention, stayed the lions where they could not devour Daniel because he knew that God had his back. God has got your back this morning.

Well, that's my little summation to you this morning. My word of encouragement is to let you know that *God got this*.

CALL TO WORSHIP

Let us prepare now to move into our worship. As we prepare, we want you to know the Lord is listening, this morning. Anybody got some praise and worship in you this morning? For God is listening and He is ready to receive His worship and His praise. Let me just tell you *the*

Lord is in His Holy temple, let the Earth keep silent before Him. Yet, you don't have the right to remain silent, because the redeemed of the Lord ought to say so. Amen.

So, at this time we're going to ask Sis. Rose to come and bless us with a selection. Then we will return to continue further into this worship experience.

SELECTION

I Sing Praises to Your Name by Terry MacAlmon

Thank You Lord. His name is greatly to be praised. He is worthy of all our praise. We can't praise Him too much. As we prepare now to petition the very Throne of God, we ask that you pray with us and pray for us.

And just before we move into our prayer this morning, let me just make mention that at 6pm this evening a variety, or should I say a group of clergymen from all over the county of different faiths will be meeting at the Court House Square to offer prayer for a variety of things because our word, our country, our community are in vast need of prayer.

We need prayer in these dark and dismal days. We need understanding. We need knowledge. We need wisdom. We need discernment. We need a whole variety of things. There is a list of things we need. So, there will be various Pastors there praying for the Holy Spirit to intervene. We are praying for Unity. And I will be praying this evening on the area of unity. Others will be praying for victory, peace, repentance. Just name it and we will be praying that God will by His divine power and intervention will move in our Earth and bring solace, unity, and peace to all. That's going to be the topic of my sermon for today. Unity. After I received this topic, the Lord put it on my heart to just talk about unity. We need unity.

Let us now go before the Throne of Grace and beseech the Lord for His mercy and His compassion for us in these times.

PRAYER

Dear God, I come to you today in the Name of Your Son Jesus Christ. First, we want to say thank You for being our God, our Ruler, and our Sustainer, the keeper of our souls. Thank You for last night's sleep and slumber. There were times we did or did not know whether we were in the world or out of this world. But you watched over us and early this morning, you awakened us to this new day, a day that has been coming since the beginning of time. When we arose this morning and saw the bright sun shining, and we begin to feel and discover in these old clay bodies we had a reasonable portion of health and strength. And we thank you God for all of your provisions, for food, for clothing, and shelter. We even thank You for family.

And as we come before you now, we say to you, Oh God, search our hearts. And if you find anything that is not like you now, Lord, remove it even now. Make us like you. Create in us clean hearts. Renew within us right spirits. Allow the joy of our salvation to show forth as the sun in the morning light while we are yet yield and still Lord. We pray that you give us the desire and delight to worship you in the beauty of holiness. We desire to praise you today because you have done so much for us. We realize that it warrants our praise to be directed toward you.

We know when praises go up blessings come down. Send your blessing. Send your anointing. Lift your people. Many are heavy with the troubles of this world. Trouble is all over the land. People want to know what's going on. And Lord, we know you know our hearts, our thoughts, even before we think them. So, Lord we ask for a move of your hand. Speak Lord in these times. Speak on Your time. We even ask you to remember the sick, today, the suffering. If you will heal the sick, if you will lift-up the suffering, we even ask you to remember the families that have lost loved ones, whether it was natural or whether it caused by another person or an object.

We need You Lord. We need you like never before. We need you like a hand needs a glove. We need you like a thirsty Earth needs water. We need You Lord. As many people experience bereavement, we pray that you will console them. Give them comfort and peace in this hour. We ask that you protect and give them guidance. And Lord, remember America. Lord look now. We ask you to save our country. Heal her. Guide her to the light.

We pray that you touch our leaders. They need you even right now. Our police officers need you. Our communities need you. We pray for unity. We pray for peace. We pray for justice. We pray for repentance. We pray for the feeling of the Holy Spirit. We pray for love. We even pray for victory.

And Lord in Your majestic Name, a Name that is above every name, and at Your Name every knee shall bow, and every tongue shall confess that You are Lord. And Lord we pray this prayer this morning with thanksgiving. And in Jesus Name, Amen and thank God.

Thank you for sharing in that moment with us.

SERMON

And as we make ready now to delve into the Word of God, I want to direct our undivided attention to the Old Testament the book of Psalms, Chapter 133. There are only three verses in this chapter, and I want to read it in our hearing. Psalm 133, Verses 1 through 3 says,

1. *Behold, how good and how pleasant it is for brethren to dwell together in unity!*
2. *It is like the precious ointment upon the head, that ran down upon the beard, even Aaron's beard: that went down to the skirts of his garments;*
3. *As the dew of Hermon, and as the dew that descended upon the mountains of Zion: for there the Lord commanded the blessing, even life forevermore.*

So, I'm going to tag this sermon this morning, **Unity.** That's what we're going to talk about this morning.

In the year 1975, a classic song was released by a group called the O'Jays. The song title that was released was ***Unity.*** And this morning I want to share some of the song with you to build the premise for this message today.

> *Unity, we must have unity. Cause united we stand, divided we fall.*
>
> *They've played the game of divide and conquer ever since the world began.*
>
> *Tried their best to separate the people so we couldn't understand.*
>
> *Come together and show our force,*
>
> *Now's the time for all the people to speak with one voice.*
>
> *I'm talking about unity. We must have unity.*
>
> *Cause united we stand, divided we fall.*
>
> *Now's the time to follow the leader and give our full support.*
>
> *Listen to the words of faithful teachers, Let's put an end to hate and war.*
>
> *Now's the time to come together and take a stand,*
>
> *Now's the time for us to bring peace and love all over the land.*
>
> *I'm talking about unity, we must have unity*
>
> *Cause united we stand, divided we fall. We've got to come together.*
>
> *Get up, get up, get up, get up, get up, Come together. Get up.*

That song says something to us today. We need unity. We need to come together. We need to take a stand. We must have unity because united we stand, divided we fall. As we move into this message text this morning, I want to begin saying that when I look at unity, unity is stewardship. And we are to be good stewards. When I think of a steward,

I think of a manager. He oversees! He's trusted with goods. We are stewards, my brothers and sisters who enjoy God's goodness in creation. All the heavenly bodies that were created by God – Mars, Venus Pluto, Saturn, even the Earth – the Earth is the planet He has chosen. God has chosen the Earth to be His special place of activity. Earth has become the theater of the universe. For on it, the Lord demonstrated His Love, in what is known as the greatest drama ever staged.

You see, God is a planner, He chose a people, and He chose a land way back when. And there He sent His Son to live, to minister, to die, and to be raised from the dead that lost sinners might be saved. My Brothers and Sisters the Earth is God's. Everything on it and in it is God, and all the people on the Earth are God's. They are made in His image and are accountable to Him. We are accountable because we are stewards. When I read Psalm 24 it says,

> *The earth is the Lord's, and the fullness thereof; the world, and they that dwell therein. For he has founded it upon the seas, and established it upon the floods.*

And then he goes on to say,

> *Who shall ascend into the hill of the Lord?...He that hat clean hands, and a pure heart; who hath not lifted his soul unto vanity, nor sworn deceitfully. He shall receive the blessing from the Lord.*

The Earth and everything in it, and on it belongs to God. I belong to Him. You belong to Him. We all belong to God. And God has given each of us something to be accountable for. What are we accountable for? We are accountable for a family. We are accountable for a home. We are accountable for ministry. Even our very lives are accountable to God. Better yet, He has given us stewardship of unity. That's why it behooves us to work diligently, faithfully toward unity.

You see, God will hold each of us accountable as to how we have endeavored to bring unity to a world that is in disarray, disunity, and confusion. Every one of us can provide a little unity where we are. We cannot be global at the same time, but wherever our little local is, we ought to be working toward unity. If we start with unity at home, I just believe unity spreads itself abroad. The old clichés say, "Charity starts at home and spreads itself abroad." We are accountable…each are accountable for unity.

Why? God Himself is a drum major for unity in the Church, in the family, and in the community where one resides. My Brothers and Sisters, if you read Psalm 11:3, it says by the Psalmist,

If these foundations be destroyed, what can the righteous do?

The Church, family, and community, I see those as foundations. Let me just kick this one in there…government. Let me add another one…schools or education. If these foundations as the Psalmist says, be destroyed, what can the righteous do? These are some of the major foundations that cause life to flow, as well as peace, love, and compassion. If these foundations be destroyed and have not unity, then everything else is a ball of confusion. I believe that's where we are in our Earth today. There is a ball of confusion. Nobody knows what to do. They don't have a solution. *If these foundations be destroyed, what can the righteous do?* Let me tell you what the righteous can do. The righteous can start getting on their knees and praying that God will intervene, even when it looks like prayer is not working.

You heard my words of encouragement this morning. Daniel was a praying man. He prayed three times a day even though it looked like prayer would have kept Daniel out of the lions' den. But it didn't keep him out. God did through divine and supernatural powers came to where Daniel was and locked the lions' jaws. If we would start implementing prayer and be serious and sincere in our praying, I believe God can shut down some things. He can change some things and get us out of this ball of confusion.

I want to use UNITY as an acronym to show you what I believe unity ought to look like. Unity. U.N.I.T.Y. Unity.

U: There ought to be some *Understanding*. In all your getting, the Bible teaches us to get understanding. To have unity, one must have an understanding first of God, then others, and then self. God, others, and self. Just be aware of people like us, guarding others' feelings, being tolerant, being forgiving. To do this, you need insight, and you need good judgment in order to have or to keep unity. You got to have some understanding. I think that's what the O'Jays was trying to tell us.

N: Neutral. Yes, understanding, but we need not to be *Neutral*. Unity is not neutral. It's not a stand still. Neutral says, "I'm standing still, just running idle." Unity is a continuing or a perpetual working. That's what unity is about. It's a continual working or perpetuation in working. We are always busy looking for ways to keep unity moving. I don't want to be unified today and then tomorrow I am disunified. Unity is not neutral, but it is progressing, continuing, and perpetuating. It's working, moving, and doing something to keep unity alive.

I: *Integrity* is a personal quality of fairness, and then honesty. You must have some strong principles. You've got to be trustworthy. Integrity makes for unity of spirit, faith, and peace. We've got to have some integrity. And let me say it like the old people would say it, "You've got to have some class about yourself." Good character, good personality, trustworthiness…that demands unity.

T: Then there is *Truthfulness*, telling or expressing the truth honestly. We've got to tell the truth. We've got to be honest. You've got be honest with yourself first before you can be honest and truthful to you. Be true to thine own self. If a man or a woman is not true to himself or herself, then they can't be true to others. You've got to be factual, faithful, and reliable. Demonstrating these qualities also makes for unity. And when people are not expressing truth honestly and being factual, faithful, and reliable, it brings about what we call disunity. You can't be trusted. You say or allow anything to go on that is not good in the eyes of

God neither in the eyes of man, nor in your own eyes because you see yourself as not being trustworthy, truthful, helpful, factual, reliable.

Y: Lastly *Yielding*. In order to bring unity, we have to allow our will to become like God's Will. We want God's Will to make for unity between you and God first, and then to other believers or fellowman. We've got to yield our minds to God so that He can bless our will. Allow God to control, not you, but you allow God to control. Not your strength or your thoughts but allow God's strength and God's thoughts to control, in order, to produce the kind of unity we need in our Earth and world today. Paul says, *I can do all things through Christ which strengtheneth me.* In other words, I'm getting out of the way. I'm allowing God's strength through me to produce this unity in the Body of Christ, whether it's in the family, whether it's in the community, or whatever foundation and entity I am involved in. I can do all things through Christ. I've got to yield to Christ so that Christ can do it through me.

Let me get into the text and lift a few things out of there. In this text Psalm 133: 1-3, David writes this Psalm. This Psalm is classified as a song praise for shouting by shouting. He says *Behold, how good and how pleasant it is for brethren to dwell together…*how? In *unity*. It seems as if the Psalmist is shouting. *Behold* means to gaze or to observe a thing or a person, especially, if that thing that is happening is a remarkable thing. It is amazing. It is something that is beyond the norm. It is something when you can stop fighting and put aside your differences and come together in mind. This is what I believe David is saying. He says, *Behold, how good and pleasant it is for brethren to dwell together in unity.* This is worthy of seeing, observing, or something to see.

David says *how good and how pleasant*. Notice the two adjectives, the words *good* and *pleasant*. Anybody can have a good time regardless of the type of activity that you are involved in. The point is, is it right or is it wrong? Is it good or is it bad? Anybody can take wrong and say it's pleasurable. I remember Moses refused the pleasures of Egypt so that he could suffer with his people.

Some pleasures are not good pleasures as we know it. There are some people who will say you can have some pleasurable times, some good times in sin. But that's on the front end, but you don't see the back end of it. That's where the devil tricks a lot of us. He shows you the pleasurable side of things on the front end, but he doesn't show you on the back end the tragedy or the trouble that will overcome you in the end. Yes, sin is pleasurable. Some folk joke at it. But it is no joking matter. Yes, some things are pleasant. Some things are good. It depends on whether it's right or wrong, good or bad. It is only good and pleasant when you can achieve something like your dreams, you can find peace, joy, and happiness. That's good and pleasant.

This event in the nation of Israel was good and pleasing for the whole nation to come together as one. David is observing what has come about in the life of the nation of Israel. They had been separated for whatever reasons. They had their differences. But David says I'm glad to see brethren dwell together. Now when he says this, he's not just talking about males, and not including the women and the children in the process. He's talking to the whole family. He's talking to the whole Church. He's talking to the whole community. You see when the family, the Church, and the community come together benefits happen. There is unity.

Israel was twelve tribes. They had differences, but they were still family. Even though they had split into the Northern Kingdom and the Southern Kingdom, still they were family. Twelve tribes of different locales, different names, but they were still family. David says, *Behold, how good and how pleasant it is for brethren to dwell together in unity.* And when he saw the twelve tribes uniting and coming together, it was pleasant. It was good. It was good for the nation. They had allowed their differences of opinion to cause chaos and disruption. They had caused them to be divided with animosity among one another. That's why David took liberty as he saw the tribes coming together and he saw the good and pleasant in this process of coming together in unity.

David wrote this song or Psalm as a celebration because they finally discovered what unity is all about. Sometimes God must pull the scales off our eyes because we can't see. In some cases, we don't want to see. But God sees.

Before anyone can have unity, something must take place. What is it Reverend that must take place? I'm glad you asked me that. Before anyone can have unity, you must have an attitude adjustment. You must be willing to commit and work together as one. In Verse 2, David describes to us what happens when brethren dwell together in unity. David says it's like *precious ointment*. Anybody got anything that is precious to you, that has worth, that has significance, that has value? Unity has value. It has worth. David says seeing brethren dwell together is good and pleasant when we are together in unity. It's like *precious ointment upon the head, that ran down upon the beard, even Aaron's beard: that went down to the skirts of his garments*. And then he says, *As the dew of Hermon, and as the dew that descended upon the mountains of Zion: for there the Lord commanded the blessing, even life for evermore.* It's like an ointment. It's like dew. It's like the ointment, the oil that is poured. It is like the dew that is fallen. That's what unity looks like. David is looking at the priestly order. He sees the oil that is used to anoint priests, and that it was a symbol of God's blessing. Precious ointment is a symbol of God's blessing.

And none of us wants to miss anything that God has for us. I just believe this morning that God could pour out more on us if we just knew how to come together. God wants to bless, but because we haven't made any adjustments or want to make an adjustment, so that God could send the anointing so this anointing can run down on us like Aaron's beard, even from the beard all the way down the skirt of his garment. That's how the anointing runs. Let me just say it this way; from head to toe and all in between. The Lord commanded the blessing in Verse 3. God commanded the blessings. I always say *I ain't got nothing* I want to miss that God has for me by having the wrong attitude. My Brothers and Sisters, God looks at our attitude. When I say attitude, I mean heart. He looks at the heart. He knows what's in our hearts. He made us so, He knows what's in us, and He knows what's not in us. So, the Psalmist gives us a picture of the oil in such a large quantity that flows. The manner in which it flows on Aaron signifies when God's people work together in unity, they can't help but experience what God has. And when we think about the dew, we think about what goes on or falls upon the grass. Have you ever walked out on an early morning, and you saw the dew on the grass or the roses? David describes it as flowing from a high mountain that moisturizes the land. Just like the dew that falls from the mountain, this is what happens when brethren come together in unity. God sends down a flow of dew from the high place, the elevated places. The blessing flows down to the people. And all David is saying is Oh how good, how pleasant it is just to come together.

As I prepare to close this morning, none of us can afford to miss the oil and the dew of God because it gives life. The oil gives life to beautiful personalities. The dew gives life to grass, and your house and my house, your Church and my Church, your community and my community can be blessed.

My Brothers and Sisters, even Jesus in His death on the cross was showing how unity works. It works like this. Man had alienated himself from God. There was a big gap or a big gulf between God and man. And God needed a go between. He needed somebody to stand in the gap. He needed somebody who could go the way. The only person who was able and was willing to take that step was Jesus Himself. And Jesus came and died. And through His death to bring unity, He brought a sinning and a sinful man to a righteous and a Holy God. And He brought them together. And my brothers and sisters do you know what that is called? That is called reconciliation. God through Christ brought sinful man to a Holy God. And with His power we have you in unity. With His power, we can love one another. With His power, we can stand together. With His power, we can be one, with His power. I didn't say your power. I said with His power we can be one. Thank you, Lord!

I hope I have said something this morning that will bring unity. That's what we will be praying for Unity around this world, around this country, around the community and everywhere. We need help. God never intended for it to be this way. But it just so happened to be, and it's all because the world needs to adjust its attitude. And when I say world, I don't mean the astrophysical as we see it, but humanity. God's created beings have got to change - our actions, our attitudes – before something stellar can come to humanity. Thank God for Jesus.

CALL TO DISCIPLESHIP

I want to open the doors to the Church. Somebody needs the Lord today. Whoever you are, wherever you are, you can ask Him to come into your life, into your heart, even right now. All you have to do is tell Him, "Lord, I'm sorry for my sins. Lord, forgive me of my sins. Lord, save me. I believe in you. I believe your Word. I believe you are the Son of God." And if you can believe it and confess it with your mouth, you're saved. A – Acknowledge, B – Believe, C – Confess. It's as simple as A, B, C. Ask for that transformation. Ask for that change. He can do it today, even right now. Today, He said, *the day that you hear my voice, harden not your heart.*

So that is my message to you today. You're saved. If you believe that, you're saved. And you can live the life that Christ wants you to live now because there's been a change or a transformation in you. God Bless you. Thank you so much.

Sister Jarrett is going to come back and sing for us. I'll be back with closing remarks, and then we will be done for the morning. Amen.

SELECTION

***We've Come This Far by Faith* by Albert Goodson**

CLOSING REMARKS

Praise God. We have come this far by faith, trusting in His Holy Word. His Word can be trusted. Am I right this morning? His Word can be trusted. No matter what the people say, God's Word will never pass away. God bless you. Thank you for tuning in this morning and sharing in this worship experience. We pray that you have been blessed by the message, and we pray that it has been a source of strength and comfort to you in this very hour. Amen.

Thank you so much. We've come to the close now. I pray that I have said something that has been a blessing to you this morning.

CLOSING PRAYER

Now unto Him who is able to keep you from falling, and to present you faultless before His presence, to Him be dominion, power, glory, honor, and majesty now and forever. And all the people said Amen. God bless you. Thank you. And we're going to close out with Sis. Cassetta Baker George again. As I stated earlier, she was our Pastor's daughter who sang with the Caravans.

A Father with a Purpose
Sunday, June 21, 2020

OPENING REMARKS

Prayer will change things. All we've got to do is tell the Lord all about what we need and pray about it. Faith is the key to the Kingdom of God and opening the door to whatever we need. Good morning! Good morning, St. Mark, Good morning, Church Community, and all my friends that are watching this morning. We are so glad you joined us for morning worship. The thing I want to tell the Lord is to God be the Glory for the things that He has done for us. Thank Him for the joy He has given us, and that the joy that I have the world can't take it away. This joy I have, the world didn't give it and certainly it can't take it away.

Well, today is Father's Day. Amen. It is Father's Day, and I want to take a moment and say to all the fathers out there, Happy Father's Day. Happy Father's Day. I hope you enjoy your day, and that this will be a memorable day in your life. Amen. It's a wonderful thing to be a father. God has given us that fatherhood, and we ought to honor it. We ought to respect it because it is a privilege, it is an honor to be called father by your sons and your daughters. Amen. Just like God is our Father we ought to be honored to just be His children and know that we have a Heavenly Father who is a blessing to us and does so many wonderful things for us. Amen. So, fathers enjoy your day. Children honor your fathers today. Show them some love. Give them some kudos because if you have a wonderful father in your life, I tell you you've got a jewel. So, honor them today. Amen.

WORDS OF ENCOURAGEMENT

Well, I've got a word of encouragement for us on this morning. I want us to listen to what I have to share in words of encouragement this morning. I'm going to look at a passage of scripture that is found in the Psalms. Psalms 62 and Verse 5, I want us to listen to it very attentively. This is a man that is talking to his own soul. He's encouraging his soul. Listen to him: *My soul, wait thou only upon God; for my expectation is from Him.* Does anybody out there have some expectation; you have some things you are looking out for, you are praying about, you are waiting eagerly and anticipating something wonderful is going to come out of just having to wait upon the Lord. *My soul, wait thou only upon God; for my expectation is from Him* – Verse 5 of the 62nd Psalm.

The Psalmist challenges his soul to wait upon the Lord. He encourages himself to trust in his God. You see the hardest part of life is waiting. This thing called waiting renders us helpless. How often have we gotten ourselves into some trouble because we refused to wait? We couldn't wait. We were antsy. We just had to go on and do it our way without waiting for instructions.

You see the waiting game is a very difficult thing for most of us. It is difficult. We can look through the Bible to find that many of God's children got into trouble for not waiting. The first sin that ever occurred happened due to Eve's failing to wait. You may be asking, "How could this have been?" Well, if Eve would have waited upon the Lord and talked with Him, conversed with Him, the serpent by chance would have never encouraged her or motivated her to eat of the forbidden fruit.

Other characters are Abraham and Sarah. If they had waited for God's timing for the promised son Isaac, their home would not have experienced turmoil. They couldn't wait. They couldn't trust God. They went ahead and did it their way, and it caused turmoil in their home.

I wonder if you may be battling the waiting game. If this is true, you need to understand the rules. The best rule to understand would be this: Don't worry about what you can't control or handle. If you feel the urge to worry, will it make whatever you are worrying about happen any faster? Will it change the outcome? We must learn to let patience control our lives. This patience that I am talking about comes directly from God, from the very throne of God.

You see we must let patience have its free course. Now, this is Godly patience – one that promotes trusting. It is not every man or woman who is willing to wait on the Lord. Often, we make wrong decisions because we fail to wait. We have settled for things that end up being worse or being wrong because of our failure to wait on God. In all reality, failure to wait upon God, to me, is disobedience. It disrupts God's plan or purpose for us. It often leads to defeat in life. So, that is why we should ask the Lord to give us this great virtue called patience and wait with all patience. It doesn't mean that you stop and do nothing. Patience means that you continue to work diligently but wait on God for His answer or the move of God. Amen.

In the coming days you may face situations, obstacles, challenges. But you know what? We're just going to have to wait. You go ahead and wait. You may have to ask Him for patience and perseverance through whatever and allow that patience that is in you to be stirred with the Holy faith of God, and just watch God in His own timing move in your direction. Listen to David again, the Psalmist: *My soul, wait thou only upon God; for my expectation is from Him.*

God bless you. That's my word of encouragement to you this morning in terms of encouragement. We need encouragement in these times in which we live. Amen. We're just going to have to wait on the Lord, and when He comes through…guess what…you are going to say I am glad I waited on the Lord. Amen. Amen.

Now we're going to ask Sister Rose to come, and she's going to lead us in a song preparing us for worship. Again Fathers, we thank God for you, and we pray that you have a blessed day.

SELELCTION

Blessed Assurance by Fannie Crosby and Phoebe Knapp

Anybody out there got a story. All of us ought to have a story to tell because the Lord has done so many things in our lives. We ought to just tell our story…just how He has cared for us, how He has saved us…and how He is continuing to preserve us in this pandemic and rioting and death and so many things. We ought to have a story to tell. We ought to look back and say this is my story. Amen. "*Blessed Assurance*". This is a beautiful hymn of the Church

CALL TO WORSHIP

Now let us prepare our minds and our hearts as we go to the Throne of God and just pray and ask the Lord to intervene into some areas, situations that are currently and have taken place in our lives. We know that God will hear us. He'll answer our prayers. God will give us some of the desires of our hearts. That's what the Psalmist says. There are some things we want. There are some things we need, special things. If we pray and pray rightly, God will just add those things as extras. And God is a God of more than enough. He is not limited in what He can do and in how much He can give because He is unlimited Himself. He's unlimited in power. He's unlimited in knowledge. He's just a God of more than enough. I just believe that if things got low, He could just speak and create more. He has already spoken what we see in existence. And I just believe that He can do even the more. Thank you. Shall we go to the Throne?

PRAYER

Dear Heavenly Father, It is again you who have allowed us to come into your presence to give Your Name praise and glory. We want to thank you for last night's sleep and slumber. Thank You for awakening us to see this day. Thank you for another Father's Day, as fathers will be honored by their children that you have blessed them with. They are a gift from you, Oh God.

And Lord, you have been our Father. You have provided for us. You have met all our physical and spiritual needs. You have been there for us in the good times and even in the bad times. Lord we ask you to forgive us our debts, as we forgive our debtors. Without your forgiveness and your mercies, we will not know what love is nor understand a touch of kindness.

Lord, we pray today that you will lift those with broken spirits. Lift those battered bodies that have been dashed with pain. We come also lifting those that are dealing with physical issues. You know who they are, and you know where they are. So, today we say have your way.

Lord, we pray and ask you to keep our Church Family. Watch over them by day and by night. Take care of every one of their needs. Keep us by your might, and by your power. Most Gracious Father, Most Gracious Father that you are, Lord, just covers us with your special graces and with your choice blessings because you are just that kind of Father.

And God we pray for our health professionals who minister in all our communities helping others to recover, to be healed, and to be strengthened. Keep them covered, Oh God. Keep our pastors as they minister to their flocks. And many Lord who have reopened the Church houses to minister their flocks. We pray that you protect them because we realize Lord that this pandemic is not over. Many are still being infected by it. Continue, Oh God, as this unseen disease rage in most of our cities and towns. Help us to do the right thing. Help us to help spare the least amount of the spread of this disease.

Lord, we ask that you look upon our country. Look upon its leadership. Speak Lord this morning in the hearts of those who lead. Speak with power, and Lord we'll be forever grateful, thankful and give you glory and praise for all that you do and all that you plan to do. And we pray this prayer this morning with a heart of thanksgiving, and it's in your Son's Name that we ask it all. Amen and Amen. Amen.

Thank you so much for sharing in that moment of prayer with us. I just believe that prayer works, as always, and it will continue to work for us.

SERMON

Now as we prepare for the message this morning, there is a passage I want to share with you this morning from Mark's Gospel. It is found in Chapter 9 of the said gospel. And due to the fact that this is Father's Day, I want to talk to fathers this morning. Let's begin our reading at Verse 14.

> 14. *And when he came to his disciples, he saw a great multitude about them, and the scribes questioning with them.*
>
> 15. *And straightway all the people, when they beheld him, were greatly amazed, and running to him saluted him.*
>
> 16. *And he asked the scribes, What question ye with them*
>
> 17. *And one of the multitude answered and said, Master, I have brought unto thee my son, which hath a dumb spirit;*
>
> 18. *And wheresoever he taketh him, he teareth him: and he foameth, and gnasheth with with his teeth, and pineth away: and I spake to thy disciples that they should cast him out; and they could not.*
>
> 19. *He answereth him, and saith, O faithless generation, how long shall I be with you? how long shall I suffer you? bring him unto me.*
>
> 20. *And they brought him unto him: and when he saw him, straightway the spirit tare him; and he fell on the ground, and wallowed foaming.*

21. *And he asked his father, How long is it ago since this came unto him? And he said, of a child.*

22. *And ofttimes it hath cast him into the fire, and into the waters, to destroy him: but if thou canst do any thing, have compassion on us, and help us.*

23. *Jesus said unto him, If thou canst believe, all things are possible to him that believeth.*

24. *And straightway the father of the child cried out, and said with tears, Lord, I Believe; help thou mine unbelief.*

25. *When Jesus saw that the people came running together, he rebuked the foul spirit, saying unto him, Thou dumb and deaf spirit, I charge thee, come out of him, and enter no more into him.*

26. *And the spirit cried, and rent him sore, and came out of him: and he was as one dead; insomuch that many said, He is dead.*

27. *But Jesus took him by the hand, and lifted him up; and he arose.*

This morning I want to tag this short message **A Father with A Purpose.** Let me begin this by asking a question. What is life without purpose? Robert Burns says that *life without purpose is a life without destination.* You see having purpose refers to the reason why some things are done, or for something that is existing. So, I have another question. What is your purpose in life? All of us ought to ask ourselves, "What is my purpose in life?" And if you are like Robert Burns who says that *life without purpose is a life without a destination*, you don't know where you are going; and you don't know how you are going to get to your desired end. As fathers, what is your God-given purpose? Why did God bless you, or why did God bless us with sons and daughters?

Unknown to many fathers, who become fathers, is that being a father is a calling, and with the calling comes responsibilities and purpose. When we look at an example of a father, we first need to look at God. I didn't say look at man. But our first purpose is to look at God. See, God

Himself is a responsible man, a responsible father. He is responsible for creating everything that was created. Whether it is visible or invisible, He created it. Not only did He create it, but He cared for it. And He protected it. How? By His Wisdom and His Power.

I know that in life we fail, we fumble, we stumble as fathers. Oh yes, we do. We fail sometimes. We fail to take responsibility. We fail to protect our families, and we leave responsibilities as fathers many times to the children's mother or mothers. Why? Because we are in pursuit of other things that have our interest. The greatest thing, which is teaching and mentoring, many times is left undone. I believe that as a father we have a purpose in-spite of the things that pull at us, and the things that sometimes grip us. We have responsibilities, and we have purpose. Sometimes we are pursuing and grappling after things that really have no merit. Sometimes it's just stuff we to gratify our curiosities, and the greater things, the weightier things are left undone – and that is taking care of our responsibilities of our families and certainly our children.

You see we sometimes find ourselves in what are seemingly impossible situations. Try as we do in some situations and some things become dilemmas, and these dilemmas we try to evade. But because dilemmas are a part of the fabric of our life when desperation comes, we must draw upon what our experiences have taught us. God is able to deliver us. He has the power to deliver us from those things that we feel are weightier…those things that are pulling after us and brings us self-gratification…those things, as I say at St. Mark, "Some matters just don't matter." We've got to be a father with a purpose. We've got rely upon Jesus who is our conquering King. You see He is our power in weakness. With Him there is no situation or problem, no circumstance, no dilemma that is too hard for Him.

Sometimes the weighty things we leave undone and the enemy, the devil, comes in and takes control, takes charge of the lives of our children and do our children harm a lot of times because we are not paying attention as to what is happening even in our children's lives because we are in pursuit of things that bring us gratification and we are not there with purpose and responsibility to see to our children being nurtured and mentored so that they can become strong and productive persons in society.

See a father with purpose pays attention to most things – the behavior and activities of our sons and daughters. And I'm sure that as we move into this text this morning, we're going to see a man who had given attention to his son because when things were happening in his son's life that were not the norm. There were some things that were driving this young boy, and this boy was being tormented. He was tortured. We have young men and young women out there today that are being tortured. They are going through some things, and it behooves the parents of these children, whether they are sons or daughters, to see what's going on. We realize that we can't do anything about it but there is a power. There is a God who is bigger than the situation that's going on in our children's lives. They're hurting. They're going through some stuff. Let's look at our text this morning.

In our text we find that there are some things that seem impossible for man, but it was possible with God. We're going to see Jesus' power unfold with the father who is seeking help from Jesus for his son. This man when Jesus did come to him, his son is being tormented, bothered day and night, week after week, month after years, and the father is in as much pain as the son. When Jesus does come to him, Jesus says, "What can I do for you?" The father says, "Lord can you have mercy upon me and my son". In other words, the father is saying as much as my son is hurting, I'm hurting too. As much as my son is going through, I'm going through too. My Brothers and Sisters, whatever is affecting our children, it ought to be affecting us in some form or fashion. And we ought to be trying to seek some help for them. Sometimes there are some things that we ought to be sick and tired of. It's happening over and repeatedly. Sick and tired of being sick and tired.

We see Jesus' power unfold with a father seeking mercy for his son from Jesus. We see this father in the text has an unknown name. He is just called father. He has a heart-wrenching dilemma. Because this father in the text is without a name, you ought to just put your name there. It could be any father. It could be me. It could be you. A father with a heart-wrenching dilemma. Perhaps this was his only son because the text does not give us any other names of other children or tell us if he had other children. He said, "my son." His son was controlled by a demon. How did this demon get there? We don't have a clue, but we do know from the text that this demon had invaded this boy's life, had invaded his space. This demon had forced himself into the life of this boy. This demon was driving this young man wherever. The Bible says he takes him. This demon was tearing him. It was causing him to foam at the mouth. It was causing him to gnash with his teeth. It says he was pining away, tormented, troubled. Can I say this parenthetically today? Demonic forces are still in operation today. And these demons are operating in our world, and they are on a mission to destroy the family. And they are most certainly out to destroy our sons and our daughters.

It behooves parents, fathers especially, to pay attention to your sons. Pay attention to your daughters. Look at their behavior. Look at what's happening in them. When you see behavior that is not of the norm, you ought to speak. All of us can witness as we look out over life, and as we observe humanity, certainly our generation that is here today we see some things that are out of the norm. We see some behavior. We see some characters. We see some personalities that do not equal the norm. And we won't be judging by what we see if it's out of the norm...if it's not the right things. We won't be judging because the Bible says that a tree is known by the that fruit it bears. You are just being a fruit picker and not a judge. We're not judging. We don't understand what judging is. Judging is when you size up or prize yourself above something. You make some critical decision. But whatever is there is there.

Demons are operative today, and they are invading people's lives. They are forcing and tearing away at the very souls of humanity. But my brothers and sisters, when we see these forces that are invading spaces that should be off limits, we ought to be like the father of our text. We should seek some help, and cry out if we must, to Jesus. We ought to converge on His Word. By that I mean shake the Word. Pull on His Word, Jerk on the Word. Step back and watch Jesus take hold of the devil's attempt to kill, steal, and destroy.

When we see things that are not of the norm, we ought to take it to the Lord. This father observed his child. He saw what was happening to him. He says this thing is bigger than I can handle. I got to take it to somebody that's bigger than that problem. See we ought to be taking our children to the Lord, praying for the children even that are not ours. We ought to be encouraging and motivating children.

But as this father comes, there are three things I want to lift from this text this morning. As the father comes to the area where Jesus was, there were others there. There was a crowd there. In that crowd was a great multitude about them Verse 14 says that the scribes were there. The scribes were there, but what were they doing? They were questioning them. And the first point I want to make this morning is **a *hindering crowd.***

If you read Matthew's account, Jesus, Peter, James, and John were up on the Mount of Transfiguration. They had been there and experienced a transforming glory. Three disciples with Jesus and nine were left down in the valley. As Jesus was coming down to the other nine, He meets the crowd. In the crowd were the scribes – these great teachers of the law. Guess what they were doing? They were arguing. They were disputing with the nine because they could not do anything with the father-son situation. That's the way it is sometimes. We spend too much time fussing and arguing. We can't do anything about the problems that we're facing. There are problems that are taking people out of here. Because we spend too much time fussing and arguing over nothing, we are giving the devil free reign.

The scribes were questioning the power and the doctrine of Jesus and the failure of the disciples. They could do nothing themselves because they were also powerless against the demons. They opposed Jesus, but never reached out to help the boy. Isn't that the way it is? We don't try to help the situation. And here this father is standing in their midst with this son that is going through in his spirit, in his body. He's got to stand there and listen to them argue back and forth. I'm sure he wasn't happy. I wouldn't have been happy either.

Let me tell you about crowds. Crowds are always trying to hinder God and those who are trying to get God's will done in their lives. The crowd is sitting there arguing, talking about everything except what they need to be talking about. We're trying to get some help, and you are over here talking about something else. And then the problem also is that the crowd will always try to find fault in what you are doing and never help. Jesus comes along, and He asks the scribes, "What are you questioning them for? Why are you arguing with them?" I'm sure the father was pleased at the presence of Jesus. He said, "I need somebody with some sense to come and let me talk to them because I'm not getting any sense out of these folks over here are saying. They seem to be unhappy, yet they are teachers of the law. They are supposed to be the elites of society. But what I am seeing I am ashamed." I'm so sure the man said, "I'm so glad to see you Lord. I feel like I can get something done now sense you are here." You see when dilemmas come in your life, and when Jesus shows up at the right time you can be assured that He will make a difference in what's going on. That's what the hindering crowd will do. But you've got to wait on Jesus.

The second thing I want to lift out of this text is *a helpless father, but a desperate father.* He's got a purpose in mind. "I'm purposing healing for my son. I'm purposing for a new life for my son. I'm purposing for a future for my son. I know what the past has been like. The past has been hard. It's been tough. It's been rugged. I'm ready to see some glory take place." He's a helpless father, but a desperate father. I can't do anything, but I'm desperate because I know who can. And I'm sure you all know that are fathers, especially, understand the situation of the father in the text. Your only son, your only child, desperate, enslaved by a demon force, desperate, and all you can do is watch helplessly, desperate, hoping and praying for divine intervention. Presently he's saying, "I'm looking for help from above."

Presently many of our sons and many of our daughters are being enslaved in an ill society. And a lot of us as parents are at a loss as to what to do. Well, I've got what I believe is a solution. If you don't know what to do, this is what you need to do. Take it to Jesus and let Him put His hands on it. Let Him speak to it and watch Him change things.

You see there is no other record of him even trying to find help in the past. Maybe he had done so, but the scripture does not give us that indication. I can only imagine what and how he's feeling. Helpless but desperate as the father gives the report of what was happening in his son's life. He had been observant of his son. He wasn't one of those fathers that look on and look off. He was one of those fathers who looked on and looked in. As the father reports what happens, he says that the demons were not playing games with this boy. And let me tell you the devil don't play. He's out to get you. These demons were tormenting him. Wherever they attacked him, they would throw him down. He would foam at the mouth. He was gnashing his teeth. Often, he falls in the fire and falls into the water to destroy him. Fire can burn you up. Water can drown you. Listen to all these things, these detrimental things that can come upon you as a result being controlled by demonic forces.

I can hear this father saying to Jesus while he's helpless but he's desperate, "Lord, if you can just do anything." That's desperate. "If you can just do anything, have compassion on us and help us." A concerned father. A responsible father. A caring father. A protecting father. He's interested in what's going on in-spite of. On this Father's Day how many fathers today need help because the outside forces have taken over? They have taken over causing children to go astray. They have taken over causing children to go contrary to the home training and their Christian upbringing if they got anything at all. Let me just tell you, it's not too late. Because as long as they are walking, breathing and talking, just like the father in the text, we can cry, "Help Lord! Help now! Send help!" This is the season. This is the right season for the family to call for help. No greater time in history of the Church age is to call on the name of the Lord. It's time.

Our young fathers, when I say your fathers – the 18-year-olds to 20-year-olds – who are fathers of children, we need to get in our sons' and daughters' lives. Don't just hit and miss. But you've got to get involved. You've got to get the Lord involved early because we don't want to continue to bring young men into this crazy world. We especially don't want to continue to bring our African American men into this world and just let them hang out without training or mentoring. We need to help them because they don't know, and they won't listen to any body. So, you better get involved now. If you don't get involved while they are babies, little toddlers, and so forth and so on the enemy is going to invade and steal and kill who they are and what they were created to be.

It's time now young men. You 20-year-old and 30-year-old fathers, don't be just a father or daddy, let me say it that way, with a pair of pants on. That doesn't make you a father. A father is one who has a purpose. A father is one who has responsibilities. And if you are a father, you want to make sure that your sons, your daughters are cared for. It doesn't matter if you are in the house with them or out of the house with them. Take care of them because they are yours. You've got to be responsible. And don't leave that responsibility to somebody else. You be the first responsible person in their life. And they will grow up to respect you. If you don't show responsibility and purpose, they have a special word out there that they call you, and I don't want to say it. I can say this. They call you just a donor. You don't want to be labeled just a donor. You want to be labeled father because it's a privilege to be called father. Let me move to my last outline.

It seems that this was a ***hopeless son***. But if you have a responsible father who is praying and who is looking out for your well-being, who is responsible and who has a purpose, you may be hopeless now, but you won't be hopeless for long. We have talked about the hindering crowd, the helpless father, desperate father. Now we need to see the ***hopeless son***. But his hopelessness will be turned into hope.

This desperate father one day longed to see his son's afflictions and torments be turned around because it had been too many days of him being afflicted. It had been too long watching him being tormented. The son could not help himself, and his daddy couldn't help him. But the father knew how to get him to Jesus. Look at Verse 24: *And straightway the father of the child cried out, and said with tears, Lord, I believe; help thou my unbelief.* The father may feel, "I believe there may be something in the back of my mind that is not helping me to believe totally. Lord, if there is any doubt in the back of my mind, help my unbelief." And that was all that Jesus needed for him to say. Help! Help! Help!

And this is what Jesus told him after he had said help. Jesus said to him, "Bring the boy to me." And at the sight of Jesus the demon inside of him was determined to cause the boy much more pain. The demon knew that this was his last opportunity. And you must understand that the demon is no match for Jesus. This is what happened to the boy; the demon cried with a spirit and rent and came out and the boy became as dead. My brothers and sisters Jesus spoke healing to this boy. He spoke to the evil spirits and commanded them to come out. This shows us today that Jesus has power over demons. He has power over Satan.

The healing Christ is a very present help in time of need. He's omnipresent. He's everywhere at the same time healing with his all-powerful healing hand. Yes, He is an all-powerful Christ. Healing is part of His business, because when He came into the world He came preaching, teaching, and healing. His trifold ministry was to preach, teach, and to heal. And He did what He came to do. He was faithful to His calling. He was merciful with His grace. He was loving and just with His compassion. Oh, I tell you this healing Christ is all we need Him to be today. Thank God for His healing power today. Thank God for His changing power today. Thank God for His delivering power today. He has not lost any power. He has not relinquished His power. If He did what He did for the boy in the text in His day, think about what He can do in our time. He has not downgraded. He's still just as powerful. All you got to do is just trust Him.

Whatever you are going through, whatever your family is going through, just take it to the Lord in prayer. Be responsible. Men you've got to be responsible. Young men you've got to be responsible. If you want to be a father, then play the father's role. Be caring. Be loving. Be there for your children. Be there for your sons. Be there for your daughters. Be an example. Clean up your life. If your life is messed up, tore up from the floor up, then clean up your life so that you can be an asset, a mentor, and an example to your children. We can turn some of the mess around that we're dealing within the world if we get the right information. When we don't have the right information, we don't act right. We need the right information. I don't mean to come across sounding harsh, but it's the truth. And we've got to get the truth told.

If we want to see a better world, and if we want to see lives changed, then somebody's got to tell the truth. I could be right here this morning telling you how to be blessed. But I need to tell you how to be who we have been called and designed to be right now because we are going through some turbulent times. We need to know how to live because it is our sons that are being destroyed. We've got to teach them how to be young men that have fathers. Too many of our young men are dying in the streets and leaving children that they never had the privilege of raising. Momma has got to raise them. Grandparents have got to raise them, and everybody else has got to chip in. We are losing our lives sometimes senselessly, other times maybe because of somebody's ignorance.

I hope I have some young fathers out there listening. Be a father with a purpose. Be responsible. Get a plan for your life. If you fail to plan, you plan to fail. Get a plan. And God's got a plan for you. This is my message to you this morning. This is what the Lord put on my heart today to say and I've got to say it. I can sleep like a baby tonight, because when the Lord puts it on me, I've got to say it. Remember what Robert Burn said: *Life without purpose is a life without destination.*

CALL TO DISCIPLESHIP

God bless you this morning. I'm going to open the doors of the Church. Right where you are, if anyone out there today heard this sermon or this message, and you are not saved, and you want to be saved, all you have to do is open your heart and say, "Lord come into my life. Save me." And if you ask Him in, He will come in at your welcome. And He will come in and He will sup with you and you with Him. He will come in. He will change your life. All you have to do is A – Acknowledge, B – Believe, and C – Confess. "I acknowledge you as my Lord and my Savior. I acknowledge that I am a sinner. I believe you died for me. I confess my sins. Forgive me of my sins. Cleanse me from all my unjust ways." And He will come. If you believe it, trust it, and receive it, you are saved right now.

My brothers and sisters, at this time, we have a song of dedication. This is dedicated to all the fathers out there. Amen. To the fathers who are out there, you are special. So, now act like you are special. Live like you are special. And you know what? You will be special. You are special. Thank you, Jesus. The title of the song is ***It's Your Time***. Listen to it.

SELECTION OF DECICATION

It's Your Mind **by Luther Barnes**

Amen. That's to all the fathers out there. We dedicate that number to you today. For your faithfulness and for your dedication. God's going to reward you for your faithfulness. He does reward faithfulness.

Thank all of you for wishing me a Happy Father's Day. Thank you so kindly for your congratulatory remarks. Thank you so much. This is going to bring us to today's conclusion of this beautiful Father's Day Celebration. We are appreciative for you tuning in with us. All of you my friends out there, thank you so much. Boy, I've got friends in faraway places. Thank everybody. Thank you. Thank you. What I'm going to do now is give the benediction, and then we will sound off.

CLOSING PRAYER

Now may the grace of God, the Love of God, and the fellowship of the Holy Spirit, may He now rest, rule, and abide in the hearts of this Thine people now and forever, and all the people said together, Amen.

Staying Positive in a Negative World
Sunday, June 28, 2020

OPENING REMARKS

Good morning! Good morning! This is a good morning, Church Family and Friends. It's good to be here and to be blessed of the Lord another day. The song writer says, "I woke up this morning with my mind stayed on Jesus. I'm walking and talking with my mind stayed on Jesus." The song goes further to say, "It's no harm to keep your mind stayed on Jesus."

I want to thank God for His amazing grace, His amazing grace. Every day of my life, God's grace becomes more amazing. And you know when I think about the grace of God, that amazing grace, I think about this. Grace is God's redemptive act at Christ's expense. You just take the word: ***G – God's, R – Redemptive Act, A – At, C – Christ's, E – Expense.*** Isn't it wonderful to know that GRACE is ***God's Redemptive Act At Christ's Expense***? Why don't you just give God a thumbs up or a great big heart right now and just thank God for His amazing grace. God's Redemptive Act At Christ's Expense. It is amazing. Let's thank Him right now. Thank you, thank you, thank you so much for tuning in with us this Sunday Morning. Thank you for getting up, taking care of your morning chores, and then tuning in with us at this particular hour for worship and praise. I want to thank you this morning.

WORDS OF ENCOURAGEMENT

Let me give you a thought for today. My thought for the day will be coming from Matthew 28. I want us to look at the 20th Verse – the ***b*** part of the verse, the very last phrase in that verse. This is what that phrase says*: and lo, I am with you always, even 'til the end of the world.* And He closes it out with a great big *Amen.* Amen. *And lo, I am with you always, even 'til the end of the world (or the age). Amen.*

This has been an extremely difficult year for the Christian Church, America, and the whole wide world. You see there are families that have encountered physical sickness and death due to Covid-19. And there are a lot more in between all those two encounters. There are others who are experiencing strange relationships or are in strange relationships. There are believers who will quickly testify that if it had not been for the Lord on our side, they would not have been able to stand the trials and the difficulty of the tough moments we are now in.

Just as the spirit of God lifted David as he mourned his family member's loss. You know he lost a son, and it became a dark season in the life of David. He mourned and put on sackcloth and ashes and just sat out in the middle of the street. Think about the Apostle Paul. Paul was reassured of his weakest hour when he had a thorn in his flesh. He prayed three times to remove it. But this was God's reply, "My grace is sufficient." We also have been sustained by God's eternal presence in our life's situations in this year 2020. When difficult times were upon us this year, God was there. He still is. He was only a prayer away. All we had to do was just pray right where we were. I know you can recall how the Lord lifted a burden from your shoulder and gave you renewed strength in midst of your weakness. And I'm sure you can say even now to God, "To God be the glory for the things that He has done."

You know He has done great things. He has done some marvelous things even through these events in our time. When Jesus told His disciples *lo, I'll be with you always,* that means exactly what it says. He meant that. He planned to be with us consistently, continuously. How long…*even 'til the end of the age.* We don't have to worry about our being alone in midst of whatever that is transpiring in our lives. You're not in it alone. You're not by yourself. God is with us even 'til the very end. And as He closes out that phrase, that statement, He concluded with Amen. So, you ought to just go on and say Amen. I'm not by myself. Amen. These are my words to you this morning. A thought for us as we move forward in the remainder of this day and the rest of this week, the rest of this month, the rest of this year, and the rest of your life. Guess what? You are not alone. Jesus is with us. God Bless you. Thank you. My thought for you today.

CALL TO WORSHIP

At this time, I'm going to ask Sister Rose to come and bless us with a song, and I'll be back to share further in this worship experience. Prepare your hearts now for prayer, the word, and song.

SELECTION

Praise Is What I do by William Murphy III

Praise is what I do. I tell you there is nothing like praise, the praise of God. Amen. We know this morning that the Lord deserves all our praise. My brothers and sisters if you've got another praise in you this morning, why don't you go on and give a thumbs up to show you have a praise in you. This is a moment of witness. Can you witness this morning? I know you can't say Amen. You can't high five anybody. You can't touch your neighbor. But at least you can give a thumbs up or a great big heart. Let God know that praise is what I do. Praise is deserved of God. Amen. He deserves our praise.

Thank you, Sister Jarrett for that beautiful, beautiful number this morning. My heart is overjoyed this morning. I woke up this morning with my mind stayed on Jesus. My Brothers and Sisters, it's no harm to keep your mind stayed on Jesus.

It is prayer time. We need prayer this morning. We ought to pray every opportunity we get. Just utter prayers because we need prayer around the world. We need prayer all over this world today. We even need it in our hearts, even in our homes and families, our churches, our government, our schools. Whatever the entity, we need prayer. Let us go to the Throne of Grace now and just have a little talk with Jesus. I believe if we talk to Him, He's going to make everything alright. Does anybody know that just a little talk with Jesus makes everything alright? Amen. It appeases our cases before the Almighty Throne of God. So, let us bow where we are and go to Him in prayer.

PRAYER

Gracious God Our Father, we come now boldly to Thy Throne of Grace, humbly bowed, and we come because you have given us the privilege to come. We come because you said man ought to always pray and not faint. And as we come, we pray that you forgive our sins, cleanse our hearts, renew within us right spirits so that we can love you and our neighbors. We can love even the unlovely.

We praise you Oh God for the Son of Thy Love, for Jesus who died and is now gone above. And as your people gather around your Word and worship to the only true and wise God, give us power, power that only comes from Heaven that gives us strength day by day. And day by day Oh God we pray that you help us along the journey called life. And as the old saints would sing in the words of a hymn, *Walk with me while I'm on this tedious journey, hold my hand while I walk along this journey, Don't leave me alone because I don't want to walk this journey Oh God by myself.*

We pray today Oh Lord that you *lift us up where we belong because the road is long, there are mountains in our way, but still, we climb higher every day.* Lord today we pray those who are sick. Touch their bodies. Heal if you will. You know what they need. And we know God that you can supply our every need. Heal in your precious name because we know that there is healing and deliverance in your Name. We know that you can. There's nothing too hard for you to do for your believing children. While we pray, we pray for the bereaved families this morning. We pray for those who are experiencing the virus that continues to spike and yet, taking lives. Lord, they need you, and we need you now. Keep your hand upon us.

Oh God, teach and touch our leaders. Show them how to lead in midst of a crisis. But we pray that you will take charge because we realize that there is so much misunderstanding and confusion. So, Lord we depend on you, for you alone is able to do that which is exceedingly abundantly above all that we can imagine or think. Our faith and our hope are in you. So, touch and keep your people, and Lord, surround your Church with grace and protection from the evil one, Satan himself who goes about seeking whom he may devour.

And so, we pray that you bless your creation. Bless right now. This is your world, and we are your people. We are the sheep of your pasture. And we know God that we're just living on borrowed time. But we ask Lord that the time that you have allotted us that we will redeem that time and get in a hurry to do your will as you have allotted us. And so, we want to say to you right now thank you Lord. Thank you for every blessing. Thank you for every healing. Thank you for everything you have done for us, and what you are continually going to do. And Lord we pray this prayer today in precious, promising, and powerful Name of Our Lord and Savior Jesus Christ. Amen.

SERMON

As we make ready now to move into the message, we trust that you will be blessed by the Word today. My message this morning will be coming from Paul's Epistle to the Church at Philippi or to the Philippian Christians. Certainly, this is one of Paul's prison Epistles as he was waiting to go before the Emperor at Rome. Paul did not allow his incarceration to hinder his spiritual growth or his spiritual endeavor for the Lord to just lay waste even though he's in prison. He's on lockdown. He was still reaching the Church, touching the Church, encouraging the Church, motivating the Church to continue in their calling. God had called them to a great, great work. So, Paul is teaching them to stay the course. That's my encouragement to us. We are not in the Church house, but we still got to stay the course. We are separated. We are apart, but we've got to stay the course. We can't give up. We can't go without being informed on what thus saith the Lord. In spite of we still must be encouraged.

Let me move on into the message. Philippians 4:6-9. You will find these words in Verses 6-9. Paul says,

6. *Be careful for nothing; but in everything by prayer and supplication with thanksgiving let your requests be made known unto God.*

7. *And the peace of God, which passeth all understanding, shall keep your hearts and minds through Christ Jesus.*

8. *Finally, brethren, whatsoever things are true, whatsoever things are honest, whatsoever things are just, whatsoever things are pure, whatsoever things are lovely, whatsoever things are of good report; if there be any virtue, and if there be any praise, think upon these things.*

9. *Those things, which ye have both learned, and received, and heard, and seen in me, do: and the God of peace shall be with you.*

Amen. Just keep talking about the peace of God. I want to use for a theme, a thought, or a subject this morning: **Staying Positive in a Negative World.** My brothers and sisters we must stay positive as we are surrounded by negativity that is in our world.

Now, we must keep in mind that when we talk about the world, we are not talking about the astrophysical world where we see the sky, the moon, and the stars because they are doing everything God told them to do. They have been doing it since creation. The sun has been rising every morning and setting every evening as God commanded it to do. Amen. The stars have been shining out of their silvery sockets every night. The moon has been shining. When I say world, we're talking about humanity. Humanity has become negative. But we're going to stay positive in a world of negative humanity.

This is what the Apostle Paul is addressing and encouraging the Philippian Church congregation concerning the negativity that was invading the Church community. It appeared that the negativity was getting next to the believers. They were allowing the negativity to come into its quarters, and it was penetrating the minds of individuals. Paul is saying don't pay that no mind. Get that stuff out of your mind. You don't need to be thinking on the negativity.

So, the Church was under attack. They were suffering from some persecution. They were facing disturbances. Their fellowship was under attack. They were encountering false teachers, and some of the believers were struggling to maintain their spiritual sanity. There was little else that could confront these Philippian Christians as they were facing trial after trial and temptation after temptation imaginable. The kind of trouble that we experience, and we see on a day-to-day basis, if we're not careful, those temptations and trials bring about anxiety and worry. Now, in midst of their circumstances the only way a person can keep from having an anxiety attack is to receive a spiritual injection of God's supernatural powers. God will enable the believer to conquer anxiety by injecting the peace of God. My Brothers and Sisters we need an injection of peace from God.

You see, in Verse 7 God is saying to the Church *and the peace of God which passeth all understanding shall keep your hearts and your minds through Jesus Christ.* That's where we must stay focused. That's why we must stay in tune with the Lord. Look at the negativity that's coming from on the outside and from every source. All we hear is negativity, down beating, and brow beating on others. They are sometimes just planning nonsense stuff that doesn't have any merit. It can take your peace away from you. But I hear Paul say if you *keep your mind stayed on Jesus, allow the peace of God which passeth all understanding, He will keep your heart and mind through Jesus Christ.*

In this 21st Century, we live in a negative world. This negative world has many problems. We are affected by the world's troubles. Let me just name a few of the things that are happening in your world and in my world: violence in our streets, crime against property, senseless killings of another, inhumane treatment, kidnapping of babies and young women, drug trafficking, squabbles between political parties, social divides. All this stuff if we are not careful, we can allow it to bombard our minds and get us off track. We focus on this stuff, and it ends up infiltrating our thought process. Our minds become lame with all this stuff. We need the peace of God. We need an injection of God's supernatural power to help flush out some of this stuff. Paul will tell us later in the text what we need to focus on in order to keep a fresh mind and to stay positive. But evidently this is the kind of world we live in compounded along with Covid-19 pandemic. Yes, as of today, even as I speak there is a surge of more than 126,000 deaths as the result of Covid-19. Yes, compounded upon all the other stuff that we are dealing with.

How do we keep a sound mind? How do we keep from going through anxiety attacks? How do we keep from worrying about what's going on around us? *Let the peace of God that surpasses your understanding keep your heart and keep your mind.* That's how we've got to focus. As Christians, we are not supposed to be negative people. We're supposed to be the rejoicing people. In Verse 4 Paul tells the Church to *rejoice in the Lord always, and again I say rejoice.* How can you rejoice in midst all this negativity? We do it by keeping our focus on positive thoughts and praise. That's how you do it.

Paul says in Verse 8 as he was concluding his discussion with the Church. He says *finally, brethren whatsoever things are true, whatsoever things are honest, whatsoever things are just, whatsoever things are pure, whatsoever things are lovely, whatsoever things are of good report, if there be any virtue, if there be any praise, think on these things.* I just gave you a catalog of things that Paul says that you ought to stay focused on that will keep you in a positive atmosphere.

Then he takes them to Verse 9. He says *Those things, which ye have both learned, and received, and heard, and seen in me, do.* You know I'm jail. I'm incarcerated. I'm lying between a quadrant of soldiers who are guarding me every day. But you know what? I'm still focused. I'm not letting my incarceration get me down and cause me to be in a state of anxiety or worry. But my mind is stayed on Jesus because that's my true deliverance. Not only that, but I've been injected with the supernatural powers of God that's going to keep me. The God of peace will keep you; yet some Christians can allow negativity to get into them. But we've got to stay positive in this negative world. Well, I've got three things I want to share from this text because I need to break these things down for us a little bit.

The first step to staying positive in a negative world is **not to worry.** What is worry? This Greek word translated to worry is anxiety or being careful. In Verse 6 this word anxiety or worry or careful means to be pulled in different directions. See, when you start worrying and you are not focused on God, what you're worrying about is pulling you in a different direction from where God is trying to get you to. So, you need to stay focused. You need to keep your eyes focused these things that he says in Verse 8: things that are true, honest, just, pure, lovely, good report, virtue. If we keep our eyes focused on those things, we won't be pulled into a different direction.

You see, worry can pull you in a different direction. You see our hopes pull us the direction of God, but our fears pull us in another direction. When we're going in another direction, rather than the direction God is trying to take us to, what happens is we become pulled apart. That's where we are in this negative world. We're just being pulled apart. As races we're being pulled apart. We're no longer together.

Can I give you another word or meaning for worry? Worry also means to strangle. If you have ever worried, you know how it strangles a person. In fact, worry has definite physical consequences. Worry brings on physical illnesses. Worry can raise your blood pressure. Worry can give you heart issues. Worry will give you a stroke. Worry will put pain in your body, pain and arthritis that you didn't know you could get. It comes from worrying. We're being strangled with this thing called worry.

Can I tell you something else that worry does to us? Worry affects the way we think. Now look at this from a spiritual point of view. Worry is wrong thinking and wrong feelings about circumstances. It could be people, or it could be things. I tell you this morning that worry is the greatest thief of all joy. It steals your joy. Worry steals your joy. You can be happy this moment, then you hear something the next moment and it just comes in and it just takes your joy out of you because now you want to focus on the worry. You've got to erase that stuff. You can't let it lodge in your psyche. That's what the enemy wants. He wants you to stay in a state of worry. It's not enough for us to tell ourselves quit worrying, because that will never put the handcuffs on the thief called worry. And that's what the thief wants to cause you to do. He wants to handcuff you and cause you to surrender.

Worry is an inside job, and it takes more than just good intentions to get the victory. The key to worry is to have a sound mind. Let's go back to Verse 7 because Paul is helping us. And I'm just trying to unpack it for you so you can see where the enemy tries to take us in our thoughts. He says *and the peace of God…* the key to worry is to have a sound mind. *And the peace of God shall keep your hearts and your minds through Jesus Christ.* I hope you are getting this. God's wants us to have a sound mind. Let me tell you what happens when you have a sound mind. When you have a sound mind, the peace of God guards you, and the God of peace guides you.

Look at Verse 9. Now you need to pay attention to *Those things, which ye have both learned, and received, and heard, and seen in me, do: and the peace of God shall be with you.* So, the peace of God, what it does is He guards you. He guides you. Look what God does with peace. He gives us that protection. So why worry if we are to conquer those things called worry by having a sound mind. When we have the peace of God that is guarding us, guiding us, and protecting us, and we have sound mind, we must meet three conditions that the Lord laid down. It's in the text. We're going to go back and we going to unpack the point. There are three conditions laid down in these short four verses.

In order, to have the peace of God, first, you must do some right praying. How do you know, Reverend? Let's go back to the verse. Verse 6 and Verse 7: He says

> 6. *Be careful for nothing; but in everything by prayer and supplication with thanksgiving let your requests be made known unto God.*
>
> 7. *And the peace of God, which passeth all understanding, shall keep your hearts and minds through Christ Jesus.*

We've got to do some right praying. We've got to learn to pray right. We've got to learn what to pray for in order to get this peace of God that keeps us positive even in negative environments. We've got to stay prayed up. And when we pray up, we stay positive even when we encounter the negative vibes, the negative innuendos that come from all the sources that surround us. We've got to do some right praying.

The second condition we've got to meet, in order, to have peace in the midst of negativity is we must have some right thinking. Yes, do some right praying, but there's got to be some right thinking. Where did you get that from Reverend? In Verse 8 Paul says,

> 8. *Finally, brethren, whatsoever things are true, whatsoever things are honest, whatsoever things are just, whatsoever things are pure, whatsoever things are lovely, whatsoever things are of good report; if there be any virtue, and if there be any praise, we need to think on these things.*

We've got to do some right thinking. We're living in a world where folks aren't thinking of ways of being true, being honest, being just, (which means just trying to do the right thing, being in right standing), things that are pure (things that are genuine), things that are lovely (living among unlovely people – hate), no good reports anymore. If there be any virtue, if there be any praise we need to thing on these things. We've got to have right praying and right thinking. This is what helps us to stay positive in a negative world.

Lastly, the condition that we've got to meet in order to have peace and to stay in the right frame of mind in a negative environment is we've got to do some right living. We've got to do some right praying. We got to do some right thinking. But we've got to do some right living. Where do you see that Reverend? It's in Verse 9. See when you've been told some things, when you have learned some things, when you have received the truth (and the truth doesn't need any props or a crutch), you just operate in those things. He says it right here. If you do those things which you have both learned and received, things you've heard, the things you have seen in me, do it because it's right. And the peace of God will be with you if you just do it.

Do it and you will see that you are staying on the good side of things. You're not on the negative side, but you're on the positive side. It matters not what goes on around you. You can go to bed at night and sleep because you've got the peace of God. You see, peace of God doesn't mean absence of conflict. The peace of God is when I can rest in my integrity, when I can rest in my good character, when I can rest in my values – the right values – not just any values, and I can find solace, and I can find comfort. That's what it means, not just absence of conflict. You can be at peace with yourself. You can be at peace with God, and you can be at peace with others because you are holding up a standard. God's wants us to hold up a standard in midst of it all. God needs some warriors, saintly warriors that represent Him in midst of all the chaos, confusion, and infusion of stuff that comes at us.

Let me move on quickly. Let me go back to Verse 6. I'm just unfolding, unraveling, uncovering some things. In Verse 6 Paul says, *Be careful for nothing*. Don't worry about nothing. Don't be anxious for nothing. *but in everything by prayer and supplication with thanksgiving let your requests be made known unto God*. You see, *nothing* carries the idea of *not one thing*. The Christian is to pray about everything. Nothing is too small to pray about. Nothing is too big to pray for. You see the word prayer here refers to the special times which we share in the period of devotion and worship. We are to have set times that we especially set aside for just specific worship and devotion. Remember right praying.

And then that word supplication in that verse refers to prayers that are focused on special needs. Anybody got some special needs out there? Do you know some people with some special needs? So why don't we supplicate so those needs can be met in our lives and in the lives of others and not just about me, my and mine. Supplicate and focus on those needs. You see, we feel a deep, intense need. We go before God and we supplicate. We pour it out before the Lord just like a child. Children, when they really want something, they want it. They don't mind asking. It doesn't matter how much it cost. They don't have any idea what the cost is. "I just want it." God is saying, "You are just like my child. And you've got me supplicating. Pray about it. Ask me for it. It's not too big. It's not too little. God's got ways of answering our prayers: yes, no, wait a while. He's got His own timing for whatever.

I'm reminded of a story of a little boy and his father went to this particular store this day. As they were in the store, they were walking down the aisles and the little boy was fascinated with all the various toys that were in the toy aisle. He would pick up a toy and say, "Daddy." Daddy would look back and say, "Come on boy. Come on. Put it down." They kept walking. They went around to another aisle. The boy saw another toy. "Daddy." He said, "Boy, put it down. Come on. Let's go. Come on. Come on." And they went down another aisle. And when they got down this aisle, the little boy saw a baseball and a bat. And he stood there with the ball and the bat in his hand. The daddy was far in advance of the boy. He made another sharp turn down an aisle, and he was looking for his son. The son was not behind him. So, he stopped and said, "Where is that boy?" So, he goes back around the aisle where the boy was. The little boy was standing with the bat and ball in his hand, and tears were running down his face. The daddy says, "Now he really wants this." See the other toys that he had seen prior didn't mean that much to him. But when he got to the bat and ball, that meant the world to him to the point that he was willing to shed tears that his daddy might get this for him. Daddy knew right off, "Now he really wants that." And that's the way it is with us. There are some things we pray and ask God for that we really don't want it. We're just asking for what we don't know. But when we really want something from God, we will go with every intent; if it means crying, if it means pleading, or if it means begging God.

And then Paul says in the same verse we ought to do it with thanksgiving. Whatever your daddy does for you, whatever your daddy gives you, you ought to give some thanks because "thanks" is also giving. The word thanks and giving are in the same word. Yes, it is Thanksgiving. And see you got to think, in order, to thank. Thank and praise God for all that He has done, for all that He is doing, and all that He's about to do, your requests – meaning specific and definite requests. You've got to be specific with God. Our praying is not to be generalized but specific. We lay before God exactly what is needed, and we're not to fear that we are being too detailed with God or bothering God. Your child, when they come to you, they don't care about you being bothered. Yeah, bother them. If it means waking you up if it's something they want, "Wake up. Momma I need this. Daddy, I need this." They are persistent. They don't fear being too detailed. They want what they want, when they want it, and as long as they want it.

This is what happens when you pray, and you supplicate and thank God Verse 7 says; *the peace of God passeth all understanding shall keep your heart and your mind through Christ Jesus.* Let me move on. Let me share the second thing with you quickly.

The second thing we must do to stay positive in this negative world, we've got to reprogram the way we think. We must reprogram our thinking. There is so much stuff out there that is competing for our mind. There is so much stuff that is vying for our minds and our thoughts. Just watching TV, they are competing for our minds. They have commercials for every kind of thing trying to get you, get your mind to do this, to do that, and to do the other. I am trying to tell us this morning that we are constantly bombarded by a negative messaging. We are in a constant and instant communication age, and through this communication age the bad and the negative reports, they come to us…how…in breaking news breaks. Breaking news! Breaking news! Breaking news! The news comes on…Breaking news! You can be watching your favorite tv show…Breaking news! Some of it is okay, and others are negative. These negative reports are coming because they want our minds. They want our attention. Better yet, we've got texting, emails, tweets, negative stuff. Every time you turn around, negative stuff, if it's not coming through emails, tweets, texts, and breaking news, it's word of mouth. It just keeps coming at us bombarding our minds and sometimes it overtakes, overshadows our thinking, thus getting us out of a positive state.

But Verse 8 tells us how to stay positive. Paul says, *Finally brethren, if you want to stay positive, focus on these things; things that are true; things that are honest; things that are just; things that are pure; things that are lovely; things that are of good report;* not breaking news or bad reports; *if there be any virtue, if there be any praise think on these things.* These things help us to stay positive in a negative world.

If one is to maintain a positive attitude in a negative world, one must have some faith building inputs. We've got to find some inputs. I know he (Paul) just gave us a catalog of things. But let me add some more to it to help us stay positive. We've got to develop a devotional life. We've got to spend some time with God. We've got to get up in the morning and spend some time with God. If you don't have time in the morning, and you are going to work, before the day ends spend some time with God. If you got something urgent that you are doing and you got to get up and get out, but make sure before the day ends that you spend some devotional time with God because it will help you to stay focused. When you approach the Word of God you ought to ask God in the Word when you read that Word God what are you saying to me through this passage. Allow the Holy Spirit to bring it to your knowledge, to your understanding. Spend some time with Him. You've got to have a devotional life.

The second input we ought to have ... is Bible reading and prayer. Spend some time in prayer. That's an input. You've got to have some input if you are going to maintain an attitude of goodness. You've got to spend some time with Him at all costs. Then, the third input, this input you need to have also, and this input is every day you ought to have a thankful heart. Every day you get up you ought to thank God. Lord Thank You for another day. You didn't have to let me live. Thank You for my health. Thank You for my strength. Thank You Lord. You've got to have a thankful heart. Nothing is too small to be thankful for. These are little inputs that help us to stay positive. And lastly, expecting God to come through for you in every situation you are confronted with. Amen.

The third point I want to make is we must stay positive in a negative world. One must set positive examples. When you can set positive examples, then there are some desires to do well because you want to be positive. There are some people that don't have it quite together, but you must stay positive. You must set positive examples for those who are not positive. You must have some desires because there are some people who don't have the desire to be positive. You must set the example to be positive.

Can you prove it Reverend? Yes, I can. Where is the proof? It is in Verse 9. Paul says, in order to be a positive example, you've got to do *those things, which* you *have* (what)…*have learned, received, and heard, and seen me do.* Paul says that did it. I show you a good example. Now that I have shown you a good example, you learn the example, you receive it, you hear it, and you do it because you have seen me do it. And He says that if you do those things, *the God of peace shall be with you.* All these things you have heard, Paul is saying that he has set the example for them by teaching them what it means to be true, what it means to be honest, what it means to be just, what it means to be pure, and what it means to be lovely. And the peace of God will come through for you and you will be positive.

I've never known a man that was so positive and that's Jesus Christ. Even in His death, He was positive. Even while they were killing Him, He was still positive. He looked out over the audience that stood around the old, rugged cross, and He says to them *Father forgive them, for they know not what they do.* If that isn't positivity among negativity, then I don't know what is positive. When you can look at others and how they are treating Him, doing Him badly, saying false things *(if you be the Son of God, come on down, save yourself, save us, he's calling for*

Elias, let's see if Elias is going to come and deliver him), they weren't nice to Him. But He stayed positive even in death. My brothers and sisters that's the way we have the peace of God when we can stay positive even when people are just at their worst. But you must stay positive.

You know what, He went on and died that cruel death on the cross. They put Him in a borrowed grave and said He's not going to get up. We've got Him. We've Got Him. But they didn't realize that on the third day He was going to get up. When He got up, He got up with all power in Heaven and Earth entrusted in His hands. That's the power that we've got to inject ourselves with. Remember, I said earlier in the text that we've got to inject ourselves with the supernatural power of God. That gives us conquering power, victory over whatever comes our way. The peace of God will keep you.

CALL TO DISCIPLESHIP

The door of the Church is open for accepting members if there be one today who is listening to me it doesn't matter where you are you can be five miles away. You can be a hundred miles away. You can be a thousand miles away. If you are hearing me this morning if you can believe that Jesus Christ, the Lord Jesus is the Son of God, if you can believe that He died for your sins that you might have the peace of God in your heart, you can receive Him today by acknowledging I'm a sinner, believe that Jesus Christ died for sinners, confess Jesus Christ you can be saved right where you are. Just ask Him in your heart Lord, I'm a sinner, I need saving, save me right now. I believe you died. I believe you rose again. I'm willing to trust you for the rest of my life. I give you me, my whole soul, body, mind, and spirit. If you can believe it and receive it, you're saved. You find a Church somewhere that you can carry out a personal relationship with Him.

God bless you. Thank you. This is my message for you today. I hope that it was a help. I hope that it is what you needed for this week and the days to come. For it is in Jesus' Name we do thank you. Amen.

Sister Rose is going to come and sing once more. I'll be back, and we will close this out. Amen.

SELECTION

***How Great is Our God* by Chris Tomlin, Jesse Reeves, & Ed Cash**

CLOSING REMARKS

How Great is Our God! There is none like Him, for there is no other God. He's a God all by Himself. He's in a class all by Himself. Who can equal God? Who can come up to God? He is the God of this world and this universe. I know man has claimed it, but he doesn't own anything. He doesn't even own himself. *The Earth is the Lord's and the fullness thereof and they that dwell therein for He has founded it upon the sea and established it upon the floods.* My God, when I read that, I just see the awesome power of God. *Who shall ascend into the hills of the Lord, he that hath clean hands and a pure heart who has not lifted his soul up unto vanity he shall see the blessing from the Lord.* And then the Psalmist goes on to talk about *lift up your heads or ye gates, lift them up ye everlasting doors and the King of Glory shall come in. Who is this King of Glory, the Lord of hosts? He is the King of Glory.* When I read that I get excited. When I got up this morning my mind was stayed on Jesus. God Bless you.

God bless you. Thank you. Well, well, well. This ends another worship, thank you for tuning in this morning. We hope you have a great rest of your day. Before I close out, if we were at our Church sanctuary, we would probably say, "It's the fourth Sunday. All of you that have birthdays in June, stand up and we will sing Happy Birthday to You." I know there were some birthdays in May and some birthdays in June. Let me sing to everyone who had birthdays in May and in June.

Happy Birthday to you! Happy Birthday to you!

Happy Birthday Dear Members, Happy Birthday to you!

It doesn't come no better than that y'all. Enjoy your day.

Well, the old saying goes, "All good things must come to an end." So, we're going to end our worship here, and we're going to ask you to bow for the benediction.

CLOSING PRAYER

Now may the grace of God, the love of God, and the fellowship of the Holy Spirit. May He now rest, rule, and abide in the hearts of this thine people now and forever and all of you say Amen.

God Bless you and enjoy the rest of your day. Pray continuously for the sick. Pray continuously for this country and this world. Pray that we stay with a positive attitude in a negative society or world. Thank you. God bless you. Have a great day.

Too Blessed to be Stressed

Sunday, July 5, 2020

OPENING REMARKS

You know my name. Thank God He knows our very names. Even though we each may have the same name in some parts of the country, He knows each one of us. And I'm glad He knows me and distinguishes me from any other person or personality.

Good morning, Church, Family and Friends wherever you might be. *This is the day that the Lord has made, let us rejoice and be glad in it.* You see *we have come this far by faith leaning on the Lord; Trusting in His Holy Word, He's never failed me yet.* Also, I can't turn around. We can't turn around. We have come too far to turn around now. We have come this far by faith one day at a time, one week at a time, and one month at a time.

You know my brothers and sisters; we are five days into a new month. Here it is July. We have moved into the second half of the year. You know we have come all this way by faith. We have come all this way, and we had to lean on the Lord. Trusting in His Holy Word, and He has not failed me yet. So, I can't turn around. So, come. Let's give God some praise by thumbs up or send up some bursting hearts. Let the Lord know that we thank Him for bringing us this far by faith. Somebody ought to witness this morning that you didn't get here on your own. You didn't get here because of who you are, what you know, or what you have. But you got here because it was faith that was motivating us, it was faith that was driving us by the power of the Almighty God. He deserves it this morning. Amen. Thank you so very much. We pray that you all had a beautiful 4th of July, and you're here this morning to worship the Lord in Spirit and in truth.

WORDS OF ENCOURAGEMENT

Well, as we move forward, I have a thought for you today. This thought is coming from the book of First Timothy, Chapter 4, Verse 4. The great Apostle Paul says, *"For every creature of God is good, and nothing to be refused, if it be received with thanksgiving.* Well, when we thank God for our entire plate of food, we acknowledge His goodness and His greatness. Paul says in the text, that everything God made was good, and so it is. Everything that God made it is good. If you go back to the book of Genesis, when God created the Heavens and the Earth, when He created all the elements in the Earth, and after six days and He looked back over everything He had created, He said it was good, and it was very good.

So, what am I saying this morning? Whatever God puts on our entire plate, we ought to acknowledge His goodness and His greatness. That's why the children's grace before they receive that meal, this is what they say: *God is great. God is good. God, we thank You for our food. Amen.* That's the children's grace. We thank Him for whatever is on our plate, because everything on it comes from a great and a good God.

The fact that God is good is not an issue with believers. We know that to be a fact. Just as good parents buy food and prepare it for their children some foods that are good for us even though we may not like it, but we trust God's goodness. We trust that if it's on my plate, and God prepared it then surely going to be good for me, even if it doesn't taste good.

But listen to what the Psalmist says in Psalm 107:9. It says, *For he satisfieth the longing soul, and filleth the hungry would with goodness.* The question is this morning, "What's on your plate that you don't like?" Is it a defeat in your life? Is it a disappointment? Is there an illness? Is there a loss of some valuable thing that you treasure in your heart the most? What's on your plate that you dislike? Well, when you see items on your plate that you don't like or care for, God is always good. So, whatever is on the plate will soon work out to your own good because God is good, and He's good all the time. And all the time, God is good. My thought for today. God bless you. Amen.

CALL TO WORSHIP

Let us we prepare to go into this worship celebration on this first Sunday in a new month in this beloved year 2020. We want to give God the Glory and give God the praise. Amen. The Lord is in His Holy Temple, let the Earth be silent before Him.

At this time Sister Rose will come and lead us in a song of her choice. Be blessed by the music, and later, the Word; and I'll be back.

SELECTION

Bless The Lord With Me by Darwin Hibbler

Come on and bless the Lord with me. Amen. What do I have that I can bless the Lord with? Well, I can bless Him with praise and thanksgiving. He doesn't need my money because He is rich in everything. Amen. So, all I have is praise and worship which the Lord so richly deserves. The redeemed of the Lord ought to say so. Amen. So, thank you for that beautiful number.

Well, it is time for prayer. We're going to beseech the Throne of Grace at this moment for we know that we are still in need of prayer around the country and around this world. Prayer is needed because we are yet in the middle of this pandemic, and it looks like it is not going anywhere. It is sticking around, and is yet, affecting lives. People are being infected every day, and the spike is up, even right here in our own state and community. We need the Lord. I don't know when and I don't know where the Lord is going to do it, but I just believe He's going to work it out. Paul says *we know that all things work together for good to them that love God and are called according to His purpose.* I just believe God has it worked out in His own time, and however He does it I'm going to thank the Lord. I'm going to praise the Lord. So, let us go before the Throne of Grace and invoke God's presence and power.

PRAYER

Eternal God, Our All-Wise God, Father of Our Lord and Savior Jesus Christ, Father of all mankind, and Creator of every living thing, we come this morning to tell you thank you for our lying down last night and this morning's rising. Thank you for a peaceful night; you allowed your angels to watch over us and protect us from the enemy that lurks in darkness. Oh God your Word teaches us that when we pray, we are to enter into our closets, our spiritual closets. When we enter, we are to shut the door to pray to the Father which is in secret and you *God which seeth in secret will reward us openly.*

And as we enter this morning, first we say to you forgive us our sins and blot out all of our transgressions. And as we come to your beloved throne, we present ourselves at the altar of sacrifice which is laid for all. Lord, we pray for the lonely today. We pray that you bless the sick and the afflicted. Look today upon our sick and answer their prayers of healing. Touch today, Lord. God, I'm sure there are those we are unaware of. So, we invoke you to come. Speak Lord into their spirits today. And while we are praying, we pray for the bereaved families. We pray comfort for the families. Bless, Oh God, our nation, for many are suffering from Covid-19. I pray that our people take the warning seriously. The virus has not gone anywhere, and we pray that they listen to our scientists and doctors…just be still and keep themselves and others safe. Lord, we pray you watch over our Churches that are opening. We pray for their protection. We still need You God. We need you right now. We just can't make it without you. So, Lord, be a fence around us every day. Protect us, Lord. And we give your name thanks for everything. And we want you to know Oh God that we love you, we praise you, we bless you, we adore you, we magnify, we lift your name. Great is your name in all the Earth.

And now God as we prepare for worship, give us a worshipping mind. Give us a true spirit for real worship. Now *let the words of my mouth and the meditation of my heart be acceptable in Thy sight Oh Lord my strength and my Redeemer,* we pray with thanksgiving, Amen.

SERMON

As we make ready to go into the Word, I'm going to ask if you will, to turn in your Bibles to one of my favorite Epistles, Paul's epistle to the Church at Ephesus or the book of Ephesians. I want us to look at Chapter 1, Verse 3 – Ephesians 1:3. Keep your Bibles open because we will be making references to various scriptures in that chapter. As we look from the beginning through about Chapter 3 Paul talks about the richness, the riches that the believer now has in Christ. I want to show us what we have in Christ Jesus this morning. I want to use Verse 3 as our premise for the preaching text. Ephesians 1:3,

> 3. *Blessed be the God and Father of our Lord Jesus Christ, who hath blessed us with all spiritual blessings in heavenly places in Christ.*

For my theme or thought or subject this morning, I want to talk about **Too Blessed to Be Stressed.** Verse 3 states its theme as the Christian's Riches in Christ. Among all the great passages of scripture in the Bible, this is one of the greatest. Its importance can never be overstated because it deals with God's plan His eternal plan for the world. This eternal plan deals with the great blessings of God which He pours out upon those who trust His Son Jesus as their Savior. You see God's blessings are heavenly. I know we have the spiritual blessings. I know we have the material blessings. But I believe that once a person accepts Christ and receives his or her spiritual, heavenly blessings those blessings are more important than the material blessings. I'm a firm believer that if you accept Christ and receive the spiritual, heavenly blessings, my material blessings will automatically follow my spiritual blessings.

You see, throughout history, God has used two methods of blessings to deal with mankind. Before Christ, God dealt with man by blessing him with material blessings. In the old era He always blessed man with material blessings. He promised Abraham and Israel a land and wealth and fame. Remember He told Abraham, "I will bless you. You will be the father of many nations. You will be a wealthy man. You will have my promises with you." But you know what, Israel received all these blessings, but they misused and hoarded the material blessings instead of sharing the blessings with others. Israel had become isolated. She had isolated herself and claimed superiority and God-given rights over other nations. However, Christ God deals with man spiritually, blessing him with spiritual blessings. There are three things I want to note about this.

Firstly, Spiritual blessings are of the spirit. It is the spirit that controls man and the circumstances that surround him. You see, a man may feel bad. He may be down. He may be depressed or oppressed. But if his spirit is strong, his spirit can rise and give him conquering power over his or her feelings. The spirit, he controls the human body. He controls and over comes the oppression and the circumstances and gives victory to life, victory to any day. But if a man's spirit is weak, it does not matter what he is doing. He will wallow around is self-pity. He's grumbling and complaining and griping and living a life of defeat every day. Too often the day stretches into weeks and weeks into months until a person's life is down. He can't get up all because the spirit is too weak to overcome. With God are bound to be blessings that are spiritual that enables a person to control his or her life.

Secondly, Spiritual blessings are the very opposite of temporal blessings. They are the blessings of the inward man, the blessings of the immortal not the mortal but the immortal. But of all the blessings the spiritual blessings are the most satisfying. They are the blessings that erase our loneliness, our unhappiness, our easiness, our hopelessness that we are feeling. They are the blessings that give man over to the abundance of life. Oh, I choose today spiritual over material anytime, any day because I know that spiritual blessings come from the Spirit. That's why Paul could share with the Church at Ephesus that the Lord Jesus Christ who has blessed us with *all spiritual blessings in heavenly places.*

Thirdly, Spiritual blessings are always superior to any temporal and mortal blessings. Spiritual blessings are permanent. They are perfect. They are eternal. They are everlasting. They have no end to them because they represent the very nature of God. And we know that God is eternal. He is from everlasting to everlasting. He is first. He is last. He is beginning. He is end. So, God's material blessings are permanent. They are perfect. They are eternal. They are forever just like Him. Spiritual blessings exist and can be experienced on this earth, the physical dimension and the spiritual dimension which is Heaven. This morning I want you to know that I'm experiencing my spiritual blessing. I'm not talking about my material blessings. I'm talking about my spiritual blessings. I am experiencing them while I am in the Earth. Also, I am experiencing them in the heavenlies. With Christ, this morning, because I'm in a dimensional world, two dimensions, I'm in Earth but I'm also in Heaven. I'm seated with Christ in Heaven because I'm in a relationship with Him. Because He's there, I'm there, yet I'm in this old Earth.

Well, I have three things I'm going to lift from this passage. First, we need to look at the source of our blessings. Let's look at Verse 3 again. *Blessed be the God and Father of our Lord Jesus Christ.* God the Father has made me rich in Jesus Christ. That's the source of our blessings. How many of you out there know that you are rich, but you don't have a lot of money in the bank? But you are rich spiritually in Christ Jesus. You see, when you were born again into God's family, you were born into richness. I was born into richness through Christ. You share in the richness of God's grace. Don't let anybody fool you and tell you that you don't have wealth. You have more wealth than wealth itself. How do you know Reverend? When you read Ephesians Chapter 1, Verse 7 Paul says, *In whom we have redemption through his blood the forgiveness of sin according to the riches of his grace.* I'm rich in the grace of God. We have talked about the acronym of GRACE – God's Redemptive Act At Christ's Expense. I have been given the richness of His grace. God has transferred this toward me at Christ's expense. I'm rich this morning. I don't know how you feel about it, but I am filthy rich with His grace. His grace woke us up this morning. His grace started me on my way. I am experiencing His eternal grace even as I speak to you.

Also, I want us to look at Ephesians Chapter 2, Verse 7. It says that *in the age to come he might show the exceeding riches of his grace in his kindness toward us through Christ Jesus.* You see, our living down here in His grace, but that same grace will follow me from this dimension to my next dimension. I'm just filthy rich with His grace, can't anyone cancel that grace. You can't close that account out on me. When I write a check on that grace, that grace won't bounce. That grace is sufficient; the account is full and overflowing. I'm rich in His grace. When I think about the goodness of God, my soul gets happy. I want to tell us that Our Heavenly Father is not poor. He is rich and has made us rich in His Son. Paul explains to us and to the Church then, what these riches are and how we can obtain them to live effective and efficient Christian lives. He tells us what these riches are.

Well, if you look at Ephesians 1:18, Paul says, "the eyes of your understanding being enlightened; that you may know what is the hope of His calling, what are the riches of the glory of His inheritance in the saints". I'm rich in God's glory, in God's magnificence, in God's great beauty, in God's unfathomable presence and power. That's His glory. I can't even begin to fathom with my finite mind of the richness of His glory. All I know is that I'm just showered with the richness of His glory. Paul says in Ephesians 2:4, he shares with us God's mercy. He says, *But God who is rich in mercy for his great love, wherewith he loved us.* I've got His mercy. I'm rich in His mercy. I don't deserve anything. I don't deserve it. I don't deserve this inheritance that He's given me, but I'm glad He's given me what I don't deserve. That's His rich mercy. God's mercy.

Ephesians 3:8 Paul is trying to help us by showing us how blessed we are. We shouldn't be walking around here all stressed out. We are too blessed. We are just too blessed. We're blessed with His glory. We're blessed with His mercy. We're blessed with His unsearchable riches in Christ, and yet, we don't even know the source of our blessings. We're too blessed to be stressed. In Ephesians 3:8 the writer says, *Unto me, who am less than the least of all saints, is this grace given.* Oh, I tell you this grace that we are experiencing *is given, that I should preach among the Gentiles the unsearchable riches of Christ.* I don't deserve to be who I am, but I am what I am because of the grace of God. This is why Paul is saying I feel like that I'm the least of the less, or the least in the least of the saints. I don't have a reason to boast, but because God has sought favor in me, He has given me this gift to share in the unsearchable riches of Christ.

Oh, there are some unsearchable riches. God has some unsearchable stuff that we don't even know about that He just wants to bestow, shower, and relinquish upon us. We don't know what we have because we are not searching. We're not looking. We are not trying with intense effort to know what we have in Christ. You're rich and you don't know it. Out of all the richest men and women in the world and their billions of dollars in wealth, all their wealth is but pennies when compared with the spiritual wealth we have in Christ. Let them brag about their abundance of the material, the mundane because that stuff is temporal. It's not lasting. The economy can be up today and down tomorrow. We can be in economic downturn. The stock market could drop or bottom out. But I'm still rich. God's economy never fails. God's economy is continuously building up, mounting up with such unsearchable riches. In this letter Paul explains what these unsearchable riches are and how we may draw on them for effective Christian living.

Coming to our second point, we have looked at the source of our blessing; now, let's look at the scope of our blessings. We find the scope of our blessings in Ephesians 1:3. Paul says *we have,* how many, *all spiritual blessings*. What's on the other side of all? Nothing, because all is all. There is nothing beyond all. We have all spiritual blessings. That can be translated all the blessings of the Spirit. That's what he's trying to tell us. We have all the blessings of the Spirit. What Spirit? We're talking about the Holy Spirit of God. In the Old Testament God promised Israel material blessings as a reward of their obedience. That's what God did in the Old Testament.

God says to them, and you read this in the book of Deuteronomy, God says that if you obey me, then you shall be blessed and not cursed. If you disobey me, you shall be cursed and not be blessed. How did God say that He would bless them with the materialistic things? It was out of an act of obedience to God. God says that if you obey me, you will be blessed where? You will be blessed in your fields. They were agricultural unlike we are living in a technological age. They were agricultural, they were blessed in their fields and in their crops. They were blessed on the vines which grew the grapes and the olives, the herds in the field, and then the cattle. And then He said that I will bless you in your bodies. He said that I will bless you going in. Bless, you coming out. You will be blessed if you obey me. That's what will happen. Your fields will be fruitful. Your vines will be fruitful. Your herds will multiply. Your body will be well if you obey me.

Now there's a flip side to that. If you obey me not, you will be cursed in the like manner in your fields. Your crops won't grow. Your vines will not produce the olives and the grapes. Your herds will not multiply. Your bodies will become deformed, ill, or sick. God did not promise them protection from the curse of poverty and pain. There must be an act of obedience to God to receive the blessings from God. That's the scope of our blessings. He says in the text, *Blessed be the God and Father of our Lord Jesus Christ, who hath blessed us with all spiritual blessings in heavenly places in Christ.* In other words, God has the scope of our blessings. Then there is a part we must play, in order, to get the scope of His blessings. God has promised the Church, He has promised Israel, and He has promised us today that if we will be obedient to what we have been told to do, we will receive the scope of His blessings.

To everything there is a principle, and many of us don't like to follow the principle. There's a principle to blessings. He promised us that He would *supply our every need according to His riches in glory by Christ Jesus.* This God has given us every blessing of the Spirit for everything we need for success and everything we need for satisfying Christian life. Again, the spiritual is far more important than the material. If a man has not the Spirit of Christ, the Bible says he is none of His. The Spirit is the blessing. This phrase is translated *all blessing of the spirit.*

Now, if man does not have the Spirit of God or Christ, he is not in Him. Unless you have the presence and the witness of the Spirit, you cannot draw on the richness or the riches of the Spirit. You've got to have His Spirit. If you're going to be born again, it's the Holy Spirit that gives you birth into this spiritual realm and gives you the spiritual blessings that flow from the reservoir of God.

We've looked at the source of our blessings. We've looked at the scope of our blessings. Thirdly, we need to look at the sphere of our blessings. Our blessings are in heavenly places. Perhaps a clear translation would be *in the heavenlies in Christ.* You see the unsaved person is only interested in the earthly stuff because this is where he lives. This is the sphere in which he lives. Jesus refers to those who are earthly and that are not in the heavenlies as *the children of this world.* I know that all of us have been children of the world before we knew Christ. We know this because when Paul talks to the Church at Ephesus in Chapter 2, he talks to them about the way they were before they knew Christ. He tells them, "You were alienated from Him. You were estranged from Him. But now that you have accepted Christ, you are a different person." I am not a child of the world. I am in the world, but I am not of the world.

The Christian life is centered in Heaven. My citizenship is in Heaven. I'm laboring for the Lord, but my citizenship is in Heaven. I am an ambassador here as a representative of another country and this country that I'm talking about is heavenly. The one that Abraham said he was going to look forward to. I'm a citizen of another country, and my name is written down in Heaven. It is written in the Lamb's Book of Life. The heavenlies literal translation describes that place where Jesus is right now. The text says, *who hath blessed us with all spiritual blessings in heavenly places in Christ,* thus meaning that Jesus is in the heavenlies. As a believer, I am seated with Him in the heavenlies because my stock is in Heaven. My stock is not in this world because this world is fleeting. This world is going out of business. I need to serve notice on you. Don't put all your stock in this world like you're going to be here all your days. No, you're just a pilgrim passing through this unfriendly world. You better put some stock in Heaven. You better find out where your riches are. I know we operate in the two spheres. We operate in the human and the Divine. I'm human, but I'm divine. I've got a human side of me, but there is a Godly side. I've got a part of God that's in me. I'm visible, but I'm also invisible. You can see my outward man, but the inward man you can't see him physically. This outward man is decaying every day, but the inward man is being strengthened, he's made stronger every day. Praise the Lord this morning! I'm on the Earth, but I'm also seated in the heavenlies with Christ. Likewise, if you are in Christ, you are here in a body. But you are also seated in the Spirit with Christ in the heavens. Therefore, I have no reason to be stressed because I'm too blessed with all I have in Christ Jesus. The basis for this life, I live, is Him. The Him that I'm talking about is Christ.

As I hurry to a close, Christians have no reason to be stressed when you are blessed of God through the Holy Spirit. You notice that there are Christians who seem to be majoring in becoming depressed. They are despondent. They are doubtful. They are dispirited, and all this stuff just leads to stress. Remember a few weeks ago I told you stress brings on a whole lot of stuff: high blood pressure, diabetes. Sometimes it can bring death to us because our poor hearts can't take it. The heart becomes too stressed. You just don't know the blessing you have. You need to crack the Book this morning and see where your blessings lie.

Too many of us are depressed. Too many of us are despondent. Too many of us are doubtful. Too many of us are dispirited and stressed. We seem to look for something to be upset about. It bothers me when I see Christians looking for something to be upset about. Just as they get over one problem, they look for another problem. I *ain't* looking for anything because I don't have to go looking for problems, problems come to me. When I see the problem coming to me, I put up my hand and say, "Nope. You can't have me. Get away. Go somewhere. I *ain't* got time for that. I *ain't* looking for nothing to be stressed over."

I'm stressing trying to get to heaven because I know that's where my possessions lie. That's where my riches are. I'm going to be with the Lord. I *ain't* looking for any problems. Too many of us are despondent, doubtful, dispirited, upset, looking for problems. We can't even smile. We can't praise God with our mouth because we're too stressed out over nothing, and I don't know why. Too many of us are negative. You ask them how they feel - I'm sick. How are you doing - I'm hurting. How are you getting along? I'm having a tough time. Can I tell you this morning, you are too blessed to be stressed?

Can I just give you a few things? Let me show you how blessed you are. If you are living this morning, if you are breathing this morning, every breath you breathe is a blessing. You ought to count it as a blessing. Every step you and I take, it may be a short step but guess what…it's a blessing just to step. Every day that you and I live, and we are on top of planet Earth and planet Earth is not on top of us, guess what? It's a blessing. Why are you stressing? Can I tell somebody this morning that every bill you are blessed to pay, you're blessed? Every meal you are able to eat and it's not through a feeding tube it's a blessing.

How can one be stressed when you are blessed like that? As a matter of fact, we are better than blessed. How do you know that you are better than blessed? Well, I'm saved. I'm blessed. What else Reverend? I've been forgiven. Look at all my spiritual blessings. I'm saved! I've been forgiven! My name has been written in the Lamb's Book of Life! I'm blessed! I'm blessed because God has never let me down. Blessed! I've let God down so many times. There is so much more that I could have done for Him that I didn't do. But He didn't take me out. I'm blessed! God forbid that I should feel sorry for myself and have a pity party when I have more than I deserve. I don't have time to have a pity party. I need to be telling the Lord how blessed I am. Just to know Him is a blessing.

Let me help somebody to get over being stressed. How do you get over stress? I believe we should pray fervent prayers. When I say fervent prayer, this word fervent carries the idea of warm prayers or hot prayers. If we start praying some hot, meaningful, and sincere prayers and start thinking of how good God is, start thanking Him every chance we have for all He's done (and He has done everything), I think we will come out of our state of stress. God has been too good.

The second thing you can do to come out of stress is to look in His Word. Know what you have in His Word. When you come out of your own ignorance and get in God's Word so that you can become knowledgeable and informed of what's there. You will find that God's power will lift you out of your stress. You will be an overcomer of your stress.

The last thing is to remember what His Word says, because this is great assurance from God. There is just one word in Philippians 4:19 that should give us great assurance. He says *I will supply all of your needs according to his riches in glory.* That one little word, *will*, gives us great assurance. God says He *will*. And if He says He *will*, He *will*. So why stress when He says He *will*? He will do what He says. And if you're like David, if you know the Lord, you won't get stressed. What did David say? *The Lord is. The Lord is my shepherd.* He is. He is. He is. *The Lord is.* And He is your shepherd. What is the role of a shepherd? What is He supposed to do for His sheep? Be there for them. Heal them. Lead them. Take them to still waters. Take them through the path of righteousness. Walk through the shadows of death with them. Anoint their heads with oil. Give them His assurance, mercy, and protection. Then you have those twins that are following. *Surely goodness and mercy shall follow me.* Why are you stressing when you have all this going on for you? He will. **Too Blessed to Be Stressed.**

God bless you. I pray that what the Lord has given me to say has been an uplifting to you, for you, and through you. I'm just doing what He tells me to do. If I only help one person, then what I do is not in vain. I can't help everybody, but if I can help somebody – one somebody- then what I am doing is not in vain. Maybe this wasn't for you. Maybe this is just a reassurance to you, then well and good. But it may have been a help to somebody that we don't know. That's how God works. We don't ever know to whom we are talking. But God knows and He uses us as servants and His voice, His conduit to say what He wants them to hear for such a time as this. God bless you.

CALL TO DISCIPLESHIP

The door of the Church is open for anyone out there who wants to receive the Lord in their heart. All you have to do is say Lord I want to receive you as my Savior. Lord I need salvation. Lord, save me. And I am a sinner. And I confess that I'm a sinner. And I believe that you died for me. If you can say that to the Lord and believe it in your heart, realistically, He can do it right where you are. And guess what – you are saved. Go on and receive Him in your heart. Just ask Him in your heart. And He will come in and do the rest. Amen.

Sister Jarrett is going to come at this time.

SELECTION

Oh, How I Love Jesus by Frederick Whitfield

CLOSING REMARKS

Anybody out there love the Lord today? Just because He first loved me, us, He was so obsessed with us. How do you know He was obsessed with us? I read John 3:16. It says *for God so loved the world.* That's obsession. So indescribable of how much He loved us. We ought to love Him back. If you love the Lord, just give Him some praise. If you really love the Lord, give the Lord what the Lord deserves Praise and worship.

Thank God for another worship experience. Thank Him for the presence and power of His Spirit as He shared and spoke through us this morning. I'm just grateful that I have His Spirit that speaks, leads, and guided and even brings some things to my remembrance. That's the working, the operation of the Holy Spirit in us today. Thank God for Him.

Don't forget to send your tithes and offering. I know you all are probably saying, "You talk too much about that tithe and offering." But this is a part of who we are in the kingdom. We are not begging, but this is what the Lord asks us to do. And we ought to do it deliberately because it is God's way of taking care of the God-things of His kingdom building, of His Church especially. We want to say to you do your part. Do your part. Those of you who have not, do your part. Do your part and watch God do His.

Remember I told you, you must work the principles. But if you don't follow the principles, you're going to get it wrong. You're going to mess up so follow the principles. Amen. Amen.

Thank you so much for tuning in today. I see some people from across the country who are tuning in with us. Thank you for sharing with a little ole country preacher back in the forest. Amen. Thank you for thinking enough of us to tune in and watch us.

It is our hope that you will obey the CDC rules. You know what the rules are. Mask up if you're going out in public. Keep yourself safe. Keep others safe. If each of us would do unto others as we would have them do unto us, we won't go wrong. Make sure you try to stay your distance. Stay your distance. Make sure that you keep your hands washed. This thing called Covid-19 is not gone anywhere. As a matter of fact, he is raising his head again, and we can't be too careful. I can't stress it enough. Those of you who are not obeying, you are in violation. You need to act right. You need to do the right thing. Do you hear me?

You need to do the right thing. Don't give it to your momma. Don't give it to your grandmother, granddaddy, you old aunt, or whoever. And you young folks, you're thinking you're getting by. No, you are not. You have the symptoms. You may not be showing it, but you are taking it to other people who can become infected. So, do the right thing. And if everybody does the right thing, there will be less cases and perhaps this thing could be out of here. But if we keep going at the rate, we are going it will be here the entire summer into the fall and probably into next year if we're not careful. Do the right thing. Act right. *Ain't* nothing like doing right. I'm going to get off my soap box. Don't send me any ugly messages. If you do, I'm going to sic the Lord on you. You don't want to mess with Him.

CLOSING PRAYER

And now the Lord bless and keep you. May the Lord make His face to shine upon you and be gracious unto you. The Lord lifts up His light of His countenance upon you and give you peace both now and forever. Amen.

I'm Down, But I'm Not Out

Sunday, July 12, 2020

OPENING REMARKS

Anybody know anything about that name Jesus? Oh, what a mighty name He has. There's no other name like the name of Jesus. Demons tremble at that Magnificent Name of Jesus. Good morning, saints, friends, and family. I'm excited this morning. The Lord has given me another chance. He woke me up this morning on this side of time and eternity. You know I could have slept on away from here last night and been over in what we call eternity. But He left me on this side of time and eternity one more time. Can I get a witness out there this morning that the Lord has given you another chance? Well, He didn't let me sleep too late either. He woke me up this morning right on time. Can I tell you He is blessing me right now…right now! I know He's blessing you as well. Amen. I'm glad you joined me for worship today. It is Sunday, the first day of the week. This is the day the Christians worship our Risen Savior Jesus Christ who is worthy of our worship. It is He who died that we might live, we might enjoy this time in history. Amen. Amen. God bless you.

WORDS OF ENCOURAGEMENT

Well, I've got a word of encouragement for you before we move into our worship through song, through prayer, and through the word; and I know you're going to give later. Those are some of the key elements of worship. Amen. Singing, praying, preaching, and giving…these are acts of worship.

My word of encouragement for you this morning is coming from the 90th Psalm, verse 14. This Psalm, we hear it read at funerals, but in actuality this particular Psalm that I'm going to quote from Verse 14 is Moses's prayer. This is Moses's prayer. It was the man of God who prayed this lengthy prayer. Go back and read it sometimes. It talks about the Lord being from everlasting to everlasting Thou art God. Before Thou formed the earth and world…He's praying to God. But he says something significant in Verse 14. Let me just quote that 14th Verse for us this morning. It says, *Satisfy us in the morning with your unfailing love.* He has already satisfied me this morning with His unfailing love. He woke me up this morning and that was unfailing on the part of God because He loves us. And then he goes on to say, *that we may sing for joy and be glad all of our days.* Oh, I've got a song in my spirit this morning. It is a song of joy. It is a song that has brought me gladness. I'm going to take that song with me all day and every day of my life. That's the Psalmist, the writer, the prophet, the man of God. Moses was praying, "*Satisfy us in the morning with your unfailing love that we may sing for joy and be glad all of our days.* That verse is quoted in the NIV version. It's simplified for us to really understand.

But let me say this. If things in your life were a little bit better, my question is would you be happy. Would you be happy if things were just a little bit better? What's better? What do you want better? Better job? Better house? Better health? Better relationship? The truth is it only takes one thing for you to be happy. And to be happy it takes a made-up mind. That's right. It takes a made-up mind. You have to decide that you are going to be happy regardless of the circumstance and regardless of the situation. You may have some obstacles to overcome, but don't let that steal your joy. You need to go on and sing for joy and be glad all your days. Amen. You see, if you begin the day thinking of all the things you have to be thankful for, and we've got so much to be thankful for. But we've got to be like David the king of Israel who decided each morning to declare that *this is the day that the Lord hath made. I will rejoice and be glad in it.* That's the attitude that David had.

You see, if you don't get happy where you are, you will never get to where God wants you to be. For you to get there, you've got to have the right kind of mind. You've got to have the right kind of thinking. It all begins with a grateful attitude. You've got to have a grateful attitude. Let me encourage you. Sometimes we need to be content right where we are in the current circumstance that we find ourselves in. When you have an attitude of gratitude, God will take you from victory to victory. Then He will give you the things that it takes for you to live in your abundant life, a joyful life. God has a joyful life already stored up for you. He's already got that taken care of. So, as Moses said, *Satisfy us in the morning with your unfailing love.* He's satisfying us this morning. Is anyone out there satisfied with His unfailing love? Alright! If you're satisfied, then you have no right to remain silent. You ought to just tell the Lord, "I'm just satisfied with Jesus, and Jesus alone." Oh Lord, you ought to have a song. I'm going to sing joy and gladness *all my days*. God bless you. This is our word of encouragement to you out there this morning.

CALL TO WORSHIP

I'm going to ask Sis. Rose to come and bless us with a song. This is worship also. Amen. So come on Rose and sing for us.

SELECTION

Soon and Very Soon by Andre Crouch

Praise God. We are someday, one day going to see the King. Amen. The King of Kings and the Lord of Lords. We're going to see Him. But, in order, to see Him, you've got to know Him. You've got to have experienced Him. You've got to have a personal relationship with Him. You've got to know Him for yourself. Amen. We're going to the King.

Let us now go before the King by way of prayer, another form of worship by way of prayer. We want to petition His throne of grace this morning on behalf of the sick, the bereaved, those that are experiencing difficulties in their lives right. We know our country, our nation is feeling the effects of this virus, and it is spiking the more every day. People are becoming infected with this disease. We want to pray and continue to pray that God will by His divine power move in a very methodical way. We know He's going to move in His own time someway and somehow. But we must continue to have faith and trust in the Almighty God. Trust in His power, His Sovereign power. We know that He has the power. If we've got the faith, He's got the power. The people of faith must pray in faith, with faith that God will move. And if people will pray enough, stop worrying about getting out there and being adventurous and having a good time, maybe this is a time that God is saying relax. Stand still and see the salvation of the Lord.

That's what He told Moses at the Red Sea when they saw no way across. There were mountains on every side. The sea was before them and a marching, mad army was behind them. They didn't see a way out. All they could see was, "They're going to take us out." But I heard the Lord say, "Moses, you've got something in your hand. All I need for you to do is just stretch it out." When Moses stretched the rod, the sea divided. The waters congealed on both sides. The Lord sent an East wind to blow down the sea and gave it a rock dry bottom. And they went across on the other side. Sometimes we're looking for the miracle somewhere else, and the miracle is right there with you. It's right there at your hand…in your hand. The miracle is right there.

You remember the boy who had the little sack lunch. They didn't have to go anywhere looking for food. There was a little lad that had what Jesus needed to feed a multitude. He took the two little fish and five barley loaves and fed a multitude. Gideon didn't need a large army. All he needed was the pictures and a cry of the voice. God has our answer. But are we praying by faith? Let us go to the throne of grace.

PRAYER

Gracious God Our Father, we gather in Your Name this morning to give that Great Name Honor. Your Name is sweet I know. Your Name is Great and greatly to be praised. You are Jehovah-jireh. You are Our Provider. You are Jehovah-nissi. You are Our Healer. You are Jehovah-shalom. You are Our Peace. Thank you for being all that we need. And Oh God, you have been there for us in all our situations. You have been more than enough. Even when we didn't deserve it, Lord, you were there.

And even when we were in our sins and shame, you sent us Your Son Jesus to die for us. And so, we declare unequivocally this morning, thank you God for Your gift of salvation that came through your Son who gave Himself freely. We even thank You for our eternal home after this life is over. Thank you that we've got someplace to go. We even thank you this morning for family and friends. We even thank You for our enemies that sometimes pushes us to our very knees to pray harder, to pray mightily.

And Lord, we need you down here in our world of tears and sorrow, a world where love has waxed cold. Men's hearts have become callus and hardened. We pray that you lift burdens right now and regulate confused minds. Where the enemy has taken joy, we pray God that you will restore joy and gladness again. God, we ask you today to touch sick bodies. Touch where they have been torn and have become feeble. We ask that you bless by Thy mighty hand and power. Lord, strengthen and keep them and place your loving arms around their families. We pray for Your Divine intervention. Oh God we lift the bereaved families. We pray that you will comfort them in this hour. Lord we just pray for all those who have lost loved ones over this country. Death is running rampant. But I know that you are in control, and you don't do anything wrong. You can't do wrong because you are God.

This morning God we lift our youth and young adults today that you will steer them in right paths. Even look on our aged and old with wisdom and insight, they who have lived through some unbearable conditions. We just pray that they will be able to share of your goodness and your mercy and your grace that sustains us as we grow older. And that grace given us will give us a chance every day to tell somebody about your goodness, how you have kept us, and how you have provided for us.

And Lord, keep a covering over our nation and those that lead us. Keep your covering over your Church as she, this morning, lifts you up in praise and worship all over this country. It doesn't matter whether it's a storefront Church, a Church house, or it's a cathedral. It may be a mosque, whatever and wherever Lord, let your Word go forth.

And God when we too like others have come to the end of our journey, we want to hear your welcoming voice say well done thy good and faithful servants. You've been faithful over a few things. Come on up higher and I will make you ruler of many. Lord it's in your mighty name we pray with thanksgiving. Amen.

SERMON

God bless you and thank you. Now as we prepare for the Word, we're in another element of worship through the Word, I pray that today's message will be a blessing to someone out there who is listening. I pray that it's just someone, but it be a blessing to everyone who will tune in, who will be listening.

My message this *morning* will be coming from Paul's Second Epistle to the Church at Corinth, or the Corinthians - 2 Corinthians, Chapter 4, Verses 8 and 9. I want to read those two verses in your hearing. This is a very familiar passage. It reads,

> 8. *We are troubled on every side, yet not distressed; we are perplexed, but not in despair;*
>
> 9. *Persecuted, but not forsaken; cast down, but not destroyed.*

From these two verses I want to use for a theme or a subject, **I'm Down, But I'm Not Out.** Let me begin this message this morning by saying that you and I live in a day of compromise, a day of expediency, a day when we seem to measure a man by how popular he is or by how many friends he might have. The late Dr. Robert Shuler whose TV ministry was called **The Hour of Power,** once said, "I measure a man by the enemies he has." My brothers and sisters, listening to that, it's important to make the right kinds of enemies. You see, Jesus said that if we would love Him and follow Him, the world would hate us. The world is not our friend. So, that means that the world is our enemy, and the enemy hates us. Paul himself had the right kind of enemies. And I'm sure that I have the right kind of enemies, also. And if you are a believer in Christ Jesus, you have enemies also.

Christians are not afraid to suffer. Don't be afraid to suffer. Jesus says that the world will hate us if we are following Him, Him being Christ. It is wonderful to take our place with Christ in these days in which we live. If the Church is going to be effective in ministry in this age of the Christian Church, the one thing she must do is get the message of Christ to the unsaved. That's the only way they are going to hear about Christ. The Church, the messenger of Christ, must take the message to the unsaved or to the masses. The Church must have both an aim and a vision to reach them. If you don't have an aim or a vision, not much is going to happen. When we aim, we must aim at the target. You've got to aim to reach the target. And sometimes to aim you must shoot up higher, in order, to reach your target. If we don't have an aim, we won't reach the target. If we have no vision, the prophet says that the people will perish. *Where there is no vision, the people will perish.* The reason it needs an aim, and a vision is because we can see the plight and the disorder that exist in our times.

The world is disturbed and out of control. Disturbances are felt in every age of life. It's not just one age anymore. Every age is feeling the disturbed and disturbances that are out there in the world today. Can I serve notice on you today? You see, the spirit of Satan is running rampart in every community. It's in the urban areas. It's in the rural areas. Satan is acting up everywhere. He doesn't have a certain locale or location to cause a problem. He's running rampant, and all of us are feeling the effects and the disturbances that are happening in communities. When you see and witness little children are being neglected and destroyed at the hands of adults and their tender lives are cut short, nipped in the bud of life, oh, I tell you that's disturbing. These little children are dying at the hands of men, adults, women, or whomever. They are not given the privilege of growing up to understand what life is about. Nor do they really know God, their Creator, and the gift of their salvation. That's disturbing.

Today, our babies are born in a crazy world, a world of hate, of disease. And not only disease but dis-ease amidst all the disturbances that wage against the morals of society. When we hear of teens and young adults engaged in gun violence it's disturbing. If lives matter, if Black Lives Matter why are we destroying Black lives? If they matter, why are we destroying them? Lives matter because God is the only one able to give life. If God is the giver of life, no one has the right to take life God created in His image and after His likeness. That doesn't give you the right. If we take a life that is created in God's image without a

I'm Down, But I'm Not Out

justifiable reason or cause, we are in violation of God's rule of law. And what does the rule of law say? *Thou shalt not kill.*

With all the killing, this tells me that we are living in a distorted, disordered, and disturbed world. We've got our values wrong. We've got life wrong. We've got it all mixed up. Because we are mixed up, we are messed up. Many must contend every day with forces for which we ourselves are no match. Our efforts must be supported by and from a source outside of ourselves. We need God's help today.

All of you out there today, I'm sure you will agree with me that all the conflict that people are engaged in is a breakdown of a society. It is rooted in Satan's scheme to destroy man and to make him miserable. That's what is happening in your community and in my community. It's a scheme. It is a scheme of the evil one, the wicked one, Satan. His apparatus is to destroy and to make mankind miserable, but I come by to say this morning, I may be down, but I'm sure not out.

Listen to Paul. Paul says, *When I would do good, evil is present on every hand.* What is Paul saying? Paul is saying evil is present with me. It's almost like where can I escape this evil when it just seems like this evil is like the thickness of darkness. It's all around me. When I would do good, when I want to do the right thing, this thing called evil is there on every hand. When you look at what Paul is saying in that verse, you will discover that the competition of life is stronger and varied. The competition will weaken us unless we have access to God's resources and know how to tap into His resources and know how to deal with this thing the business of life. Can I tell somebody out there this morning that living is a very serious business? You don't get but one life, one chance to live. We better discover what it is and try to live it to the best of our ability. We've got to get that ability from God as to how to live that life because it is serious.

Listen to Paul again. Paul says, When I want to do the right thing…I want to do the right thing… but this thing called evil is present on my every hand, my every side. My Brothers and Sisters, you don't have to go looking for trouble. I've found out that trouble will find you. As I hear Paul keep saying in this verse evil is present on every hand. It's on every hand. I don't have to go looking for it. It's right there.

This Old Testament saint by the name of Job tells us in Chapter 14, Verse 1, he says, *Man that is born of a woman is of a few days...* and he says it's what... *and is full of trouble.* There is nothing any truer than that. Trouble is a common denominator of mankind, and all of us have trouble. If you don't have it right now, just keep on living. Keep waiting. It's coming.

But in that same book, a good friend of Job by the name of Eliphaz, Job's friend, his close confidant, one of his counselors which is found in Job 5:7, he says this about trouble, yet *man is born in trouble as sparks fly upward.* Trouble is a language that humanity knows about. Trouble here, trouble there, trouble everywhere. It's a human language that affects us all. As Eliphaz tells Job that trouble is *as sparks fly up,* we know that sparks occur when there is a fire somewhere (or you chunk the fire as they would say in the old school days) the sparks fly everywhere. So, in other words, trouble is everywhere. It's a human language. Let me get into the text this morning.

In our text today, Paul says it this way, *we are troubled on every side.* We *are perplexed.* We *are persecuted.* And we are *cast down, but not destroyed.* I'm perplexed. I'm troubled. I'm persecuted. I'm cast down. But I'm not destroyed. It is not only Paul having trouble, because when you listen to the language of the text, he includes us. He says that it's not just me, but we. I want us to see the we in there. Paul is inclusive. We are troubled on every side. We are perplexed. We are persecuted. Paul is trying to get us to see what we are. We make us apart of this fiasco of trouble. But not destroyed.

Can I just serve notice on you this morning that many of us have experienced many troubling moments in our lives? All our troubling moments may not be the same. But we have experienced trouble at some given point and time in our lives. All of us are going to experience some trouble – some troubling moments. All of us in here have been knocked down. You may as well go on and say Amen out there. You've been knocked down. You've been set back. You've been trampled upon. You've been walked on. You've been stomped on. You've been persecuted. Somebody has violated you. Somebody has ridiculed you. Somebody has dogged you out at some point in time. You've got some trouble. You've had some trouble. Guess what? You're going to have some more trouble. We are troubled, not just me. We are troubled. We are perplexed. We are persecuted. We are cast down. But not destroyed. The enemy has been on all our tracks.

Can I just go on a little further? We have felt the sting of words from somebody on the outside. We have felt cutting remarks of the enemy behind our back. We have felt the foot of our oppressors upon our necks. Yes, there have been many who were knocked down in every round of life. Seems like when you get over one thing, you get knocked down again. When you get over that you get knocked down again. The rounds just keep on coming. What are some of the things that knock us down or knock us back against the ropes? Lost jobs, broken relationships, failures, disappointments, deaths, and lost opportunities have given us a knockout punch. But you're not out yet. That's the good part. Yes, I've been punched, and I've been knocked against the ropes. Sometimes I've been floored, and I've been nailed. But guess what? I'm not out yet. I'm not cast down.

Can I go a little further? See, sometimes knockout punches from whatever it is that is troubling us or coming at us, blind sighted, we don't see the left hook, we don't see the upper cut, but we felt the wind from it. Maybe the wind from it or maybe just the swing itself put us to the canvas. And it can happen not only to the weaker Christians, but even to the stronger Christians are sometimes put to the canvas, so many look on at us because there are spectators in the arena that come to see the fight. They come to see you get knocked out. They see you knocked down in every round and they say, "Ain't no way he can come back and win this fight." They believe that because we're down so many times in the fight that it's over for us. But let me tell those who are at the fight don't leave the arena. Don't walk out and say that he doesn't have a chance. Yes, I'm down, but what you don't know is that I'm not out yet. Don't leave. It ain't over until it's over. Down, but I am surely not out.

I have had some stuff that has had me on the canvas…had my back against the rope. I wasn't like Muhammad Ali. I didn't have a "rope-a-dope". But I had one who could come to my corner and say, "Yes, you've been hit. You've got the bruises. You've got a black eye. You've got a busted nose. But it ain't over yet. You still got some fight in you." Just like Paul who said, "I'm troubled. I'm perplexed. I'm persecuted. I'm cast down, but I'm not out." I'm not out of the fight yet. Paul, in your own words can you tell us about some of the troubles that you have gone through? Well, let's hear it from Paul's own lips.

Paul says, "It was in Macedonia. I had some unrest; my flesh was unrestful. I had some trouble. I spent a night in a Philippian jail. They thought it was over for me, but God heard my prayers. I just got on my knees and started praying. I started singing the Zion songs, and heaven heard me. Heaven sent an earthquake and shook the ground. It shook the jail. Shook the door and shook the locks on my hands and my feet. I'm a free man because they thought I was down. If you think that was something, of the Jews five times I received stripes. Save one on my back. They beat me with rods. They stoned me one time. I was shivering when I spent a night and a day in the deep of the sea. Do you know how I survived? Do you know how a came to get up out of my troubles? The Lord said to me, Paul not a life will be lost even at sea. Just grab hold of a broken piece."

My brothers and my sisters, sometimes life crumbles around us. Everything around us falls. But we need just grab a broken piece. Some of us know about broken pieces. We have lived through some broken stuff, broken money. Just broke. Didn't have enough food, broke, broke down houses, broke down cars, but we made it. Here we are. We made it on broken pieces. God can get you to the safety zone if you just hold on. Even on broken stuff, God will get you out of it.

Let me tell you this since it's on my heart; when Paul and the prisoners got to the shoreline, they were wet, they were cold, and they were tired, they made a fire. See one trouble after another. They were warming by the fire, and a viper leaped out of the flames and attached itself to Paul's hand. He just shook it off. Everybody stood around looking to see Paul fall out and die. But I heard Paul say, "No harm!" Sometimes, when others stand around and say it's over, it ain't over. No harm! I got my troubles now. I'm down, but I ain't out. Shipwrecked, survived on broken pieces, got out of the ship on the shorelines, bitten by a viper but he didn't die. And it ain't over yet. He's got some more troubles.

Now, he's got to go before the emperor. While he's in the prison, God watched over him, and put him under house arrest. No harm. He still went on for the Lord. Paul says in his journey, often he was in perils. He was in perils of robbers, perils of his own countrymen, peril of weariness, and perils of pain. Sometimes he was naked. He was sleeping in a cold jail cell. He had trouble on every side. I just catching all this hell, I'm down, but I'm not out. I'm going through, but I'm not out.

Somebody out there this morning is going through, but you're not out. Don't count yourself out. Don't let anyone around you, in the arenas of life, look on you in your downward moment that you're going to stay down. If you're down, God can pick you up. God can turn that situation around for you. Paul, you told me from your own lips of some of your troubles. But I've got another question. How did your troubles affect you? Did they have an undercurrent that caused you some emotional problems or some issues that you couldn't deal with? What was your attitude, Paul?

Well, Paul says, "Since you're interviewing me, I was troubled on every side, which means in every imaginable way and place and thing. But I wasn't distressed. I kept a good attitude. Even though I was cast down, I was pressed against the walls of life. But since you're interviewing me, I didn't feel hemmed in at all. Yes, there were sometimes that I am little bit perplexed, but I wasn't in despair. Yes, there were perplexities all around me. Sometimes it seemed like things were not going to work itself out. I wasn't certain about tomorrow, even baffled sometimes but never in despair. I never gave up hope, nor did I lose my faith." Well, Brother Paul, you said some very helpful things.

So, let's conclude this scenario. He was persecuted. As we said earlier this is a familiar language. Trouble is a familiar language. Everybody understands troubles. Foes come. Foes go. They will persecute, not just one time, but many times. But we've got to keep standing of the promises of God. Paul tells us, "Yes, we go through, but we are not forsaken." We're never left alone to bear these burdens by ourselves. Our Savior, Jesus Himself, left on record that when you are going through life situations, *Come unto me, all you that labour and are heavy laden, and I will give you rest. Take my yoke upon you, and learn of me; for I am meek and lowly in heart: and ye shall find rest unto your souls. For my yoke is easy, and my burden is light.* Come on to me!

My brothers and sisters I come by to tell you this morning on my way to Heaven that if you've got troubles this morning and they've got you down, don't count yourself out. You can get back up again. Don't spend your time looking back at your bad days. Don't let your day of trouble keep you from your tomorrow. I just come to tell you that your future looks better than your past. Yes, when you know you've got a better future coming you can look back at your battlefield scars and say, "Well you know what? I *sho' was* in the fight. I've the scars, the trophies to *show for what* I've been through." Anybody got some trophies this morning to show that you have been through some things?

If you think those trophies look good to you, think about what you're going to get on the other side. What's on the other side? I'm hearing Paul again. Paul says to young Timothy who just entered into the battle arena, "I want you to know young man *I have fought a good fight. I have finished my course. I kept the faith.*" My Brothers and Sisters we all are in a fight. Sometimes we get knocked down, but never out. Paul says that this is the kind of fight I was in. I was in a good fight. I kept the faith. Not only that but I've got another trophy that is waiting on me. I know there is a crown laid up for me. I've got something better than this earthly trophy. Yes, I've been down, but I'm not out yet.

Come here Jesus. Jesus will tell you, "It was one Friday. They led me to Calvary's hill. And up on Calvary, oh, they treated me ill. They pierced my body. Yes, they did. They nailed my hands. They said, 'We're going to get rid of him. We're going to put him down. We're going to knock him out. And we won't see him anymore.' But they failed to realize what was said beforehand. If you crucify me, if you kill me, in three days I'm going to get up again. I'm going to be down, but I'm going to get up again." They did not realize what they were saying.

They fooled around and they killed Him. Yes. Then they took Him down and buried Him in a borrowed tomb. Yes, they laid Him down on Friday night. He was down, and He was out. All day Saturday, He was down, and He was out. All night Saturday night, He was down, and He was out. But God bless your soul, early Sunday morning, the down Jesus got up out of a dusty grave. When He got up, He stood on Resurrection ground, and He declared with these words, "*Oh grave, where is your victory. Oh death, where is your sting.* I was down, but I'm not down any longer. I'm up because I got all power in my hand. Anybody know He's got power to bring you back when you've been down? Anybody been down, but you knew about that Resurrection power of Jesus that is able to lift you out of dead situations, dead circumstances, from around dead people, dead stuff and give you a living hope that this too shall pass? Yes, I'm down, but I'm not out.

Oh, bless His Name this morning. He is a mighty God. Won't He take care of you? Won't He see you through whatever you're going through? Somebody out there may feel down this morning. You feel like you've gone to your last minute. You've reached your depths, your end. Don't count yourself out. Just go to Jesus. *Come unto me, all you that labour.* I'll take care of you. I'll give you solace. This is my word to you this morning. I pray that this has been a blessing, that this has been an encourager. Down, but not out.

CALL TO DISCIPLESHIP

And if you out there that have been listening, if you are not a part of a Church home or Church family, I encourage you to get with someone about getting in a Church home or a Church family. If you're unsaved this morning, and you don't know Jesus as your personal Savior, I encourage you to receive Him in your life right now by A – Acknowledging that you're a sinner; B – Believe that He is the Son of God that is He who died for your sins that you might have life more abundantly, you can be saved; C – Confess that He is the Christ the Son of the living God. And if you can believe it and confess it with your mouth, you can be saved. Then you need to connect to some Church, call some Pastor or some Deacon of some Church to get you in the right direction where you can make this public profession to someone who can help you to further your spiritual knowledge and growth. I pray that you will do that this morning, right now. Salvation is instantaneous, but then it is also a process. I've been saved. I'm being saved. And one day I will be ultimately saved, delivered out of this cruel, evil, and troubled world. I will be secured, safe with the Savior, the Master, the Lord Himself. I hope that you will take this seriously and do it because it is right. It is necessary. Come on Rose and sing for us.

SELECTION

There is Something About That Name **by Gloria Gaither**

CLOSING REMARKS

We are yet singing and praying and preaching about that great Name, that wonderful Name of Jesus. You just can't bypass Jesus that wonderful

Name. We pray that through the prayer, through the singing, through the Word that you have gotten your daily necessities met spiritually. Amen. We need our spiritual diet each day to get us through these troubled days in which we live. This is what will sustain us. This is what will keep us filled, fed, and going in the right direction. We must keep prayer at the forefront of all that we do because we want success in anything, we do that is spiritual. You'd better tag it with prayer because they are like a hand and glove. Just like a relationship with male and female. You can't have one without the other. Prayer and singing got to go together. The prayer and the Word they've got to go together. Whatever you're doing, it's got to be mingled together. And whatsoever God has joined together, nobody ought to separate it. Prayer and singing…prayer and preaching…prayer and whatever, it's got to work together. God Bless you. Amen.

Well, God bless you. Thank you for tuning in with us on today. Have a great rest of today. Be safe. Remember the criteria to stay healthy, to stay safe from this virus. We know our county numbers are continuing to escalate, going up and up and up. So, we're going to ask that you mask up, continue social distancing, and also keep those hands sanitized or soap washed. This is going to be our vehicle to get us out of this and to stay safe. I'm asking you, begging you let's stay as safe as possible.

I want to wish anybody and everybody out there a happy birthday on today. My mother's birthday will be on Tuesday, July 14th. I'm not going to tell her age but however we're going to give her a shout out even now and on Tuesday. Anyone out there who is celebrating a birthday God bless you. You may be having an anniversary, kudos to you too.

CLOSING PRAYER

The Lord is in His greatness. May He bless you and keep you. The Lord will make His face to shine upon you. And may the Lord be gracious to you. May the Lord lift His light of His countenance upon you. And may the Lord give you peace both now and forever, in the Name of Jesus we pray with a heart of thanksgiving. We also pray that you will bless the giving that will be rendered unto or ministry. Bless it in Jesus Name we pray. Amen.

For the Glory of God

Sunday, July 19, 2020

OPENING REMARKS

Well, well, well. I can call Him in the morning, and your morning just might be today. Good morning! Good morning church family, community, and friends. It is with Jesus' joy I greet you this morning. It is a beautiful morning in the neighborhood. The sun is shining bright, and we can feel its warmth and heat. It is a good morning. So, I am both grateful and thankful just to be here. You see, God's grace and mercy has kept me another day. My Brothers and Sisters, if you are happy and you know it just give God a handclap of praise right where you are. Go on and give God praise for this beautiful morning.

Reflecting and thinking back over our Church days, I remember years back our Junior Choir use to sing a song, and probably many of you were in that choir. You sang this song. The song says, "I don't know what you come to do, but I come to clap my hands. I don't know what you come to do, but I come to shout for joy." King David says, "The joy of the Lord is my strength." As the blood of Jesus gives us strength from day to day, so does His joy give us strength from day to day. So, we just want to honor God today in our worship and in our praise, and to thank Him for another day of joy.

WORDS OF ENCOURAGEMENT

Well, I have a thought for you today. My scripture will be coming from Hebrews Chapter 11, Verse 6, a familiar verse. And the scripture reads, *But without faith it is impossible to please him: for he that cometh to God must believe that he is, and that he is a rewarder of them that diligently seek him.*

You see the greatest key to abundant life and abundant living is a life that is filled with God's blessings and favor to keep Him first in our lives. Notice who God rewards, He does not reward people who half-heartedly seek Him when only they have problems. David says something in Psalm 34, Verse 10. He says, "*The young lions do lack, and suffer hunger: but they that seek the Lord shall not want any good thing.* Why? Notice the Psalmist says *good things*. If you seek the good things, you won't be able to outrun the good things of God. God has rewards waiting to just release upon us. But you must meet the requirements of the Lord. And God makes it so easy for us to meet the requirements. "If you seek me…if you will get up in the morning and thank me, search my word, and make an effort to please me, I will give you the rewards." That's what the Lord wants to reward us with; us seeking Him and seeking His favor upon our lives. My thought for you today. God bless you.

Oh, come on and bless that wonderful Name of Jesus. There is no other name like the name of Jesus. When you call on that Name, demons tremble at that Name. At the Name of Jesus, knees bow. At the name of Jesus, confessions are made because there is power in that magnificent Name.

CALL TO WORSHIP

So at this time we're going to ask Sister Rose to lead us in music ministry. I want to thank her again for her beautiful gift of music. We want you to enjoy this morning. As we fore stated, we come to give God praise, praising Him with clapping of our hands. Whatever means you have to praise Him, just go on and praise Him. Come on Rose.

SELECTION
Bless That Wonderful Name of Jesus
Well, let's beseech the throne of grace now. It's prayer time. And certainly, we want to go before the throne of God because He has given us that wonderful privilege to come before Him boldly to the throne of grace. We can just prostrate before Him. We can bow before Him. We can stand before Him. However, you choose to come, just come into His presence. Well, let us talk to the Lord now.

PRAYER

Our Father who art in Heaven, hallowed be Thy name, Thy Kingdom come. Thy Will be done in Earth as it is done in Heaven. God, we thank you, and we praise you now for who you are. You are Holy. You're great. You are gracious. And first, we just want to ask you to forgive us for our many sins. We ask you, oh God, to wash us and cleanse us from all that is not like you. Create in us clean hearts. We ask for renewed spirits.

Lord, we thank you for all that you are doing and are about to do in our lives. You have done so much for us. We can't even begin to count all that you've done. But we can say you have supplied all of our physical and spiritual needs. You have been our daily bread. You have quenched our every thirst. You are just that kind of a Father. So, now Lord, continue to anoint us with your Holy Spirit and power, that He leads and guide us in paths of righteousness and spiritual truths.

Oh Lord we come now asking that you remember our sick and shut in. Shower them with your special graces and your mercies. Shower your favors today and lift them all. We lift the families before you today who have lost loved ones. Strengthen them. So many have expired because of Covid-19, so many lives were lost, but Lord we realize that it's got to be tough for so many. Lord, you alone are able to reach and to comfort. Lord, look today on all people and touch and bless.

Most of all God, we pray that you would unite our country. There is so much division. And you said in Your Word anything that's divided against itself cannot stand. And these are your words. So, Lord, help us in this season of indifferences. Touch now those hearts that are cold and indifferent to love.

And Lord it seems as if love has waxed cold. But teach us to love with a fervent and warm love, love that is not touchy, that is not puffed up. And you taught us in your Word to have faith, to have hope, and to have love. But you said of all of these virtues that love is the greatest. So, God we pray that we will learn who love is. And when we learn to know who love is and what love is about, then I believe we will learn and start to love.

So, we praise you oh God for the Son of Thy Love, for Jesus who died and is now gone above. We thank you for His gift of salvation to us. He loved us so much that He gave His all. He gave His life. So, we just tell you now thank you Lord. We thank you for these petitions that we ask of you. And God we just pray that you will grant it in Jesus' name. And we pray it with a heart of thanksgiving. Amen and thank God. Amen.

SERMON

Thank you for sharing in that prayer moment with us. We need prayer all over our land and all over our world. If we're going to get through what we're going through, it's going to take prayer. *If my people, that are called by my name, will humble themselves and pray, and seek my face, turn from their wicked ways; then will I hear from heaven, and will forgive their sin, and will heal their land.*

Alright it's time for a Word now. I'm going to ask you to turn in your Bibles to John's Gospel, Chapter 9. I'm going to read the first ten verses, and of course, we are going to utilizing some of the remaining verses to deal with the points we'll be sharing in this text and message. But let me read the first ten verses for us. This will be the launching pad for what's to come.

1. *And as Jesus passed by, he saw a man which was blind from birth.*
2. *And his disciples asked him, saying, Master, who did sin, this man, or his parents, that he was born blind?*
3. *Jesus answered, Neither hath this man sinned, nor his parents: but that the works of God should be made manifest in him.*
4. *I must work the works of him that sent me, while it is day: the night cometh, when no man can work.*
5. *As long as I am in the world, I am the light of the world.*
6. *When he had thus spoken, he spat on the ground, and made clay of the spittle, and he anointed the eyes of the blind man with the clay,*
7. *And said unto him, Go wash in the pool of Siloam, (which is by interpretation, Sent.) He went his way therefore, and washed, and came seeing.*
8. *Thy neighbours therefore, and they which before had seen him that he was blind, said, Is not that he that sat and begged?*
9. *Some said, This is he: others said, He is like him: but he said, I am he.*
10. *Therefore, said they unto him, How were thine eyes opened?*
11. *He answered and said, A man is called Jesus made clay, and anointed mine eyes, and said unto me, Go to the pool of Siloam, and wash; and I went and washed, and I received sight.*

I want to talk from this subject this morning, **For The Glory of God.** This man's miraculous healing was for the glory of God, so that God's work could be made manifest.

This text this morning starts out as John records it. It says *And as Jesus passed by, he saw a man who was blind from his birth.* As Jesus passed by, he saw…What did he see? He saw a man who had been blind from birth. I just want to inform someone out there this morning that Jesus is still passing by. I don't know this morning who, where God is passing by your way, but I want you to know wherever you are if He's passing by, He sees you. He still sees those who cannot see Him. This young man was born with a physical impairment. He was born this way. He was birthed into the world. He was blind; therefore, he could not see. He couldn't see Jesus, but Jesus could see him.

May I just serve notice on all of us, when all of us were born into this world, this world of chaos and confusion; we were born blind as well because we were born in sin. We have been blind since birth until we came to the Light to know who Jesus really is. He took the scales off our eyes. I know someone is saying this morning, "I wasn't born blind." Yes, you had your physical sight, but you didn't have Spiritual sight or insight. Yes, you had the 20/20 vision. You could see from the natural perspective. But Spiritually Jesus passed by, and He anointed and opened your eyes. I want you to know this morning that Jesus is able to open the eyes of the blind. No one, no matter who you are or where you are this morning and you are not spiritual, God can open your spiritual eye and retina and give you eyesight.

My Brothers and Sisters, the teaching in this text this morning of the healing of the blind man teaches us that those who do not believe in Jesus are the ones who are truly blind. You need spiritual eyesight because when I read Verse 18 the Jews did believe concerning him, this man that was blind. They didn't believe that he had been blind and received his sight until they called the parents of him that received his sight. I'm talking about the blind man. I believe that they were in disbelief because they did not want to attribute the miracle to Jesus. They had issues. They had problems with Jesus. Do understand this is the sabbath day, and Jesus has healed this man on the sabbath day. This posed a problem with them. So, they are really trying to discredit Jesus. So, they use this against Jesus and the man himself. "We don't believe that he was blind." They see the evidence, and now, they must go and question this young man's parents of how he received his sight if he was blind. This miracle and healing of the blind man is a record of the good news that Jesus can do in our lives what no one else can do. What no other doctor can do. What no other medicine can do. This Jesus can do the unthinkable for us. Let me move into this text by using three principles, three points.

The first point I want to make is Jesus saw the blind man. Verse 1 says, *And Jesus passed by and saw him.* And He saw him in his blind state. Everybody is looking on at this man. Jesus saw him. He saw his circumstance. But guess what? The disciples saw the man also. But when they looked on the man and saw him, they saw a question to be asked. They asked the question, "Who did sin?" Then they started pointing the blame for the man's blindness. "Who did sin? This man or his parents?" That isn't the way Jesus saw it. I'm glad that Jesus doesn't see things the way man sees them. You see, when Jesus saw him, He saw a need to be met. They saw him for who sinned. Isn't that the way people are today? They don't see you for who you can be and what you can become. They just see you for who you are. But I'm glad that Jesus made it clear that this man's blindness was not a result of sin. My Brothers and Sisters we cannot equate people's problems and faults and sicknesses and illnesses or their handicaps with sin. Then we are becoming judges of others.

Let me tell you why some things are the way they are; Jesus wanted them to know that this man was born this way to be a platform for God's glory to be displayed. If you look at Verse 3 Jesus says to them, "*Neither hath this man sinned, nor his parents: but that the works of God should be made manifest in him.* And that's why I'm saying this man's blindness was a platform for God's glory to be displayed. Some things that happen in people's lives or the way people are … God allows it, so that He can demonstrate who He really is. God wants to work. Sometimes the work of God must be demonstrated through humanity for others to see the glory and the goodness of God. Do I have any help, out there this morning?

Jesus goes on further in the text. Jesus says in Verse 4, *I must work the works of him that sent me, while it is day: the night cometh, when no man can work.* "I've got work to do. I come to demonstrate and to show you the power of God; and how it can manifest itself and transform people from one state of being to another." It's transforming power in Jesus Christ. Once Jesus gets ready to heal this man, He says in Verse 5, *As long as I am in the world, I am the light of the world.* What does this young man need? He's living in darkness. He doesn't have eyesight. He cannot see, and Jesus is saying to the crowd, "Yes, Light has come. I'm in the world, and I'm going to demonstrate Light in the midst of darkness." This young man has lived all of his life. The Bible doesn't five us his age, but we do know that he was born blind. He was in darkness. He could not see, but light has come. Jesus has come to give Light in the midst of darkness. "I'm the Light of the world. I'm the Light of the world. I am the Light of the world." For those of us who have come out of darkness into the marvelous Light, Jesus says, "You have become light also. You are the light of the world. You are a city that sits on a hill that cannot be hidden." Somebody ought to be spreading a little light today to the dark areas and people that are in darkness. Jesus used this platform to demonstrate God's glory so that it could be displayed.

What we need to understand about John and his writings is that his whole book is about believing Jesus Christ. If you believe Him, then you can have eternal life. It's all about believing. You read throughout this book of John, you just hear the word believe, believe, believe, believe, believe. So, he is trying to get people to believe. So, he's using this man's situation to allow others to see the works, the power, and the miracles of God working in this young man. Some things that happen in our lives, they happen so that God can get a display, and then He can bring some glory to His Name. So, don't curse everything that has happened to you in your life because somebody out there needs to see. Somebody out there needs to believe. God needs somebody that He can use as a conduit to get His message across…to get His message across…get His blessings across…get salvation across. So, Jesus is getting ready now to do a little display.

The man is blind. What did Jesus do? He spat on the ground, and He made some mud from the saliva. Then He took it and mixed it together like a salve. Look at my Miracle Worker. Then He comes to the man and started to bathe his eyes with the saliva and mud mixture. He anointed the man's eyes with it, and told him, "Now go wash in the pool of Siloam." And the Bible says, *and he went his way and washed and received his sight.* Let me say to you quickly, eyesight is not in mud and spit. You see, if we don't follow orders, if we don't follow directives and prerequisites of Jesus, nothing is going to happen in our lives. The healing of the blind man and the sight that came into his eyes was not because of the mud and the saliva. His eyesight came because he believed what Jesus said and obeyed Jesus and went as he was told to the pool of Siloam and washed. When he obeyed, when he followed Jesus' command, he received his sight. The power of Jesus and obedience is what gets miracles. Power and obedience are what gets healing. Power and obedience are what gets salvation. It is all to the glory of God…for the glory of God…for the glory of God…for the glory of God.

Let me just fast forward to Chapter 11. We all know the story of Lazarus in Chapter 11. You know about Lazarus, Mary, and Martha. You know Lazarus got sick, and Lazarus died. They sent for Jesus because He was out of town. When Jesus got the word that *he whom thou lovest is sick* and you need to come to town, Jesus stayed away three days until Lazarus died. And after three days Jesus went back to Bethany to Mary and Martha. They were weeping and crying and mourning. The community was mourning and weeping with this family at Lazarus's death. When Jesus did come back to town, you know the story. The sister came to Him and said *If you had been here, our brother would not have died.* Jesus said show me where you laid him. And they take Him to Lazarus's tomb. You know the rest of the story. Jesus wanted them to know that He was going to raise Lazarus from the dead. Not to prove anything, but to show them and those who stood around and cause them to believe. This Gospel of John is about believing. Believe that He was the Son of God, and that God would get the glory for raising up Lazarus so that somebody would come to know Christ. That's what it's all about…to believe. Go to Chapter 14, He says, "*Let not your heart be troubled, ye believe in God believe also in me.* It's about believing. Let me go to my second point.

Remember, the first thing is Jesus saw the blind man, and the disciples saw the blind man. They all asked questions: Who did sin? This man or his parents? The second thing is his neighbors saw a healed man. The disciples saw a blind man. Jesus saw an opportunity to glorify God. Look at Verse 8. Verse 8 says, "*Thy neighbours therefore, and they which before had seen him.* When they had seen him before he was a blind man. Now they see a different man. He's seeing. He's walking. He's not the man they had previously seen sitting and begging. When God does something wonderful in your life, when you've been out there at the disposal of others, you have to depend upon others to lead you and take you places and fix your food and do all of these things that are necessary, now when you can do it yourself. It's glorious when you can do it for yourself, and you don't have to depend on other people. These folks, they saw a healed man and once the blind man's neighbors saw him, they did not know what to think. Yes, they recognized him as the one who said he was blind, the one who use to sit and ask and beg for things.

Others were not sure. When you read Verse 9 he kept saying when they asked him, "Are you the one that was blind?" He kept saying, "I am the man. I am the man." They wanted to know, "How did your eyes become open?" He declared that Jesus did it. Jesus did it. My Brothers and Sisters when Jesus has done something in your life don't keep it to yourself. All he could say was that Jesus did it. He didn't know anything about Jesus. But he knew one thing. It was Jesus. What did Jesus do? Jesus had done something marvelous. Jesus had done something magnanimous. Jesus had done a miracle in his life. My Brothers and Sisters, if Jesus has opened your blinded eyes, there ought to be something different about you. You should not be ashamed to testify about what God has done in your life. I don't care what others say.

Others were thinking who was this man? He kept saying, "I am he. I'm the man. I'm the one that was blind. My eyes are now opened." He declared, "It was Jesus who did it. It was Jesus. It was Jesus who healed me." When God does something wonderful in your life, don't hold it. Put it on display because there is always somebody watching you. They know your flaws. They know everything about you. When they see something different about you, now they want to know how did it happen? Who did it? You were this way. You were that way. Yes, that's the way I use to be. I used to beg. I used to sit. But now I am a different person. I'm changed. I'm changed from the inside out. I'm no longer the same.

When God does something wonderful, testify about what He's done. Don't keep it to yourself. That's what a testimony is. It's a test. Something you have been tried, but you have been proven that you are authentic. So, brothers and sisters, don't take someone else's testimony and try to use it for your benefit. My testimony won't work for you. Your testimony won't work for me. I know where God has brought me from. I know what He has brought me through. I have a testimony, and I'm not ashamed of my testimony. I'm not ashamed to testify about what the Lord has done in my life. You see, if we are ashamed after God has done so much for us, it would have been and indictment on this man who has been blind all of his life and then Jesus gives him his sight and he be dismissive. But I hear him say, "It was Jesus. It was Jesus. I don't know a whole lot about Jesus, but I know it was Him. They say His name was Jesus. I haven't known Him long enough to really know Him. I don't know all about Him." My Brothers and Sisters we don't know all there is about the Lord either, but that I do know I am willing to tell it. I'm not ashamed about what I do know about Him, and that I don't know, I ought to be asking God to help me to know and to understand. Give me understanding. Give me revelation so that Lord the more I know the greater my testimony. The greater my witness will be.

As I come to the last point, we looked at Jesus saw the man. The disciples saw the man. The neighbors saw a healed man. Now the third thing in the text, there was another crowd there. That was the religious crowd. The religious crowd couldn't see anything. Isn't that ironic? Some folks can see, and others can't. Look at Verse 13 through 15. Verse 13 begins, "*They brought to the Pharisees him that aforetime (formally) was blind. And it was(on) the sabbath day when Jesus made the clay and opened his eyes. Then again, the Pharisees also asked him how he had received his sight. He said unto them, He put clay upon mine eyes, and I washed, and do see.* You see the crowd; they couldn't see anything. That's the way it is today. There are folks who can't see anything. They can't see the signs of time. They can't see the handwriting on the wall. They were shocked not because the man was blind and couldn't see. They were shocked because Jesus had healed him on the sabbath day.

They are asking him how did he receive his sight? Now the blind man can testify about Jesus. This left the religious leaders, the Pharisees, divided. Some started arguing that He has healed on the sabbath day. Others how could a sinner do such signs. They are talking about Jesus. They are calling Him a sinner. Religious folks. Religious crowd denounced the credibility of Jesus because they are hung up in their religious rules and their religious laws. They couldn't see the power of God at work in every aspect. Blind. Couldn't see anything. Can't see God. They have scales on their eyes.

Jesus says that if the blind leads the blind, won't they both fall in a ditch? This is what's happening to these religious Pharisees. They are blind, and they are trying to lead the blind. They are at the sabbath day, but they can't see God. And yet, they are trying to tell people about God. They can't see the powers and the workings of God. Hear Jesus say, *I must be about the works of my Father.* Jesus says that "I'm working while it's day. I know night is coming. So, I'm going to spend my time working for the Master." They couldn't see the workings of God. If I could ask you this question, who were the blind folks in this text? It certainly wasn't Jesus. It was the folks who could not see beyond their nose.

They are continuing to question this young man. They are interrogating him. They're badgering him for the miracle that has been wrought in his life. All at the same time they are discrediting Jesus, and they are putting Jesus on the same level with sinners. This is the Savior of the world who has come to save sinners. I need us to look at Verse 32. Jesus says this, *Since the world began was it not heard that any man opened the eyes of one that was born blind.* Yet they couldn't believe in Jesus.

My Brothers and Sisters don't let unbelief blind you to the power of One who is able to open blinded eyes. My God is able to do whatever He wants. Sometimes God sets up things just to get us to see His power – get us to see His work. And I just believe through this Covid-19 that God is going to get some glory out of this. Yes, many have lost their lives, and there are those who are yet losing their lives, but I truly, deeply believe from looking at the Word of God that those who have and the Covid virus, and many have been at the point of death, yet lived to say, "I made it through, I got over it", God is going to use those voices as display as a platform so that God can get glory and be a witness to somebody out there that God can bring you through anything if you just believe and obey Him. I just believe that through Covid-19 God is going to get some glory out of it. Somebody is going to get off their bed of affliction. Somebody is going to come up off their death bed say, "If it had not been for the Lord who was on my side, I never would have made it. It got rough. It got tough. It was hard. But I kept praying. I kept the faith, and God has brought me through. I'm a living testimony that He's able." Somebody is going to have that testimony. They are going to be bold and vivacious and stand up and say to God be the Glory.

This didn't just happen. It happened for a reason. If God didn't want it to happen, it wouldn't have happened. He has that kind of power. It happened. It's here. We're dealing with it. God can do miraculous things through matters of this type…these things we're experiencing. Even through the protests and the Black Lives Matter Movement, God will get some glory out of it. We can already begin to see some of the fruits. I have to say it because the Spirit is pressing me to say it.

As I get ready to leave you this morning, this is not the time for unbelief. You see, this religious crowd couldn't see anything. The Pharisees were settled in their unbelief. They concluded that this man was not blind. It's in Verse 23. They keep questioning and the keep advocating, "Were you blind?" They called for the man's parents. They ask the parents, "Is this your son? Was he blind? Better yet, who opened his eyes?" The parents were a little hesitant or reserved in answering the question because they did not want to be excommunicated from the temple or synagogue worship. They didn't want to face the religious leaders. They did not want repercussions from these unbelievers, this religious crowd, this "show off group". So, the parents didn't want to go against the grain. As they were asking, "Is this boy your son? Was he born this way? Who opened his eyes?", the parents just simply said, "Well, he's of age, you ask him. He can tell you better than we can tell you. We don't want any problems with you. So, we will let him tell you how, who, and when." They did not want confrontation. When it comes to blessings, if it was one of my family members…if it was my child and I knew my child was in the shape and condition he was in and he had to sit and he had to go out and beg every day, would have been a slight case of embarrassment for me, but I would have been more than happy, I would have been elated, I would have been glad to say, "Yes, it was Jesus who did it. So, if you want to put me out of your house, put me out. But I'm not going to denounce what Jesus has done. I'm not going to discredit the power of God working in my child's life."

Look at Verse 24. They call the man in again for questioning. They just keep questioning. They said to him, "Give God the praise. We know that this man is a sinner. Don't give Jesus any credit but give God the credit." Talking about Jesus, little did they know who Jesus was. Jesus was God manifested in the flesh. It was Jesus who said in John's Gospel, "*when you see the Father, you see me. I and my Father are one.* "We work that way. I'm God just wrapped up in human flesh. They are telling this man to give God the praise. Give God the glory. This man that you received this miracle from is a sinner. He doesn't know God. He has no relationship with God. That's what a sinner is. A sinner is alienated from God because his sins have him separated. In other words, they are calling Jesus a sinner. But when God has brought about a miraculous and magnanimous deed in your life, and then when others try to denigrate and tear apart what good has happened to you because of Jesus, you have to stand up with a Holy boldness from within, I see it in this man. This man, he's got to testify now. He says, "I don't know what you are talking about. You call him a sinner. All I know is His name is Jesus. One thing I do know, I was blind, but I can see now. And what I am seeing through my eyes right about now it looks good to me. I've never seen any of it before. I've never seen my parents before. I've never seen you guys before, and what I'm seeing it looks good. I'm looking at God's creation. I can see the beauty of God. I can see the beauty that exists."

I thank God for Jesus this morning. I come to testify when I was lost and couldn't find my way, my pathway was dark. But Jesus, the Light of the world, came, pulled the scales from my eyes. He showed me how beautiful things can be in having a relationship with Him. I'm like the blind man, all I know is I was blind, but now I see. I can see clearly now. I'm like the song writer now. *Amazing grace, how sweet the sound, that saved a wretch like me. I once was lost but now I'm found. I was once blind but now I see.* What was it Reverend? It was grace that brought me safe thus far. If I move any further, grace will lead me.

Somebody ought to give Him praise and thanks for His grace this morning. Somebody ought to just give God the glory this morning because whatever happened in your life, it was to his glory. It can bring glory. It can not only bring glory, but it can bring grace, mercy, and salvation to so many others through whatever is happening in your life.

I say this all the time. Don't curse the things that happen in your life. Some things happen in our lives so that God can get the glory. God knows who He can trust. He knows who will get out there and tell the story. He knows who will say that it was nobody but the Lord. Some people are just too afraid, too ashamed to just mention His name. He knows who will stand up boldly and give His name Holy praise. This brings me to the conclusion of today's message: **For the Glory of God.** Thank You Lord for this day. Thank You for Jesus who hung, bled, and died on the cross that you and I might have this rightful privilege.

CALL TO DISCIPLESHIP

There is someone out there today who has heard this short, but I believe impactful message…if you can believe the word today…if you can believe that a miracle can happen to you…if you will accept the gift of salvation this morning, that could be the greatest miracle for you today. If you can believe that Jesus died, was buried, and was raised the third day…if you can confess with your mouth and believe it in your heart, then you are saved. A – acknowledge, B – believe, C – confess… Acknowledge you sins, believe that Jesus died, Confess Him. Say it. Say what it is, and you're saved. Get hooked up with somebody that you know is saved, and let them know, "I've accepted Christ as my Savior." God Bless you this morning. Thank you so much. We're going to have Rose come and bless us with a beautiful number. And we'll see you in a few minutes.

SELECTION

He Looked Beyond My Faults and Saw My Needs **by Dottie Rambo**

CLOSING REMARKS

Praise God. He looked beyond all my faults and saw my needs. Isn't that what we said in the message today? When Jesus passed by and saw a man who had been blind from birth, He saw a need. Others had questions of who did sin, the man, or his parents. The neighbors saw a healed man. The religious crowd didn't see anything. They questioned the parents. They questioned everybody, and even discredited Jesus. Thank God He looked beyond my faults and saw my needs. God bless you. Thank you for your participation in today in out worship. We pray that your rest of the day will be just as great as the morning part of your day has been.

CLOSING PRAYER

Now unto Him that is able to keep you from falling, and to present you before His presence with exceedingly great joy, now unto Him be dominion, power, glory, honor, and majesty now and forever…and all the people said Amen, and oh God do bless the gifts that will be coming in. We ask it in Jesus's Name. Amen.

Zacchaeus's Conversion
Sunday, July 26, 2020

OPENING REMARKS

All I need is You. My brothers and sisters we need the Lord on this day. Every breath I breathe, I need the Lord. Every wink of the eye, I need the Lord. Every time I move, I need the Lord. I need Him. You need Him. We all need Him. Thank God that we have needs, and the Lord supplies. He meets our every need. Whether they are physical needs, spiritual needs, social needs, financial needs, psychological needs, every need the Lord meets for each one of us.

Well! Good morning! Good morning church family. I'm so happy and so elated to see you chiming in this morning. I see a number who have tuned in with us. Some of you are tuned in secretly; however, we are just so glad you could tune in with us - our Church family, our Church community, our friends whether they are near or far. Amen. We are so glad you chose to tune in with the St. Mark Church family and the Church community - the Faith community. Amen. All believers, it does not matter your Church denomination or affiliation might be this morning. We're just here to spread the Good News of the Gospel of Jesus Christ because it is needed for such a time as this.

Well, I've got another blessing today. Reverend, what is that blessing? I'm yet alive. That's a blessing isn't it just to be alive. And the Lord has showered me with that blessing. The Lord has kept me another day and to know it. See there are a lot of people who are alive this morning, but they don't know it. For some physical reason they don't know they're alive. But I am alive, and I know it. Somebody ought to just say, "He's keeping me alive." Amen. That's an old song from back in the day. He's keeping me alive. Amen. I can't do it myself. I told you, I need Thee every breath I take. He's keeping me alive. It's a joy to just greet you this morning in the Name of our Lord and Savior Jesus Christ. I am glad you could join me so we can worship and praise the only Wise God for there is no other God. How do you know Reverend? The Psalmist tells me for the Lord is great, a great King above all gods. So, I invite you today to lift and exalt His Name, the only God, the only Wise God. So, let's give Him a hearts-up or a thumbs up for being a great God, and a great King above all gods. This is our form of praise. We can't touch one another. We can't high five one another. But at least we can thumbs-up or hearts up, just letting the Lord know that He is great. I see you. I see you. And I love what I see. God bless you.

WORDS OF ENCOURAGEMENT

Well, I have a word of encouragement for you. For those who are in the hospitals, those who are confined at home, and those confined in prisons, I want you to especially hear these words of encouragement this morning. This word of encouragement will be coming from Mark Chapter 5. This is a very familiar passage, but I'm just selecting a couple of verses to give a word of encouragement as we dissect this verse: Mark Chapter 5, Verse 27 and 28. It says *When she had heard of Jesus, came in the press behind, and touched his garment. For she said, If I may touch but his clothes, I shall be made whole.*

Just thinking over the ministry of Jesus, out of all the miracles and many healings that Jesus performed, He touched many of the people with His hand. But in the case of the woman in our text, we will classify her as the No Name Woman because she has no name, she laid her hands on Him. There was a large crowd of people that surrounded Jesus. Many that were in the crowds were in need of blessings, also. They were in need of healing or deliverance, but they did not believe like this woman believed to get their healing. This woman believed and was healed. Is anyone out there needing a touch from Jesus? Are you waiting for Him to touch you with His hands? Are you expecting a miracle? Let me serve notice on you. He's bigger than your problem. He has all power. Not some power, but He has all power.

Let me tell you what you need to do. You need to just brush up against Him and touch Him. I didn't say He touch you, but you need to touch Him. Don't be afraid. Don't wait to touch Him. You touch Him. You touch Him like the woman did. She touched the hem of His garment. You see, your faith can activate that power to do something wonderful in you. Your faith can activate God's power to do something wonderful in you. Do like the woman. Don't wait for Jesus to touch you. You touch Him and believe and see what will happen in your life or in your situation.

That's a Word to somebody in the hospital. That's a Word to someone who is confined at home. That's a Word to everybody that may be listening. Don't wait for Jesus to touch you. You touch Jesus and watch what happens in your situation. My words of encouragement to you. Amen.

CALL TO WORSHIP

Let's get ready to go further into this worship experience as we prepare our minds and our hearts. The Lord is in His Holy Temple, and let the Earth be silent before Him. Amen.

So, Sister Rose our song leader is going to come and bless us with song. We pray that you will enjoy it and that it will be blessing in your life for this moment and moments to come. Amen. Sister Rose, will you come and bring us a soul stirring, heart wrenching selection of your choice. Amen. And I'll be back to lead us further into this worship experience.

SELECTION

***Down Through the Years, The Lord Has Been Good to Me* (an old church Hymn that has been recorded by gospel artists such as: Bishop Neal Roberson, Rev. Jasper Williams, Jr. and many others).** Oh, praise His Name. The Lord has been good to me. He's been good to all of us. All of us can praise Him for that. Let's go on and give Him some praise for being a good God. Give Him a thumbs-up. That's our only way of showing our praise. Amen. A thumbs-up or a hearts-up because certainly the Lord has been good. And if you think the Lord has not been good, then oh I tell you that you're in trouble. He is good. He is good all the time, and all the time God is good. He is worthy of praise.

Thank you, sister for blessing us. Thank God I got a good song leader to help us through these worship experiences. Amen. Because if I didn't have her, we'd be suffering right now for some singing and some music. Thank God that He's always got a ram in the bush. He's always got someone who can always bring up the slack. Amen. God bless you.

Now let us prepare to go to the Throne of Grace. Remember in my words of encouragement, we talked about the woman who touched Him. Somebody needs to touch Him this morning. Not so much He touch you, but you need to touch Him so that the power that is in Him can flow from Him into you. You've got to play a part. You've got to believe that what you are touching and believing God for that it can happen to you. It doesn't matter what it is or how long you've had it.

This woman had this matter in her life for twelve long years, and it had depleted her bank account. She had no other alternative but to come and touch Jesus. She touched Him. She had a touch of faith. So, where is your faith today? Can you reach out by faith and touch Him today? Let us go to the Throne of Grace.

PRAYER

Most Gracious God Our Father, we come into Thy presence this morning to give Thee thanks and praise for another chance in life to live and to recognize your goodness and your tender mercies. Thank you for divine grace which is called forgiveness. And oh God if we have offended you in any manner, please forgive us. Extend to us your compassion one more time and deliver us from all evil for we realize without your mercy we would not know mercy and love is. Have mercy on those who stand in need of your blessings, your healing, and your deliverance today.

Lord I just want to lift before you those who need a touch of your hands even right now. Lord they are just waiting on a touch. I realize there are so many out there, and I know that you know each by name. You know what they need. They need your grace. They need your mercy. So, Lord grant healing in the Name of Jesus. Lord, touch everyone that's under the sound of my weak voice. Bless them also. Meet every need according to your riches in Glory.

And Lord as your Word goes forth today, we pray that your Word will produce faith and hope in these dark days of uncertainty. For we don't know what's lurking around the corner to overcome us or even set us back, but we know this; we know that your eyes are upon us even as your eyes are upon the sparrow. And I know you are watching over us. You are our constant friend. You are a very present help in the time of trouble. You are always there, and for that we are just so thankful.

Bless today those that are incarcerated, that are in prisons, jails all around this country. Look also upon bereaved families today, Lord those who have lost members to Covid. Lord, keep your hands upon our youth and our children as school is being discussed. Many are afraid that it's too early to send them back in our systems that they might be faced with this virus that could be transmitted back into their homes and community. Lord, keep them. Look on our teachers. Look on our workers. Look on our stewards. Keep your covering upon our country. Continue to be a shield around our Church and your pastors. Lift them today with a Word from your very Throne Room. Bless them with a spoken Word. We know you can. We believe you will because you're God.

And we're just going to go on and thank you now. And we're going to ask it in the Name of Jesus, the Name which is greatly to be praised. And we pray this prayer today and ask these blessings with thanksgiving. Amen. Amen. God bless you.

SERMON

Thank you for your participation in our prayer moment. Now it is time to indulge in the Word. My message this morning, medium size sermon this morning, will be coming from a New Testament book, Luke Chapter 19, Verses 1-10. Here is how the passage reads,

1. *And Jesus entered and passed through Jericho.*
2. *And, behold, there was a man named Zacchaeus, which was the chief among the publicans, and he was rich.*
3. *And he sought to see Jesus who he was; and could not for the press, because he was little of stature.*
4. *And he ran before, and climbed up into a sycamore tree to see him: for he was to pass that way.*

> 5. And when Jesus came to the place, he looked up, and saw him, and said unto him, Zacchaeus, make haste, and come down; for to day I must abide at thy house.
>
> 6. And he made haste, and came down, and received him joyfully.
>
> 7. And when they saw it they all murmured, saying, That he was gone to be guest with a man that is a sinner.
>
> 8. And Zacchaeus stood, and said unto the Lord; Behold, Lord, the half of my goods I give to the poor; and if I have taken any thing from any man by false accusations, I restore him fourfold.
>
> 9. And Jesus said unto him, This day is salvation come to this house, forsomuch as he also is a son of Abraham.
>
> 10. For the Son of man is come to seek and to save that which was lost.

From these ten verses I want to use for my subject, or my theme for this passage, **Zacchaeus's Conversion**. In this printed text this morning, Luke says, *and Jesus entered and passed through Jericho,* as if Jesus, when He left Heaven, had Jericho and Zacchaeus on His agenda for this specific time. But also, as Jesus enters and passes through Jericho, Jesus was on His way to Jerusalem because the Cross of Calvary is just a short time away. And as He had to enter and pass-through Jericho with an agenda, He knew Zacchaeus was there. He knew He had to stop and give Zacchaeus a visit.

The Bible says that Zacchaeus was a tax collector. He was the chief of tax collectors. During that time and era, there were three tax collecting sites. One was in Palestine. The other ones were in Jerusalem and Capernaum. Jericho was the tax capital of Palestine. Zacchaeus was the chieftain. I do understand that tax collectors were not honest people. They were rude, heartless. They cheated the people out of more of their tax monies. These tax collectors were considered traitors of the taxpayers for the Roman citizens or the Roman officials. Tax collectors, because of their ostracizing from society, because of their manner of cheating the people, and because they were despised and looked down on, they could not participate in gatherings; nor in synagogues for worship because of their thievery ways. So, they were forced out of the general population and places of worship.

My Brothers and Sisters, one must ask the question how did Zacchaeus the chieftain, the chief tax collector know about Jesus and was concerned to see Jesus? For one thing, Jesus had been busy for almost three years. He had been preaching, teaching, and healing. And His name and His fame had proceeded Him. His fame had gone around the regions. They had heard about His fellowship with those who had bad reputations, those who were sinners, and those whom society had ostracized. He came to the poor and the underprivileged. And that was His ministry. His ministry was about reaching those that were outcast, broken hearted, those who were cast down. Go back to Chapter 4 and you will find all these things. However, Jesus's fame had proceeded Him, and many were wanting just the privilege to see Him. Not so much as to talk to Him, but "We just want to see this man they call Jesus."

My Brothers and Sisters on that same note, Jesus had been hated and rejected by the religious leaders. He was criticized for eating and drinking with sinners and with the publicans. This could very well be Zacchaeus's reason for wanting to see Jesus because He was known for sitting and eating with the outcast. That's the way he felt. "I'm an outcast. I can't go to the worship places because I'm criticized. I'm jumped on. If I just try to socialize with people in the community, I'm criticized. I'm ostracized. I can't go anywhere without being humiliated. Since Jesus eats with publicans which I'm one of, and sinners – and I am a sinner – just maybe, just maybe He'll just stop by. Maybe we could just spend some time together. Maybe He will speak nicely to me. Maybe He will be more cordial. Maybe He will be more polite to me. He'll eat with me."

You see, even though Zacchaeus had heard all these innuendos and rumors about Jesus eating and drinking with sinners and with publicans, Zacchaeus feels as though he is not interested in what the people had said about Jesus, he just wants to see Him for himself. He wanted to figure out what it was that made Jesus different from everybody else. Everybody else did not take time for sinners. Everybody else was too religious, too Holy, and more Holy than the Holy Himself. Zacchaeus is trying to figure out all this stuff. "You all are so Holy, and you're talking about everybody else. Well, let me see this Jesus for myself." He wanted to figure out what made Jesus different from everybody else.

It just so happened that here this man that others had talked about, He's in town now. Zacchaeus wants to see. He's in the streets of Jericho. He has a crowd of people that have surrounded Him as He's coming down Jericho Blvd. He's walking through the streets of his (Zacchaeus) town. So, Zacchaeus is thinking, "He's in town. I've got to get to Him. I've got to find a way to see this man." Anybody out there want to see Jesus? There's a song that Edna Friend use to sing at the Church: *Oh, how I want to see Him; Just to look upon His face. And there to be forever.* Let me get into my outline. I promised you I wasn't going to be her awfully long this morning. I have three points I want to bring out of this lesson this morning about this little man called Zacchaeus.

This first thing we want to look at about this man is Zacchaeus had a handicap. What was Zacchaeus's handicap? Well, the scriptures say that he was short in stature. This little man about four feet tall or less was almost a midget. He was short physically. That was his handicapping condition. He was not only short physically, but he was short spiritually as well. And before we get on to Zacchaeus handicaps, each of us has either had one or both handicaps that Zacchaeus has at one time or another. We may not be short in stature. You may be five-eleven. You might be six feet tall. You might be seven feet tall. That's just one. But if you don't have Jesus in your life, guess what? You have a *shortness*, you're short spiritually. So, all of us, and some of us yet are physically short and somebody is physically and spiritually short at the same time. How are we short? When I read Romans 3:23 says *for all have sinned and fallen short of the glory of God.* And you know my brothers and sisters we all have fallen short. Some of us are short this morning. We are too short. Some of us were born short. All of us really were born short because all of us have sinned and fallen short of the glory. That was our handicap before we came to know Christ. We were handicapped. And all of us were born in sin. David said we *were born in sin, shapened iniquity.* We were born with these handicaps.

Zacchaeus just so happened to be handicapped. He was physically short, and he could not see Jesus because the crowd was too large and too tall over him. So, he says, "I got to see Jesus. I want to see Jesus. It's been my desire to see Jesus, and I can't miss Him today." Little did he know that Jesus was going to come to him. So, what does this little, short man do? He ran and he climbed a tree so that when Jesus would pass his way, he could get a good look at him. "I just want to see His face…to look upon His face." My question to you before we move further this morning: What is your handicap that's keeping you from seeing Jesus? Is it a bad habit that's got you to the point that you don't want to see Him? You can't see Him? Is it a relationship problem in which that relationship is not promoting you? Maybe it's a bad experience that you've had with someone? Has somebody done you wrong? Maybe you've done somebody else wrong, and it is hindering you from seeing Jesus? My Brothers and Sisters I come by to tell you not only did Zacchaeus have a handicap, but you've got a handicap.

Or maybe it is Satan himself that's got you to the point that you're handicapped? You can't function. You can't glow. You can't grow. So, what is your handicap? And if you have a handicap this morning, I come by to tell you, you need to see Jesus. You need to see Him this morning. And I just believe that if you just get a glimpse – a real glimpse – or personal contact with Him, He could change that situation for you this morning. He can break that habit. He can mend broken relationships. Relationships that were demoting you, these relationships will now promote you. These bad experiences will now turn into good experiences. To somebody that's done you wrong, you can look at them in the face and say, "You done me wrong but that's alright. I forgive you because I'm forgiven." You can get over your handicap if you just seek Jesus. And I just believe that if you ask the Lord to show up, He will come to where you are. You don't have to go to Him.

You see Zacchaeus could not hide from Jesus not to be seen but I can see Him. It's the other way around. You can't hide from Jesus. You can't hide behind your handicaps. Ask Adam and Eve. After they sinned and fallen short from the glory of God that they were created with, and they hid themselves from God. They sewed fig leaves to hide their nakedness. God didn't just come down when they sinned. He waited a while. He waited until the cool of the evening, and then He came walking through the garden. Look at God walking to man. He came to him and asked Adam, "Where art thou? Where are you, Adam? I know you're in here. I know you're in the garden. You can't hide from me."

My Brothers and Sisters just ask the Lord to show up. He'll show up, and He can change the situation. God changed that situation. Yes, they were handicapped. They had sinned. God says, "Okay. Now that you know the difference between good and evil, right and wrong, now you're going to die. But I'm going to provide a way to bring you back. Yes, you have broken the fellowship. But, in order, to bring the fellowship back, I'm going to send Jesus." And Jesus is our covering. They tried to cover themselves with fig leaves. They were going to dry up in a matter of hours or days anyway. And that was not going to keep them covered. They needed another covering. So, God killed a lamb which symbolized the lamb of God which is Jesus Christ to cover us with His blood, in order, to cover up our shortness. God has a way of covering up our shortness. Oh, bless His name today.

See Zacchaeus couldn't hide from God. Adam couldn't hide from God. You can't hide from God. He knows where you are. Nor can you hide from Him at any time. He knows your address. He knows my address. He knows my email address. He knows my Facebook account. He knows all these things about me. He knows every strand of hair that's in my head. He knows my going in and my coming out. He knows my down sittings. He knows my up risings. What is it about me that God doesn't know? God knows everything about me.

Come here David. David will tell you, "Where can I flea from God's presence?" He's everywhere at the same time. He's in Heaven. He's in the uttermost parts of the world. He's even in hell. Where can I flea from God that He can't find me or that He can't know where I am? He knows. He knows. He Knows. He knows. He knows. He knows my handicap. He knows my shortcomings. He knows my weaknesses. He knows my likes. He knows my dislikes. Thank You Lord. Before I get bogged down there, let me move on to my second outline. The first outline was *Zacchaeus Had a Handicap*.

The second outline is *Zacchaeus Had a Special Need*. Yes, he had a handicap, but he had a special need. You and I have a special need. Zacchaeus needed what only Jesus could give him. Jesus says in Matthew 9:12 that the well folks don't need a doctor, but it's the sick folks that need a doctor. Jesus is not only dealing with a physically short man but dealing with a spiritually weak and vulnerable man. He's dealing with folks on the outside who are self-righteous, and they are looking in saying that Jesus eats with sinners and publicans.

They knew that Zacchaeus was a publican. Therefore, Jesus had to answer them and say to them, "Look, you are trying to be self-righteous, so you don't see a need for Jesus." He says in the 12th Chapter and the 9th verse that it's not the well folks that need a doctor. It's the sick folks that need a doctor. Can I tell you this morning you feel fine? Your blood pressure is on the up and up. Your diabetes has leveled off. You have no other physical problems. Why would you want to go and lay up in the hospital when you are well? You're feeling good. You're not sick. The well doesn't need a doctor.

Right now, I don't need to go to the doctor. I feel pretty good this morning because I woke up this morning. I don't need to ask to go to Tipton County hospital, or Ripley hospital, or Baptist East or any of those places because I'm well right now. But if I were sick this morning, I would want to go and get the best help I can. So, Jesus is saying to them, "It is not the folks that are well that need Jesus, need salvation, and need a conversion. It's the sick folks. It's the sinners who need me. I need to be among the sinners and the publicans. I don't have time to avoid them." If we fast forward quickly to verse 10, He says,*" For the Son of man came to seek and to save that which was lost.* "I come for sick folks." The sick need the hospital. And Jesus is saying, "I am the doctor. I have the right antidote. I have the right medicine. They need me. That's why I'm coming and passing through Jericho on my way to Jerusalem to be crucified." Oh, help me today God.

Jesus wants them to know that their righteousness will suffice not for that of Christ. No, my righteousness, your righteousness cannot suffice for Christ. Jesus is seeking you. We *ain't* seeking the Lord. The Lord is seeking us. Back to verse 10, *"for the Son of man came to seek.* Jesus is seeking for you just like He sought for Zacchaeus. You must see your need for Him. You have needs only Jesus can meet. Does anybody hear me out there this morning? You have needs that only Jesus can meet.

I know you have a lot of stuff. You have all these creature comforts of life. But your needs are greater than that. Do I have any help, out there this morning? Somebody ought to give me a hearts-up. I know I'm telling the truth this morning. See, I need to tell you that your money can't meet your special needs. Your fame and your reputation cannot meet your most desperate needs. Your worldly wisdom cannot meet your special needs. Only Jesus can meet your desperate and special needs in your life. Forgiveness of iniquities, only Jesus can do that. Only Jesus can heal you from sin sickness. Can I just keep going for a minute? Only Jesus can redeem your life from destruction. Nobody else can do it. Only Jesus can crown your life with loving kindness and tender mercy. Only Jesus can do it. It is only Jesus that can satisfy your mouth with good things. Can I keep going? Only Jesus can renew your strength and make you become like a youthful eagle that can fly above stuff. Only Jesus can do that.

You must see what your special needs are. Zacchaeus need a Savior because he was lost. Can I go on and ask the question this morning? What are your needs today? Do you need a Savior? Maybe somebody out there that's listening, you are anonymous. You didn't chime in this morning, but you are listening from somewhere. My question to you this morning, "Are you in need of a Savior?" If you need a Savior, yes, He knows you're out there. You ought to come to Him. You ought to come to Him.

I just named a catalog of things that only Jesus can meet those needs in your life. But can I tell you this one thing? Zacchaeus had plenty of money. He had stolen and thieved. He was rich. He put the poor down to get himself upon life ladder. He had plenty of money, and at this point in his life his money did mean a lot. He had some special needs. What were his special needs? This man is ostracized. He can't worship. He can't go out in public. He has to go out when people are settled to get his personal needs met. He has not peace because people were whispering and pointing a finger at him, talking about him, and threatening him. He had all the money he needed.

Maybe somebody out there, you have all the creature comforts, all the money, but you still *ain't* happy. You're still lost. You're still in your sin. What did Zacchaeus need? Zacchaeus needed peace in his heart. And guess who is coming to his house? The Prince of Peace. He needed joy in his life. Guess who was coming to his house. The Joy Supplier. He needed hope. Guess who is coming to his house. The Hope of Glory was coming to his house. And only Jesus can give these things for special needs. Praise His name. I'm about to get happy up in here.

Now, number three; we've talked about one and two: Zacchaeus had a handicap; Zacchaeus had a special need. But he needed this, and this was the biggie. This was the supplier of it all. *Zacchaeus Encountered a Seeking Savior.* Zacchaeus didn't have to go looking for Jesus. Jesus came looking for him. Can you look back in Verse 1 again, Jesus entered and passed through Jericho. It was on Jesus's agenda to go there anyway. The Lord knew he was there.

The Lord knew that Zacchaeus was sick and tired and sick and tired of being sick and tired of living the life that he was living. He wanted change. He wanted to be converted or changed over even though the Spirit was moving him. The Holy Spirit does come to sinners and move them. He doesn't live in them. But He does come and move us and move us to want and desire Christ. And if we don't yield to the Spirit, then the Spirit just goes on about His way. But He never gives up on us.

It was Jesus who looked up and saw him in the tree. It was Jesus who called him by name. It was Jesus who said come down from that three. It was Jesus who said I must go to your house.

This is how it all happened. Jesus made the first move. We would never be able to come to Jesus unless He comes to us first. Zacchaeus didn't waste any time getting out of the tree. He was elated to be asked down by Jesus. After the meal and the man to man talk, Verse 8 says *And Zacchaeus stood, and said unto the Lord; Behold, Lord, the half of my goods I give to the poor; and if I have taken anything from any man by false accusation, I restore him fourfold.* Zacchaeus had been impacted by his visit from Jesus. He was fully sold out to Jesus. He had a changed heart. That is what happens when a sinner meets Jesus.

> *A change, a change has come over me. He changed my life, and now I'm free. He washed away all my sins, and He made me whole. He washed me white as snow. He changed my life complete, and now I sit, I sit at His feet. To do what must be done, I'll work and work until He comes. A wonderful change has come over me. A wonderful change has come over me.*
>
> **_Lyrics by Walter Hawkins_**

Zacchaeus's decision was voluntary and flowed out of a heart of gratitude for what Jesus had done for him. Whenever Jesus meets someone, there is change.

My Brothers and Sisters, what Jesus wants to see in men and women lives today is change, a transformed heart. And the way to transforming is to have a renewed mind.

I'm not what I want to be; but I'm not what I use to be. The difference in your life and my life is we are saved. Thank You, Jesus!

CALL TO DISCIPLESHIP

Is there anyone out there who wants a new life, a changed life? Jesus is looking for you. If you can believe that Jesus died, was buried, and raised the third day…if you can confess with your mouth and believe it in your heart, then you are saved. A – acknowledge, B – believe, C – confess…Acknowledge you sins, believe that Jesus died, Confess Him. Say it. Say what it is, and you're saved. Get hooked up with somebody that you know is saved, and let them know, "I've accepted Christ as my Savior." God Bless you this morning.

CLOSING REMARKS

God bless you. Thank you for your participation in today in out worship. We pray that your rest of the day will be just as great as the morning part of your day has been.

CLOSING PRAYER

Now unto Him that is able to keep you from falling, and to present you before His presence with exceedingly great joy. Now unto Him be dominion, power, glory, honor, and majesty now and forever…and all the people said Amen, and oh God do bless the gifts that will be coming in. We ask it in Jesus' Name. Amen.

www.ingramcontent.com/pod-product-compliance
Lightning Source LLC
Chambersburg PA
CBHW071953070526
44583CB00015B/1170